The Impact of the Law

John Witte | Michael Welker (Eds.)

The Impact of the Law

On Character Formation, Ethical Education, and the Communication of Values in Late Modern Pluralistic Societies

EVANGELISCHE VERLAGSANSTALT
Leipzig

The project and the publication were supported by the Alonzo McDonald Agape Foundation and the Forschungszentrum Internationale und Interdisziplinäre Theologie (FIIT) at the University of Heidelberg.

Bibliographic information published by the Deutsche Nationalbibliothek
The Deutsche Nationalbibliothek lists this publication in the Deutsche Nationalbibliographie; detailed bibliographic data are available on the Internet at http://dnb.dnb.de.

Printed in Germany

This book is printed on ageing resistant paper.

Cover: Kai-Michael Gustmann, Leipzig
Cover picture: © persephone3d / www.fotosearch.com
Typesetting: 3w+p, Rimpar
Printing and Binding: Hubert & Co., Göttingen

ISBN 978-3-374-06801-2 // eISBN (PDF) 978-3-374-06802-9
www.eva-leipzig.de

Inhalt

Preface to the Series

Five hundred years ago, Protestant reformer Martin Luther argued that "three estates" (*drei Stände*) lie at the foundation of a just and orderly society–marital families, religious communities, and political authorities. Parents in the home; pastors in the church; magistrates in the state–these, said Luther, are the three authorities whom God appointed to represent divine justice and mercy in the world, to protect peace and liberty in earthly life. Household, church, and state –these are the three institutional pillars on which to build social systems of education and schooling, charity and social welfare, economy and architecture, art and publication. Family, faith, and freedom–these are the three things that people will die for.

In the half millennium since Luther, historians have uncovered various classical and Christian antecedents to these early Protestant views. And numerous later theorists have propounded all manner of variations and applications of this three-estates theory, many increasingly abstracted from Luther's overtly Christian worldview. Early modern covenant theologians, both Christian and Jewish, described the marital, confessional, and political covenants that God calls human beings to form, each directed to interrelated personal and public ends. Social-contract theorists differentiated the three contracts that humans enter as they move from the state of nature to an organized society protective of their natural rights–the marital contract of husband and wife; the government contract of rulers and citizens; and, for some, the religious contracts of preachers and parishioners. Early anthropologists posited three stages of development of civilization–from family-based tribes and clans, to priest-run theocracies, to fully organized states that embraced all three institutions. Sociologists distinguished three main forms of authority in an organized community–"traditional" authority that begins in the home, "charismatic" authority that is exemplified in the church, and "legal" authority that is rooted in the state. Legal historians outlined three stages of development of legal norms–from the habits and rules of the family, to the customs and canons of religion, to the statutes and codes of the state.

Already a century ago, however, scholars in different fields began to flatten out this hierarchical theory of social institutions and to emphasize the foundational role of other social institutions alongside the family, church, and state in shaping private and public life and character. Sociologists like Max Weber and Talcott Parsons emphasized the shaping powers of "technical rationality" exemplified especially in new industry, scientific education, and market economies. Legal scholars like Otto von Gierke and F. W. Maitland emphasized the critical roles of non-state legal associations (*Genossenschaften*) in maintaining a just social, political, and legal order historically and today. Catholic subsidiarity theories of Popes Leo XIII and Pius XI emphasized the essential task of mediating social units between the individual and the state to cater the full range of needs, interests, rights, and duties of individuals. Protestant theories of sphere sovereignty, inspired by Abraham Kuyper, argued that not only churches, states, and families but also the social spheres of art, labor, education, economics, agriculture, recreation, and more should enjoy a level of independence from others, especially an overreaching church or state. Various theories of social or structural pluralism, civil society, voluntary associations, the independent sector, multiculturalism, multinormativity, and other such labels have now come to the fore in the ensuing decades–both liberal and conservative, religious and secular, and featuring all manner of methods and logics.

Pluralism of all sorts is now a commonplace of late modern societies. At minimum, this means a multitude of free and equal individuals and a multitude of groups and institutions, each with very different political, moral, religious, and professional interests and orientations. It includes the sundry associations, interest groups, parties, lobbies, and social movements that often rapidly flourish and fade around a common cause, especially when aided by modern technology and various social media. Some see in this texture of plurality an enormous potential for colorful and creative development and a robust expression of human and cultural freedom. Others see a chaotic individualism and radical relativism, which endangers normative education, moral character formation, and effective cultivation of enduring values or virtues.

Pluralism viewed as vague plurality, however, focuses on only one aspect of late modern societies–the equality of individuals, and their almost unlimited freedom to participate peaceably at any time as a respected voice in the moral reasoning and civil interactions of a society. But this view does not adequately recognize that, beneath the shifting cacophony of social forms and norms that constitute modernity, pluralistic societies have heavy normative codes that shape their individual and collective values and morals, preferences and prejudices.

The sources of much of this normative coding and moral education in late modern pluralistic societies are the deep and powerful social systems that are the pillars of every advanced culture. The most powerful and pervasive of these are the social systems of law, religion, politics, science/academy, market, media, family, education, medicine, and national defense. The actual empirical forms of each of these powerful social systems can and do vary greatly, even in the relatively homogeneous societies of the late modern West. But these deeper social systems in one form or another are structurally essential and often normatively decisive in individual and communal lives.

Every advanced society has a comprehensive legal system of justice and order, religious systems of ritual and doctrine, a family system of procreation and love, an economic system of trade and value, a media system of communication and dissemination of news and information, and an educational system of preservation, application, and creation of knowledge and scientific advance. Many advanced societies also have massive systems of science, technology, health care, and national defense with vast influence over and through all of these other social systems. These pervasive social systems lie at the foundation of modern advanced societies, and they anchor the vast pluralities of associations and social interactions that might happen to exist at any given time.

Each of these social systems has internal value systems, institutionalized rationalities, and normative expectations that together help to shape each individual's morality and character. Each of these social spheres, moreover, has its own professionals and experts who shape and implement its internal structures and processes. The normative network created by these social spheres is often harder to grasp today, since late modern pluralistic societies usually do not bring these different value systems to light under the dominance of just one organization, institution, and power. And this normative network has also become more shifting and fragile, especially since traditional social systems like religion and the family have eroded in their durability and power, and other social systems like science, the market, healthcare, defense, and the media have become more powerful.

The aim of this project on "Character Formation and Moral Education in Late Modern Pluralistic Societies" is to identify the realities and potentials of these core social systems to provide moral orientation and character formation in our day. What can and should these social spheres, separately and together, do in shaping the moral character of late modern individuals who, by nature, culture, and constitutional norms, are free and equal in dignity and rights? What are and should be the core educational functions and moral responsibilities of each of these social spheres? How can we better understand and better influence the complex interactions among individualism, the normative binding powers of these social systems, and the creativity of civil groups and institutions? How can we map and measure the different hierarchies of values that govern each of these social systems, and that are also interwoven and interconnected in various ways in shaping late modern understandings of the common good? How do we negotiate the boundaries and conflicts between and among these social systems when one encroaches on the other, or imposes its values and rationalities on individuals at the cost of the other social spheres or of the common good? What and where are the intrinsic strengths of each social sphere that should be made more overt in character formation, public education, and the shaping of minds and mentalities?

These are some of the guiding questions at work in this project and in this volume. Our project aims to provide a systematic account of the role of these powerful normative codes operating in the social spheres of law, religion, the family, the market, the media, science and technology, the academy, health care, and defense in the late modern liberal West. Our focus is on selected examples and case studies drawn from Western Europe, North America, South Africa, and Australia, which together provide just enough diversity to test out broader theories of character formation and moral education. Our scholars are drawn from across the academy, with representative voices from the humanities, social sciences, and natural sciences as well as the professions of theology, law, business, medicine, and more. While most of our scholars come from the Protestant and Catholic worlds, our endeavor is to offer comparative insights that will help scholars from any profession or confession. While our laboratory is principally Western liberal societies, the modern forces of globalization will soon make these issues of moral character formation a concern for every culture and region of the world–given the power of global social media, entertainment, and sports; the pervasiveness of global finance, business, trade, and law; and the perennial global worries over food, health care, environmental degradation, and natural disasters.

This volume is focused on the impact of *law* on character formation, ethical education, and the communication of values in late modern pluralistic societies. It builds on two volumes already in print on the respective impacts of the market and religion, and these three will soon have a companion volume on the impact of academic research. Forthcoming volumes will study the respective impacts of the family, education, the media, the military/defense system, politics, and the healthcare systems. A final integrative monograph will distill the main findings of these volumes and outline some constructive responses for late modern pluralistic societies.

Michael Welker, University of Heidelberg
John Witte Jr., Emory University

Acknowledgements

This volume was made possible by a generous grant from the McDonald Agape Foundation. We give thanks to President Peter McDonald and the members of the Foundation board for their generous support and participation. We are grateful to our colleagues at the Internationales Wissenschaftsforum Heidelberg (IWH) and the Forschungszentrum Internationale und Interdisziplinäre Theologie (FIIT) in Heidelberg for generously hosting a roundtable conference in May 2019 to discuss preliminary papers. We are grateful to the editors of the *Emory Law Journal* and the *Fordham Law Review* for permission to reprint abridgements of articles by the late Professor Allan Farnsworth of Columbia Law School and the late Professor Jean Bethke Elshtain of the University of Chicago Divinity School. And we give thanks for the work on this volume by Dr. Gary S. Hauk, senior editor, and Ms. Amy Wheeler, chief of staff, in the Center for the Study of Law and Religion at Emory University. It was a privilege to learn from each of our chapter authors and to work with our editorial friends at Evangelische Verlagsanstalt in Leipzig. Warmest thanks to each of them for sharing their time and talents with us so generously.

Introduction

John Witte Jr.

> Just as man is the best of the animals when completed, when separated from law and adjudication he is the worst of all.
>
> –Aristotle, *Politics,* bk. 1, chap. 2

> Now before faith came, we were confined under the law, kept under restraint until faith should be revealed. So that the law was our schoolmaster (*paidagōgos*) until Christ came, that we might be justified by faith. But now that faith has come, we are no longer under a schoolmaster; for in Christ Jesus you are all sons of God, through faith.
>
> –Saint Paul, Galatians 3:24–26

> If men were angels, no [law or] government would be necessary. If angels were to govern men, neither external nor internal controls ... would be necessary. In framing a government which is to be administered by men over men ... experience has taught mankind the necessity of auxiliary precautions.
>
> –James Madison, Federalist Paper No. 51 (1788)

> The better the society the less law there will be. In Heaven, there will be no law, and the lion will lie down with the lamb. In Hell, there will be nothing but law, and due process will be meticulously observed.
>
> –Grant Gilmore, *The Ages of American Law* (1977)

This volume brings together seventeen distinguished scholars of law, theology, ethics, philosophy, history, and political theory. Together, they address three central questions: (1) whether, (2) how, and (3) where the *law* teaches values and shapes moral character in late modern liberal societies. While ranging across the Western tradition in addressing these questions, the chapter authors focus on four distinct liberal nations–Germany, the United States, South Africa, and Australia–from which they collectively hail. Each author recognizes the essential value of law in fostering peace, security, health, education, charity, trade, democracy, constitutionalism, justice, human rights, and many other moral goods and virtues in many late modern nations. Each author also recognizes, however, the grave betrayals of law in supporting fascism, slavery, apartheid, genocide, persecution, violence, racism, bigotry, intolerance, chauvinism, and many other forms of moral pathos and injustice. Those realities underscore the need to balance the roles and limits of state law in setting a baseline civil morality for late modern liberal societies with the rights and duties of private individuals and nonstate institutions to cultivate and enforce morals.

Creative Tensions

Three creative tensions emerge in the seventeen chapters that follow. The first concerns the various forms of law that come under discussion and the various dialectics that cut across them. Our chapter authors variously discuss natural laws of conscience, reason, and the Bible and the positive laws enacted by states, churches, and voluntary associations. Some distinguish laws that are local versus national, domestic versus international, legislative versus judge-made, written versus unwritten, codified versus customary, "condensed codes versus elaborated codes" (in Mary Douglas's phrase). Some focus in on specific types of state positive law—family law, constitutional law, criminal law, human rights law, and laws governing taxation, contracts, property, and inheritance. Some scholars differentiate the law on the books from the law in action; the rules and procedures prescribed by an authority versus the behavior by citizens, officials, and legal professionals in positive, negative, or indifferent response. Beneath these various distinctions is the reality that laws of various sorts emerge out of an evolving spectrum of normativity: acts become behaviors; behaviors become habits; habits yield customs; customs produce rules; rules beget statutes; statutes require procedures; procedures guide cases; statutes, procedures, and cases get systematized into codes; and all these forms of legality are eventually confirmed in national constitutions, if not regional conventions and international covenants.

When discussing the role of "law" in teaching values and forming moral character, it is important to be clear what kind of law is under discussion. It is a lot easier to see the moral values and influences at work in a lofty text like the Decalogue or the U.S. Constitution than in a prosaic statute on street parking or food packaging. Representing a defendant on death row has far more obvious moral valence than negotiating a contract for the sale of pencils. The moral "law written on the heart" shapes daily moral behavior far more powerfully than the local laws written in statutes or codes. Saint Paul's statement that Christians are "no longer under the law" reads very differently if the focus is on the Mosaic law as "schoolmaster" rather than the laws of state or church altogether.

A second creative tension concerns the relationship of law (however defined) and other forms of normativity. Several authors note and document the close interaction, confluence, and even integration of law, religion, and morality in earlier legal cultures of the West. But they also recognize that in late modern pluralistic societies, the state's legal system is a differentiated sphere with its own rules and rituals, its own profession and academy, its own methods and practices, its own logics and literature. The modern liberal state claims no monopoly on morality or character formation. It recognizes and supports other internal normative systems at work within families, churches, schools, corporations, charities, clubs, sports leagues, and sundry other voluntary associations. These institutions are often far more important sources of morality for individuals than the laws of the state. A parent's statement to fighting children—"We don't do that in our family!"—carries much more moral weight than the state criminal prohibition on assault and battery. The conduct codes of schools, churches, or corporations guide their members' moral lives much more directly than the bureaucratic rules of the administrative state. Today, a number of theories of subsidiarity, sphere sovereignty, social pluralism, and multinormativity help explain this complex latticework of norms and their respective interactions with state law and their impacts on private and public morality.

Third, the chapters herein point to various methods or strategies that state law in particular uses to teach values and form moral character. Despite our emphases on limited government and maximal liberty, the late modern liberal state does still operate with a number of routine "thou shalt" and "thou shalt not" commands—some of them with ancient religious and moral roots: Pay your taxes. Register your properties. Educate your children. Answer your subpoenas. Obey your conscription orders. Honor your parents. Do not kill. Do not steal. Do not bear false witness. Do not violate your neighbor's household and its members. Commands like these—both prescriptive and proscriptive—are essential to maintaining basic legal, political, social, and economic order, and to fostering the health, safety, peace, and welfare of the entire community. That's what both Aristotle and Madison were underscoring in the opening epigraphs. These state commands set a baseline civil morality, a minimum moral code for the community that the state will enforce, by coercion if necessary. In centuries past, the Western state had much longer lists of moral commands, and much more brutal forms of enforcement. Modern constitutional and cultural norms of liberty, privacy, autonomy, and self-determination have whittled down these state commands and outlawed many cruel forms of punishment. But the late modern liberal state still maintains and enforces a core moral code, a basic civil or public morality.

Between these apodictic poles of thou shalt and thou shalt not commands, the modern liberal state now often operates with softer and more subtle methods of encouraging and facilitating preferred moral behavior and discouraging or impeding immoral behavior. "Nudging" is what behavioral scientists call the common legal strategy of promoting desirable public and private goods in many areas of life. The liberal state commends, licenses, and sometimes even pays for or rewards all kinds of morally desirable behavior: think of voting in a state election, getting a free vaccine, or going to college on a state scholarship. The state imposes taxes or fines or withholds state benefits or opportunities for those who indulge in morally undesirable behavior: think of smoking, not wearing seat belts, or dropping out of school. The theory of nudging stipulates that, over time, the desirable behavior encouraged by the state will become more customary, even natural or reflexive among citizens, and the undesirable behavior will be viewed as aberrant and perhaps even stigmatized.

But the state and its laws can do only so much in the moral field. Late modern societies also need broader communities and narratives to stabilize, deepen, and exemplify the natural inclinations and rational norms of responsibility, sociability, and morality that all human beings have written on their hearts if not embedded in their genes. Even the most progressive liberal societies need models and exemplars of love and fidelity, trust and sacrifice, commitment and community to give these natural and rational teachings further content and coherence. They need the help of stable institutions beyond the state–families, neighborhoods, churches, schools, charities, hospitals, recreational, athletic, artistic, and creative associations, and much more–to form the rich moral characters and refined ethical outlooks of their citizens, and to teach both the minimal morality of duty that keeps the sinners within all of us at bay and the morality of aspiration that brings out the angels in all of us who are devoted to love of God, neighbor, and self.

Chapter Themes

The chapters in this volume are divided into three main parts–respectively addressed to whether, how, and where the law affects character formation, ethical education, and the communication of values in late modern pluralistic societies.

Part I probes, theoretically, whether the law–particularly the law of the state –can, does, and should teach values and virtues, or shape the characters and beliefs of citizens and subjects. The five chapters in this part offer a range of cautionary answers, with a repeated warning about the inherent and necessary limits of state law and the need to balance state laws with other formal and informal sources of normativity and character formation.

In the first chapter, Australian family law scholar *Patrick Parkinson* takes up the theme of "Law, Morality, and Fragility of the Western Legal Tradition." He argues that the Western legal tradition has long depended, in part, on state law to enforce and reinforce basic moral norms to promote liberty, sociability, exchange, and stability. Those moral norms are not so much creations of state law as reflections of biblical, classical, Christian, and Enlightenment teachings, which have been intermittently reformed in accordance with the changing needs and values of society. The normative power of state law, however, has long rested on three fundamental "pillars"–the autonomy of state law; the ideal of the rule of law; and the moral authority of law. The first pillar, concerning the autonomy of state law–particularly its separation from religious laws like canon law or Halacha, which might still operate independently for their voluntary faithful–remains firmly in place in late modern liberal Western societies. But the ideal of the "rule of law," of the *Rechtsstaat,* Parkinson argues, has come under growing attack with the recent rise of populist authoritarianism in the United States and in parts of Latin America and Eastern Europe. These new governments routinely flout the democratic rules of checks and balances within and across the executive, legislative, and judicial branches that are so central to a just and orderly democratic society. And they often ignore customary, equitable, and international legal standards that have proved so vital to the stabilizing the Western and non-Western world, particularly after the horrors of World Wars I and II. These attacks on the ideal of the rule of law, in turn, undermine the law's moral authority and create cynicism, scepticism, and sometimes even anarchy among citizens. To have moral power, Parkinson argues, the law must be believed in, and this belief in the legitimacy, authority, and efficacy of the law has been badly shaken in a number of late modern liberal societies. Those who believe in the Western legal tradition therefore must do everything possible to retain and restore these fundamental pillars of legality, along with other sources and institutions of normativity.

American Catholic jurist and ethicist *Cathleen Kaveny* addresses "Law's Pedagogy in a Pluralistic Society: Challenges and Opportunities." She builds on Thomas Aquinas's idea, drawn in part from Aristotle and Isidore of Seville, that just state laws are by definition teachers of virtue, even though state laws are only one form of law, and laws are only one form of normativity. One can see that teaching function of law at work still today in the socially formative objectives of such legislation in the Americans with Disabilities Act and such constitutional cases as *Brown v. Board of Education*–though, of course, other statutes and cases reflect and reinforce less appealing values. Kaveny sifts through the objections and impediments to the pedagogical function of law that come from liberal legal theory, economic analysis of law, and the critical legal studies movement. She confirms their critical calls for a basic separation of law and morality, and state and religious authority; but she also urges readers to recognize the overlapping jurisdiction and necessary points of cooperation between them. Modern state law can and should foster certain basic virtues and values, Kaveny concludes. She holds up as key examples the ideals of autonomy (defined by Joseph Raz as the capacity to be the part-author of one's life) and solidarity (understood, as Pope John Paul II understands it, as a determination to commit oneself to the common good).

American legal theorist *Brian Bix* analyzes "The Effects of (Family) Law: Frameworks, Practical Reasoning, Social Norms, and Slippage." As his title indicates, the effect of state law on character or virtue is complicated. There are grounds for wondering to what extent law *should* concern itself with such matters, with reasonable views on both sides of the question. When these complexities are added to the controversies surrounding issues like sexual expression and relationships and questions about which side is the side of good character, and to concerns about unintended consequences, the need for caution on these matters is clear. Additionally, there are ways in which legal rules–even laws that fall far short of being "evil"–can work *against* good character. Law can, as Saul Levmore observed, make "self-help, personal involvement, and teamwork less enticing." Finally, there are many ways in which legal rules can have effects far different from what the lawmakers intended, with normative slippage. This can be seen not only in the common disparity between the law on the books and the law in action, but also in the reality that the formal enactment of a legal rule sometimes triggers deliberate disobedience and organized resistance by some citizens. Think of the reaction to requiring masks or getting vaccinated during the current global Covid-19 pandemic.

The following chapter reprints an essay by the late American political theorist *Jean Bethke Elshtain*, which we had commissioned for an earlier project on law and religion. The title of the chapter underscores her cautionary message: "There Oughta be a Law on This–Not Necessarily! The Limits of Law as a Teacher of Values and Virtues." Here Elshtain contrasts Augustine's minimalist dependence on law (just enough rules to govern a "den of robbers"), with Aquinas's more robust theory (laws should serve "to foster the common good"), to even more expansive Protestant views (laws should aim for "the redemption of everyday life"). Immanuel Kant translated this earlier Protestant dependence on state law to establish and enforce Christian values and virtues into a perfectionst rule-of-law ethic for all liberal societies. That last move has sometimes proved dangerous today, Elshtain argues. It has allowed state law to reach too deeply into the interior life of all citizens, risking the tyranny of conscience. It has also allowed those in political power to establish an ever expansive and strangulating network of rules to enforce their own ultraliberal values (think of sexual liberty codes, hate crime legislation, or military operational rules) or pernicious world views (think of the extensive laws of Stalinist Russia or Nazi Germany) that threaten personal freedom and eclipse many other forms and forums of virtue and value formation.

German philosopher *Rüdiger Bittner* challenges on "The Law as Educator?" the very notion that law can and should serve as a moral landmark or steeple of virtue to orient diverse individuals holding multiple beliefs, values, and perspectives. Bittner allows that state laws can set basic rules of the road, punish violent crimes, and offer basic procedures to enforce contracts, vindicate torts, or transfer property. But beyond that, the law of the state has no capacity or remit. State law cannot form character or teach virtues or values because law is not one thing and does not aim at one thing. The term "the law" covers a vast array of diverse concerns and activities that have only a nominal unity, and this array of legal phenomena cannot muster a coherent pedagogy. Even if it could, state law also cannot be trusted to guide citizens on the right path, as too many examples of tyrannical governments and regimes, even in recent times, can attest. Law thus does not and should not have a moral commission or set about on an ethical project to form character. In the end, Bittner concludes, human beings can only trust their own judgment in figuring out what is right to do.

Part II moves from general principles to concrete cases and statutes in analyzing the roles and limits of the state law's teaching function. The eight chapters in this section offer several examples of how the law reflects and shapes, if not commands and enforces, public and private morality. Constitutions and bills of rights, and judicial opinions interpreting them, offer poignant examples of how the law defines and defends many constitutive values and moral beliefs of a community concerning power, order, justice, liberty, equality, and more. Education laws help habituate the next generation in the basic values of democratic citizenship, with public state schools sometimes teaching more expansive ethical habits of liberal citizenry and private religious schools sometimes fostering the moral formation of a child in a particular faith. Taxation laws prescribe forms and forums of distributive justice that move resources from those with "superfluous" wealth to those who need more. Criminal laws set a baseline of morality to protect each citizen's person, property, and privacy. Church laws ideally set higher moral standards for their leaders and voluntary members. The laws of contract help facilitate the voluntary relationships and consensual expectations of individuals, and offer remedies for harms that result from actions or omissions.

American constitutional scholar *James E. Fleming* takes up the question, "Are Constitutional Courts Civic Educative Institutions? If So, What Do They Teach? He argues that constitutional court opinions, in attempting to resolve conflicts between rights in "culture wars"–in particular, conflicts between gay and lesbian rights and religious liberty claims–can teach lessons to citizens concerning how to accommodate such conflicts. Court opinions can model how to secure the central range of application of each conflicting right rather than vindicating one right absolutely to the exclusion of the other, with one side winning it all. They also can teach how to speak with respect concerning both gay and lesbian rights and religious liberty. Moreover, Fleming argues, while religious freedom is a fundamental good and value for modern liberal soceities, religious exemptions for businesses from antidiscrimination laws often undercut the significant, moderating influences of trade in large commercial republics. They also undermine the salutary civic function of trade in facilitating contact, moderating difference, promoting tolerance, and securing the status of equal citizenship for all.

His fellow American constitutional scholar *Linda C. McClain*, who is also trained in theology, takes up the vexed topic of "Bigotry, Civility, and Reinvigorating Civic Education: Government's Formative Task Amidst Polarization." In the United States and globally, she argues, concerns over a decline in civility and tolerance and a surge in extremist violence motivated by hatred of religious and racial groups make preventing hatred and bigotry seem urgent. What meaning can *e pluribus unum* ("out of many, one") have in this fraught and polarized environment? In the United States, a long line of jurists, politicians, and educators have invoked civic education in public schools as vital to preserving constitutional democracy and a healthy pluralism. Civic education remains a vital means for fostering civility and decreasing contempt and prejudice, but is challenging amidst democratic discord. This chapter examines the contours of a reinvigorated civic education and best practices for addressing class- and race-based civic inequalities. Religious literacy (nonsectarian education about religion) should be a component because of the harmful effects of widespread religious *illiteracy.* Teaching students to think critically and to deliberate respectfully across differences is no easy task, as this chapter illustrates with the example of controversies over LGBTQ rights.

Jesuit priest and Australian human rights lawyer *Frank Brennan* sets out "An Australian Case Study on Law and Values: Debating a Bill of Rights." Australia is the only Western liberal nation without a national bill of rights, preferring instead to handle rights questions locally and legislatively. Brennan has been at the forefront of those advocating the adoption of a bill of rights for Australia, drawing lessons from European and American constitutional and statutory regimes and regional and international human rights instruments. National protections of human rights, Brennan argues, serve to confirm and protect the essential moral values of human dignity, liberty, equality, and fairness, particularly for racial minorities, new immigrants, and indigenous peoples who often cannot escape the tyranny of the legislative majority or the prejudices of local judicial tribunals. The gravest danger to human rights, he writes, is the constraint placed on discourse and debate about the conditions under which people can participate in shaping the kind of society in which they live, especially in relation to issues which are deemed "politically correct." In the absence of a bill of rights, Australia needs to enhance public conversation, law, and policy making in order to root out unfairness, respect the integrity and dignity of those most different from us, while extending mercy to those who most need it.

German public law scholar *Ute Mager*, briefly presents "The German Constitution as Value System." She argues that the Basic Law of Germany, forged in the aftermath of two world wars and repulsed by the horrors of the Nazi regime, strongly affirms several fundamental moral values of Western liberalism and its Christian antecedents: human dignity; equal treatment; personal freedoms; freedoms of religion, speech, assembly, and association; a guarantee of private property; and support for the welfare state and environmental protection. These are national values whose implementation and protection depend on a blend of legislative and judicial actions as well as negotiations with individual *Länder.* These basic moral values of constitutionalism pervade German public, administrative, and private law alike, and also help shape the German educational system, which promotes such values in the next generation.

The following chapter is by the late American contracts scholar *E. Allan Farnsworth*, who had prepared this text for a volume on the ethics of contract that did not come together. Titled "Parables About Promises: Religious Ethics and Contract Enforceability," this chapter calls for a sharp distinction between the much wider moral obligation and much narrow legal obligation to abide one's promises. God, the Bible records, did enforce moral obligations to abide by divinely sealed covenants. Medieval church courts used to enforce some informal moral promises as a matter of sacramental penance. But today, whether and how to honor one's promises is left primarily for individuals to sort out in accordance with the dictates of their own consciences and the duties set by their families, churches, clubs, employers, or other communities in which they voluntarily participate. Modern liberal societies embrace the fundamental right of freedom of contract, Farnsworth emphasizes, and many constitutions forbid states from "impairing" the contracts of their citizens. Liberal state courts will thus enforce contractual promises only if the parties have abided by the proper formalities of making a contract –offer, acceptance, and consideration are the main requirements of Anglo-American common law–and only if one or both parties seek relief from the court. Morality does govern the boundaries of contract law. State courts will not enforce "unconscionable" contracts that foster such immoral behavior as usury, enslavement, prostitution, organ selling, illicit drug sales, criminal conduct, and the like. Courts will work hard to ensure that both parties gave their full consent to the bargain. And they will make equitable adjustments if a contract imposes grave injustice. But beyond those moral minima the modern liberal state does not go–and should not go, Farnsworth concludes. The morality of promises is a much wider field than the legality of contracts, and he offers several parables and stories to illustrate the distinction.

German contracts scholar *Thomas Pfeiffer* reaches much the same conclusion in discussing European private laws of obligations. In "The Law of Contracts and Ethics: Interrelation in Spite of Separation," Pfeiffer argues that the state imposition of a single moral ideal of promise making or promise keeping would violate a cardinal axiom of late modern pluralistic democracies–the fundamental freedom of everyone to pursue happiness according to their own choices, including through entering into voluntary contracts with others. Pfeiffer emphasizes some of the same moral limits to contract making that Farnworth lifted up, particularly the concerns about unconscionability in contracts and protecting parties who are incapable of giving true consent to a bargain. He further emphasizes that contract law deliberately confirms and teaches society about each individual's moral agency in protecting their ability to consent and requiring them to abide by their voluntarily adopted bargain. He also suggests that reliance on the market rather than predetermined state rules to set the "just price" of a bargain further affirms the morality of economic freedom and the moral agency of all those "invisible hands" at work in the marketplace.

American tax lawyer and Scottish-trained theologian *Allen Calhoun* presents an innovative study of "Martin Luther's Vision of Redistributive Taxation." He shows how the 1523 Leisnig Ordinance of a Common Chest represents the first legislative attempt to put into practice Luther's wish that the poor and needy be helped through redistributive taxation. Redistribution as a theme in Luther's theology is based in the "happy exchange" of attributes between Christ and the believer that is central to Luther's doctrine of the *communicatio idiomatum.* The Eucharist or Lord's Supper is, for Luther, the paradigm of this happy exchange and the most salient example of how the physical world mediates God's gracious dealings with people. The Eucharist thus carries the redistributive logic of the *communicatio* out into the material realities of wealth and poverty. Just as God shares superabundant grace with all needy communicants in the church through the Eucharist, so all communicants share their superfluous property—even if only a "widow's mite"—with all those needy subjects in the community. Taxes paid to the Christian magistrate, like tithes paid to the Christian diaconate, help to express the community's and the individual's commitment to redistributing God's gracious favor, and helping the poor and needy in so doing.

American legal historian *John Witte Jr.* offers a case study of "Teaching Sexual Morality in Church and State Historically and Today." He shows that, for much of the second millennium, sexual morality and criminal law overlapped, and churches and states enforced sundry sex crimes. Today, new constitutional liberties and new reforms of family law and criminal law have dramatically reduced the roll of sex crimes and the roles of churches in maintaining sexuality morality. But sexual misconduct remains a perennial reality in modern societies, Witte documents, including notably within churches, and sex crimes inflict some of the deepest scars on their victims. Modern liberal states must thus maintain a basic standard of sexual morality in its criminal law as a restraint on harmful behavior and as a bulwark against a sexual state of nature where life is often "nasty, brutish, and short" for the most vulnerable. And liberal societies should encourage its citizens and churches to pursue a higher morality of aspiration that views sex and the sexual body as a special gift for oneself and others.

Part III of this volume takes up the question *where* the law teaches value, offering views from the bench and the bar in four final chapters.

First, Australian jurist *Reid Mortensen* presents "The Clergy of Liberalism: Lawyers' Character, Virtue, and Moral Education in Pluralized Societies." He uses Alasdair MacIntyre's description that lawyers are the clergy of liberalism, a professional group that, by and large, enables and exemplifies liberalism's values, including, notably, its promotion of individual rights and entitlements. In this sense, the role of modern lawyers is analogous to the role of the clergy in earlier Christian societies. The respective moral dispositions, habits, and discipline of these two professions sync with the moral purposes promoted by the community, and these professionals exemplify and help enforce the community's moral purposes. In late modern liberal societies, lawyers are thus required to be paradigmatic liberal citizens. This is reflected in the three main pillars of the ethical system of the legal profession: partisanship (the single-minded representation of client interests); procedural morality (promoting client legal entitlements even if they are considered unjust); and moral accountability only for failures to give effect to partisanship or procedural morality. A more complete account of lawyers' ethics should also concede that, in contemporary legal practice, these three ethical pillars may also develop moral character–but a kind of character shaped by a scheme of procedural virtues that respond to the needs of pluralized liberal societies. This kind of character also has implications for the role of the law school in developing the distinctive moral expectations of lawyers in their role as "the clergy" of liberalism.

American legal ethics expert *Robert F. Cochran Jr.* offers a meditation on "Legal Representation and the Character Formation of Lawyers and Clients." Legal representation influences the character of both lawyers and clients, he argues. Lawyers generally play a morally responsible role in the legal system or in commerce. Litigators advocate for each side and enable judges and juries to make wise decisions. Business lawyers draft documents and negotiate deals enabling businesses to employ people and meet the needs of customers. Such legal representation should employ and develop the virtues of truthfulness, courage, justice, and prudence. Nevertheless, legal representation carries moral risks. Constant advocacy for clients may cause a lawyer to become argumentative and less forthcoming in areas of life where these qualities are not justified. Legal representation can also be an occasion for moral harm or moral growth for clients. Some lawyers encourage clients to act in self-serving ways, reinforcing the selfish instincts of clients. A better role for the lawyer is that of a friend in the classical sense, initiating moral discourse between the lawyer and the client and encouraging moral growth for both of them.

South African theologian *Robert Vosloo* provides a striking reflection on "Law, Conscience, and Character Formation: A South African Case Study in Ricœurian Perspective." Against the backdrop of a court case in apartheid South Africa, as represented in the book *The Trial of Beyers Naudé: Christian Witness and the Rule of Law* (1975), his chapter calls for greater conceptual clarity regarding the relationship between law and conscience. Vosloo draws on the work of French philosopher Paul Ricœur to argue that one should guard against setting up a false dichotomy between law and conscience in which this polarity becomes a schism. Moreover, the freedom and law of conscience should not be viewed as an arbitrary faculty of the autonomous individual that functions in isolation from the law or the counsel of others. The law of conscience is not a law unto oneself. As the two halves of the word indicate, "con-science" has a profound relational and societal aspect, requiring the need to give a public account of oneself and one's claims of concience and their influence on character formation and moral behavior. Particularly when claims of conscience are used to seek exemptions from general laws that bind all others, the claimant has an obligation to explain to courts and communities the moral values and decision-making involved.

Finally, in **Chapter 17**, leading Australian high court justice *Kenneth John Crispin* reflects on "Law, Values, and Moral Influence." He argues that the laws of the state obviously reflect moral values, whether arising from religious or philosophical beliefs or the acceptance of social mores, such as support for equal rights and basic freedoms. The converse is also true, however, Crispin emphasizes. While moral consciousness and community values are more obviously influenced by enculturation, religious beliefs and political inclinations, laws also have a profound effect on the circumstances in which people mature and develop social consciences. They shape the institutions of political, economic, social and, to some extent, even family life, within which beliefs are formed and character development fostered. Laws may also be exemplars, providing information and stirring consciences by proscribing conduct that infringes moral standards and upholding the rights of individuals. Judicial rituals, in particular, offer public affirmations of values, and landmark cases provide catalysts for change. The liturgies of the courtroom are critical to confirming the justice of the law and its underlying moral foundations and values. Justice must be done not only with due process and proper representation; justice must also be seen to be done to inspire the confidence and shape the moral character of both officials and citizens, plaintiffs and defendants, the accused and their victims.

It is high time for me to stop hovering in front of these chapters and let the authors speak for themselves, which they do with eloquence and erudition on the pages that follow. Having started this introduction with several epigraphs, however, I cannot resist lifting up in conclusion two choice quotes from among many others herein. Both quotes are in Robert Vosloo's chapter 16. The first is from Cathleen Kaveny, the distinguished author of chapter 2, whose contribution builds on her signature 2012 book, *Law's Virtues.* There, Kaveny warns against "two opposite and equally damaging extremes":

> We should not make the mistake of assuming that law and morality are co-extensive, on the one hand, or of maintaining that they should have as little as possible to do with each other, on the other. In very different ways, both mistakes can be traced to the same fundamental problem: ignoring the full range of ways in which moral considerations enter into wise lawmaking.[1]

The second quote is by leading South African theologian Dirkie Smit, now at Princeton Theological Seminary. Having lived under both the brutalities of an

---

1 Cathleen Kaveny, *Law's Virtues: Fostering Autonomy and Solidarity in American Society* (Washington, DC: Georgetown University Press, 2012), 45.

apartheid legal system and the new constitutional democracy of South Africa, Smit writes about the pedagogical role of law in developing habits, customs, and eventually self-guided rules of morality. For Smit, the law can help persons and peoples become better, realizing the good within them and guided by the moral law written on their hearts by God. Smit writes:

> Law can even fulfil the role of moral education, formation and transformation. Morality changes, and very often it changes as a result of legal changes. Experience amply shows that forms of racism, sexism, homophobia, prejudice and discrimination, disregard for human dignity, violations of human rights, slavery, abuse, and in fact many practices of corruption, nepotism and exclusion often first have to be prohibited by law, before a major part of the population will change their minds to accept and share these convictions. In this sense, living in a city with just laws is indeed an important form of moral formation–as the Greek philosopher [Xenophon] already taught.[2]

---

2 Dirk J. Smit, "What abou' the lô? Adam Small on law and morality," in *Remembering Theologians–Doing Theology: Collected Essays 5*, ed. Robert Vosloo (Stellenbosch: Sun Press, 2013), 402–03.

Part One:
Does Law Teach Values and Virtues?

Law, Morality, and the Fragility of the Western Legal Tradition

Patrick Parkinson

Is Law Inherently Moral?

It is a defensible proposition in Western societies that law plays a role in character formation, ethical education, and the communication of values in late modern pluralistic societies, and that it should continue to do so. Law has played a quite fundamental role in social ordering, providing a framework for the relationship between government and governed, between husband and wife, parent and child, and employer and employee. More generally, law orders the relationships among citizens who must coexist in the villages, towns, and cities of our shared communal life. Law also establishes a framework for society's mediating institutions such as corporations, schools, universities, and community organizations.

At least to some extent, universally accepted moral norms of conduct are embedded in the law as forms of legal obligation or prohibition. The law which is written on people's hearts (Romans 2:15) is also to be found in the statute book. Prohibitions found in the Ten Commandments against such wrongs as murder, theft, and perjury are both moral and legal norms in all Western societies.

The overlap between religiously inspired moral codes and legal obligations is of course far from complete. To honor one's father and mother is a moral obligation that is given weak effect in terms of legal (and financial) obligation in many Western societies, although at least some jurisdictions give some effect to the notion of "solidarity" between generations.[1] The moral prohibition against adultery no longer has a place in most Western legal systems. Even so, the average citizen would be likely to affirm that the most basic legal rules of a society have their basis in shared moral values that are reflected in the law. Law both enforces and reinforces moral norms. For example, criminal sentencing is understood as having an educative role. A prison sentence is imposed not only to deter others but, by punishing the offender, to reinforce publicly the moral norms that are important to a society. When people refer to justice being done by the conviction and sen-

---

1 See Hugues Fulchiron, ed., *Solidarities Between Generations* (Brussels: Bruylant, 2013).

tencing of an offender, they are referring to this retributive and norm-reinforcing role of the criminal justice system.

Of course, there remains an argument about whether the law merely follows changes in social and moral attitudes or whether it has a role in educating about values.[2] There is also an argument about what the law should even seek to achieve in terms of moral education.[3] Generalizations are difficult in this area. Yet there are obvious examples of where the law could be said to have shaped social values, taking a proactive role. Consider employment law and, in particular, the issue of discrimination in employment. A hundred and fifty years ago, no one would have questioned the idea that if I owned a factory, I had the right to determine who worked in my factory and for how many hours each day. Employees served at their employer's pleasure and could be dismissed at will. In that workplace, there were no laws against unfair dismissal or discrimination on the basis of gender, race, or disability.

All that has changed. Laws restrict the basis on which people can be dismissed. A raft of antidiscrimination laws provides remedies for those with "protected attributes" who consider that they have been subject to adverse employment decisions.[4] These laws would seem to have had powerful effects on what people consider ought to be done, and on their sense of rights and entitlements. Mary Ann Glendon has identified employment rights as a new form of property.[5] The obligation not to discriminate is perhaps at the very front of all moral obligations among those committed to a progressive agenda in Western societies,[6] and it is increasingly based on an idea about the right of individuals to self-determination[7] and to dignity.[8] This belief in nondiscrimination as a moral prin-

---

2 See Brian H. Bix, chapter 3 in this volume.

3 See Rüdiger Bittner, chapter 4 in this volume.

4 See, for example, Sandra Fredman, *Discrimination Law* (Oxford: Oxford University Press, 2002).

5 Mary Ann Glendon, *The New Family and the New Property* (Toronto: Butterworths, 1981). The concept of new kinds of property right derives from Charles Reich, "The New Property," *Yale Law Journal* 73 (1964): 733–87.

6 See, for example, Cass Sunstein, "The Anticaste Principle," *Michigan Law Review* 92 (1994): 2410–55.

7 Sophia Moreau, "What is Discrimination?," *Philosophy and Public Affairs* 38 (2010): 143–79.

8 Robin Allen and Gay Moon, "Dignity Discourse in Discrimination Law: A Better Route to Equality," *European Human Rights Law Review* 6 (2006): 610–49; Jürgen Habermas, "The Concept of Human Dignity and the Realistic Utopia of Human Rights," *Metaphilosophy* 41 (2010): 464–80.

ciple seems to underlie what Alexander Somek has called a "generalizing momentum" that drives continuing expansion in the scope of antidiscrimination law.[9]

So, yes, it is a reasonable premise that law and morality have a considerable degree of overlap–in the sense that basic moral norms about how we should live in relation to others find expression in almost universal legal obligations in developed societies. Furthermore, a reasonable case can be made for the proposition that at least in some respects, changes in legal norms can influence people's perceptions about what ought to be done–what is right, and what is wrong in human relations.

Yet this is not necessarily so. How moral, for example, is the law in corrupt regimes in which those with power may murder, steal, or commit perjury with impunity, while others may be punished for crimes of political opposition to an oppressive state? Law in itself need have no moral content. That it does is almost universal, even in corrupt or totalitarian societies, and even if it is selectively and unjustly enforced; but it is possible to conceive of a society in which law is nothing more than the orders of a tyrant, an implementation of executive power over the governed. It is no answer to this possibility to withhold from such a legal system the description of it as "law"; for as law it is experienced by those oppressed by it. Law, in other words, may represent nothing more than a ruler's orders backed up with a jailer's keys and a hangman's noose. It is possible to have law without much justice; and as Augustine put it, kingdoms without justice are "but robber-bands enlarged."[10] Law can be used to serve, and even to legitimize, banditry.

Even in developed and democratic societies, we should not complacently assume that law will continue to have beneficial educative effects in communicating shared values. Nor should we assume that it will continue to be perceived as a source of moral norms. The moral quality of law, its normative power and its capacity for good, is something that our legal tradition has been imbued with, but it is not necessarily inherent.

The Origins of the Western Legal Tradition

The Western idea of law developed from a combination of Roman, Greek, and Judeo-Christian thought. These all played a role in shaping our ideas about law as a result of a revival of classical learning from the late eleventh century onwards.

Roman law, as rediscovered and interpreted by the medieval glossators and commentators in the eleventh and twelfth centuries, provided the basis for the civil-law systems of Continental Europe. However, Roman law was inextricably intertwined with Greek and Christian influences, for it was studied within the

---

9 Alexander Somek, *Engineering Equality* (Oxford: Oxford University Press, 2011), 6.

10 Augustine, *City of God Against the Pagans*, bk. 19, 13.

context of a worldview derived from Aristotelian philosophy as reinterpreted by Christian theology. It was largely through the influence of church teachers and writers that classical ideas from Greece and Rome gained so much currency. Furthermore, the methodology used to study the Roman law texts was the same methodology of Scholasticism–derived from Greek dialectical reasoning–which was used to explain, harmonize, and reconcile the scriptures and the teachings of the Church Fathers.

It was no accident that law and theology should adopt the same method. Both were working with authoritative texts. The premise of Scholasticism was that certain books were authoritative. The two major sources of authority were Aristotle and the scriptures–reason and revelation.[11] The Christian theology of revelation was thus married with the Roman and Greek ideas of natural law to form the intellectual underpinnings of the medieval legal system.

Roman law also influenced canon law, which provided for the church a vast system of law by which it was governed. It was through law that the content of the faith was laid down. It has been said that "it was the Church that first taught western man what a modern legal system is like."[12] That law should be used to govern the church reflected the worldview of the medieval period. It was thought that since God ruled the world through natural laws, it was appropriate for the church to use law to govern itself. Law had received divine approval. In this way law and theology were inextricably intertwined.

Christianity was to the formation of the Western legal tradition as the womb is to human life. The history of Western law cannot be understood in isolation from religious influences, for at every level of society, and in every aspect of social and political life, these influences were pervasive. These influences have given to the modern world as a legacy many of its foundational precepts and most commonly invoked ideas.

The Three Pillars of the Western Legal Tradition

The normative power of law in the Western legal tradition rests, I would argue, on three fundamental pillars.[13] These are, first, the autonomy of law; second, the idea of the rule of law; and, third, the moral authority of law. None of these pillars can be taken for granted in late modern pluralistic societies. All of them are vulner-

---

11 Ellen Goodman, *The Origins of the Western Legal Tradition* (Sydney: Federation Press, 1995), 213.

12 Harold Berman, *The Interaction of Law and Religion* (London: SCM Press, 1974), 59.

13 This section is derived from chapter 2 of my book *Tradition and Change in Australian Law*, 5th ed. (Sydney: Thomson Reuters, 2013).

able, not only to political earthquakes but to the slow, and perhaps largely unseen, erosion of their foundations.

The Autonomy of Law

Law in Western thought is an autonomous discipline. That is, it is conceptually distinct from custom, morality, religion, or politics. A clear differentiation is made between legal institutions and other types of institutions, and between legal rules and other kinds of rules. Moral norms and legal norms may coincide, but they are not synonymous with one another. Laws may originate in the customs of a community, and historically many of them did so,[14] but laws are distinct from customs inasmuch as not all customs are law, and not all laws originate in custom. Laws may have a religious rationale, but the source of their authority and binding nature is not religious obligation but civic duty. Thus, courts in countries of the Western legal tradition punish criminal infringements and enforce contractual obligations not merely because the majority of the population would approve of this, nor because such action is sanctioned by the teachings of a particular faith, but because the law of the land allows, and indeed instructs, the courts to act in this way. Similarly, laws may reflect the will of a government, but the will of the government is not, in itself, law, and indeed the laws of the land may at times thwart the will of a government.

Law is not autonomous in the sense of being free from the influences of politics, religion, economics, and those factors of culture, upbringing, and worldview which influence the beliefs and attitudes of individual judges. The content of law is shaped, perhaps even dictated, by the social forces which are the context of law's operation; but the values of these social forces are not simply reproduced in the Western legal tradition as legal norms. They have to be reconstructed within law and to be accepted as law. That is, the language of other disciplines and belief systems is not merely translated into law but rewritten as law, converted into legal norms of rights and obligations, and of lawful and unlawful acts.[15] The vindication of those rights occurs through legal procedures, and the law takes on a life of its own as it develops the content and scope of those rights through its normal processes of legal reasoning and the establishment of legal precedents.

The autonomy of law in Western societies is reflected in the fact that it has its own institutions, its own profession, its unique rituals, and its own university discipline, professional literature, technical language, and peculiar etiquette. The

---

14 Alan Watson, *The Evolution of Law* (Baltimore: Johns Hopkins University Press, 1985).

15 Some theorists, applying Nicklas Luhmann's theories, regard law as an "autopoietic," self-referential system which is, in certain ways, closed off from other systems. See Gunther Teubner, *Law as an Autopoietic System* (Oxford: Blackwell, 1993).

discipline of law is a distinct one. It is characterized in all Western countries by a tendency toward the formal organization of the law into categories and legal concepts, with an emphasis on consistency in the application of legal norms.

The autonomy of law seems so obvious to the Western mind that it is difficult to conceive of a civilization which does not organize itself in the same way. Yet examples abound, both historically and in the present day. Indeed, in many traditional societies, law is utterly inseparable from other aspects of life.[16] A contrast may be drawn, for example, between the Western idea of law and the concept of law in traditional Aboriginal culture in Australia. Aboriginal communities certainly have laws. However, these laws are inseparable from traditional Aboriginal cultural practices and beliefs about the universe and the place of humans within it. As Elizabeth Eggleston has written:

> Law and religion were intimately bound up in Aboriginal society ... and any attempt to identify certain segments of Aboriginal life as "legal" involves the imposition of alien categories of thought on the tribal society.[17]

Aboriginal laws require no distinctive hierarchy of judges to uphold them, nor is there a distinctive profession associated with them. This does not mean that Aboriginal customary law is any less law than the laws of Western societies. It differs from Western law, however, in that Aboriginal customary law is not autonomous.

The Rule of Law

The second pillar is the corollary of the first. Governments are subject to law and accountable to an independent judiciary. That is, law in the Western legal tradition is not merely a manifestation of political power. By binding rulers through constitutions or other legal limits, the law asserts its independence from political power and subjugates political power to its authority.

To speak of the rule of law in Western societies is not only to reflect the idea that governments are themselves subject to law. It is also to identify the central role that law plays in social ordering. Law pervades every aspect of modern soci-

---

16 Glenn describes these as "chthonic" communities: H. Patrick Glenn, *Legal Traditions of the World*, 3rd ed. (New York: Oxford University Press, 2007). He writes (p. 69): "So the law that we know is in there, in the chthonic tradition, is all mixed up with other things—how to cook, how to catch rabbits and deer, how to behave to one's family (in a very large sense), how to be honourable."

17 Elizabeth Eggleston, *Fear, Favour or Affection: Aborigines and the Criminal Law in Victoria, South Australia and Western Australia* (Canberra: Australian National University Press, 1976), 278.

ety and is a primary means of social control. This centrality of law as a source of normative coding and a means of moral education has a long history in Western legal thought. Adda Bozeman writes:

> [I]t would be difficult not to conclude from the records that law has consistently been trusted in the West as the main carrier of shared values, the most effective agent of social control, and the only reliable principle capable of moderating and reducing the reign of passion, arbitrariness and caprice in human life.[18]

Law in itself is perceived as having not only a coercive value but also an educative power. It sends messages as well as mandating particular conduct. Geoffrey Sawer emphasizes the pervasiveness of legal ordering in observing the paradox that law is seen as essential even by revolutionaries who demonstrate hostility to lawyers:

> [T]he lawyer as an individual or a type has often been exceedingly unpopular and lawyers have often been the first to suffer in revolutionary situations. Nevertheless, lawyers ... have also always been prominent in the councils of rulers and of revolutionaries alike. A respect for and even a demand for the legal approach to the structuring or ordering of social relations has kept triumphing over the periodic dissatisfactions with the particular structure or order achieved at a particular time and place.[19]

The centrality and pervasiveness of law in Western society is nonetheless far from universal. Law plays a less pronounced role in societies which can appeal to other bases for molding behavior. The appeal to Islamic tradition or to socialist values is a call to do certain things or to behave in certain ways for reasons other than adherence to legal rules. In particular, the centrality of law in Western societies may be contrasted with the tradition of Eastern cultures, such as China. Traditionally, the Chinese recognized the enacted or "positive" law, called *fa*, which meant the rules prescribed by an earthly ruler. However, traditional Confucian thought contained a general suspicion of *fa*. The preservation of harmony and order in the universe was perceived to be much better if social relations were governed by *li*, the ethics, taboos, ceremonies, and customs of the community. The distrust of *fa* is demonstrated in the introduction to the oldest datable code of law in China, the *Tso Chuan* (535 BCE), in which it was said:

---

18 Adda Bozeman, *The Future of Law in a Multicultural World* (Princeton: Princeton University Press, 1971), 38.

19 Geoffrey Sawer, "The Western Conception of Law," in *International Encyclopedia of Comparative Law* (The Hague: J. Mohr / Tubingen: Mouton, 1975), 2:47.

> The ancient kings, who weighed matters very carefully before establishing ordinances, did not [write down] their systems of punishments, fearing to awaken a litigious spirit among the people. But since all crimes cannot be prevented, they set up the barrier of righteousness, bound the people by administrative ordinances, treated them according to just usage, guarded them with good faith, and surrounded them with benevolence .... But when the people know that there are laws regulating punishments, they have no respectful fear of authority. A litigious spirit awakes, invoking the letter of the law, and trusting that evil actions will not fall under its provisions.[20]

Historically, law certainly played a role in China. However, the role of law was primarily in maintaining peace and stability and in reinforcing the power of the government. The Western concept of law being concerned with protecting individual rights was an alien notion.

The Moral Authority of Law

A third feature of the Western legal tradition is that the law commands a high level of respect in Western societies. This respect is independent of popular acceptance either of the merits of particular laws or of the level of respect shown to the lawmakers. Law, thus, is not only autonomous; it tends to be disembodied in people's consciousness from the lawmakers, and it derives authority and respect from a deep sense within the community that the law *ought to be* obeyed, not merely for fear of sanction but from a feeling of positive obligation. Law in the Western legal tradition carries inherent connotations of legitimacy.[21]

Descriptions of law as an instrument for giving effect to the policies of those in power, or as a collection of rules governing political, social, and economic relations, or in terms of law's function in regulating society, provide a wholly inadequate description of law in themselves. They miss the important element that law in the Western legal tradition is not only generally obeyed but also *believed in.*

It is not only, or even mainly, fear of sanctions which secures obedience to law (although some laws, such as speeding laws, may be an exception). People have an emotional commitment to such values as the desire for equal treatment before the law, the claim to an impartial hearing, the need for consistency in the application of rules, and the principle that governments are themselves subject to law. People appeal to their legal rights, and to the obligations of others toward them, as a standard to be adhered to in their private dealings with one another and as an

20 Quoted in Joseph Needham and Colin Ronan, *The Shorter Science and Civilization in China* (Cambridge: Cambridge University Press, 1970), chap. 16.

21 See further, Tochen Spaak, "Legal Positivism, Law's Normativity and the Normative Force of Legal Justification," *Ratio Juris* 16 (2003): 469–85.

objective indication of right conduct. Law, in popular consciousness, thus represents what one ought to do morally as well as legally. As Harold Berman writes:

> Law itself, in all societies, encourages the belief in its own sanctity. It puts forward its claim to obedience in ways that appeal not only to the material, impersonal, finite, rational interests of the people who are asked to observe it but also to their faith in a truth, a justice, that transcends social utility .... Even Joseph Stalin had to reintroduce into Soviet law elements which would make his people believe in its inherent rightness–emotional elements, sacred elements; for otherwise the persuasiveness of law would have totally vanished, and even Stalin could not rule solely by threat of force.[22]

The Legacy of History

These characteristics of the Western legal tradition–law's autonomy, the idea of the rule of law, and law's moral authority–are explicable only by the context of the birth of that tradition and the history of its development over the subsequent centuries. The autonomy of law, which had been an aspect of the Roman tradition, was reestablished when law began to be studied in its own right in the new law schools of Europe from the end of the eleventh century onwards. The medieval scholars took the laws of the late Roman empire and by dialectic analysis turned them into a system, renewed and reinterpreted to do service in the different context of medieval Europe. Although the development of the common law in England has a distinct history, the notion that law could be a coherent system and that it was founded on reason passed into the thinking of English lawyers as well as their Continental counterparts.

The centrality of law may also be traced to the origins of the Western legal tradition. The church was governed by law. The authority of rulers was limited by law, for their authority came from God, and divinely ordained law restrained the exercise of arbitrary power. Laws derived from Roman law influences, reason, and custom governed human reactions in both private and economic life. Mercantile law allowed for the growth of transnational commerce. Even international relations camc to be governed by law. International law emerged as a system of rules to govern disputes between sovereign countries.

The moral authority of the law may also be traced to its history. The close relationship between law and theology in the formation of the Western legal tradition, the belief in law as ultimately given by God, and the idea that there were natural laws which governed human relations meant that law was imbued with a certain aura of sacredness. Law, like religion, had its liturgies and rituals which

---

22 Berman, *Interaction of Law and Religion*, 29.

gave to law an impression of derivative authority from the divine. The close relationship between law and faith meant that law was believed in; for law, even in Caesar's kingdom, was an aspect of the will of God.

The experience of harsh laws and oppressive rulers did not reduce this faith in the law. Rather, it strengthened it. Disobedience to rulers could be justified in the name of law when rulers refused to be bound by its foundational moral precepts.[23]

This respect for law in Western countries, and its quasi-sacred authority in popular consciousness, reinforced by its rituals, is not universal. Indeed, in some ways, respect for law has a fragile quality. When people become alienated from a society and perceive themselves as destined to be the have-nots within a nation where levels of wealth are high, respect for the rule of law will often give way to violent and destructive tendencies. Respect for law is always dependent, ultimately, on people's sense of belonging to a society. Where law is seen purely as an instrument of repression, it ceases to be effective as a form of moral education at all.

The fracturing of Western societies, involving ever-increasing polarization and loss of faith in its institutions, is one threat to the Western legal tradition. Another is our gradual loss of memory concerning the origins of our values, and loss of a worldview that gave those values such extraordinary educative power. What happens to a society when the influences that imbue a civilization recede? For how long can the echo of fundamental religious and Renaissance values continue to reverberate down the centuries before it becomes too faint to be heard by the postmodern human ear?

Are the Pillars of the Western Legal Tradition Being Eroded?

It would be tempting to say "yes" unequivocally to this question, but to do so would be simplistic. The autonomy of law is well entrenched in Western societies. Indeed, as the influence of Christianity on the law of Western nations has receded, these societies have become ever more firmly committed to the separation of secular law from religious morality.

The notion of law's autonomy has come under attack in the universities, of course. Marxist ideas about law, feminist legal theory, the critical-legal-studies movement–all of these have sought to assert that law is little more than the manifestation of political, social, or economic power. Law is superstructure, or based upon patriarchy, or a source of oppression masked by a pretence of neutrality. These critiques come and go. They may be fashionable for a time, but they recede

23 Aquinas, *Summa Theologiae* 1–2, qu. 95 and 96.

eventually because they present such a limited and partial view of the role of law in social ordering. Road traffic laws, after all, are hardly a manifestation of patriarchy.

The rule of law is more vulnerable. It routinely comes under pressure from governments that see the courts of a jurisdiction as an obstacle to its policy or a check against governmental corruption. By and large, pressure can be brought to bear on governments that brazenly interfere with the independence of the judiciary, for example by seeking to dismiss judges of its highest court.[24] However, preventing the politicization of the judiciary becomes harder when it comes to the appointment of judges. The battle over appointments to the Supreme Court of the United States, and indeed to the lower levels of the federal judiciary in America, is testament to that. Furthermore, judicial appointments or appointments to tribunals may be used by politicians to reward friends or supporters who would not qualify on merit, in a way which borders on corruption. That is an issue in Australia and no doubt in other countries. It demonstrates a lack of respect for the rule of law and for the people whose disputes will be heard by these poorly qualified or partisan judges.

The rule of law is also fragile in jurisdictions that have little respect for the text of a constitution or for precedent. To say that a constitution is "living" may be only to say that it is malleable in the hands of judges who change its interpretation with the mood of the times or the perceived necessities of the hour. The rule of law requires respect for tradition, generally building upon the work of previous generations of judges. It requires judges to provide reasons for decisions that justify outcomes in the light of previous expositions of the law. Harlan Stone, a justice of the United States Supreme Court, once wrote:

> I can hardly see the use of writing judicial opinions unless they are to embody methods of analysis and of exposition which will serve the profession as a guide to the decision of future cases. If they are not better than an excursion ticket, good for this day and trip only, they do not serve even as protective coloration of the writer of the opinions and would much better be left unsaid.[25]

The politicization of the judiciary and lack of respect for the wisdom of previous generations as contained in precedent are in combination grave threats to the rule of law. The United States, in particular, is at risk of losing a fundamental aspect of its legal tradition. Before President Trump, attacks on the rule of law were largely

24 Francis Trinidade, "The Removal of the Malaysian Judges," *Law Quarterly Review* 106 (1990): 51–86.

25 Letter from Justice Stone to Felix Frankfurter (Feb. 25, 1936) (Stone Papers, Library of Congress), cited, inter alia, in Richard Re, "On 'A Ticket Good For One Day Only,'" *Green Bag 2nd* 16 (2013): 155 ff., at 156.

insidious and covert. That one of the major political parties in the United States has accepted without much criticism the continuing and overt attacks on the rule of law and the courts by the president ought to be cause for grave concern.

Attacks on law's autonomy and the erosion of the rule of law together impact the law's moral authority. To have moral power, the law must be believed in. It is important, but not enough, that the *content* of law be believed in. Belief in laws against murder, theft, or the sexual abuse of children is unlikely to be diminished in late modern societies. However, belief in the law, and therefore its moral authority, requires more than this. It requires that if judges are to decide great moral and social questions, such as those about same-sex marriage or abortion, they must draw on an accepted source of legal authority that stands apart from their personal beliefs and values.

If the resolution of a social or moral controversy turns on delaying consideration of a president's Supreme Court nominee until an election can be held, or if it is seen as the outcome of majority voting that tramples upon fundamental human rights, or if the courts or law enforcement officials are perceived as corrupt, or the judge who has to exercise a discretion in a difficult case is not remotely qualified to do so, all of this erodes belief in the law.

Those who believe in the Western legal tradition therefore must be particularly assertive of the importance of retaining its fundamental pillars. In the past, attacks on the law's moral authority, derived from the perception of its neutrality, have come mainly from the left of politics. In recent years these attacks–in the United States, Poland, and elsewhere–have mainly come from governments associated with the right. When these attacks are overt, they are at least identifiable and can be resisted. The covert erosion of the moral authority of law is a more existential danger to its role in character formation, ethical education, and the communication of values.

We must, for these reasons, be alert to the gradual erosion of the values that underpin the Western legal tradition and must do whatever we can to prevent it.

Law's Pedagogy in a Pluralistic Society

Challenges and Opportunities

Cathleen Kaveny

I live in the Commonwealth of Massachusetts. In March 2019, I read about a proposed law that gives drivers a new option on their licenses: instead of choosing "male" or "female," applicants could select "X" if they wanted to indicate their gender as nonbinary. Maine, Minnesota, Colorado, Oregon, California, New Jersey, and Arkansas already make this opportunity available to their residents.

What is the aim of this new option? It is not primarily to regulate a burgeoning segment of the population. By all accounts, only a small number of people describe themselves as gender-nonconforming. It is also not to provide better information to police officers. The mandatory photographs on licenses are more helpful to the police than self-reported data about height, weight, and gender.

The purpose of the bill is its new pedagogical message. Karen Spilka, the bill's sponsor, was straightforward about its moral lessons: "This is about validating and letting people be who they are.... This is a matter of civil rights." The bill's opponents also saw the bill's pedagogical message as the key issue. Jim Lyons reflected,

> "Maybe we ought to have an open and transparent discussion about what X means and what are the genders we're talking about .... I view the world as male and female. If they view it differently, then bring the argument. Discuss it."[1]

Lyons complains that Massachusetts citizens were not afforded the opportunity to debate the merits of the bill's moral message. My complaint is more fundamental. American lawmakers rarely take responsibility for the challenges involved in grappling with law's pedagogical function. Instead, they careen between two opposite poles: on one hand, when it suits them, they assume that making law is like magic—that when lawmakers pass a law that encodes a new set of standards, the

---

1 Andy Metzger, "Spilka Calls for Gender X Bill's Passage," *CommonWealth* (March 28, 2019), https://commonwealthmagazine.org/politics/spilka-calls-for-gender-x-bills-passage/.

populace will immediately conform to the new moral vision. On the other hand, when it suits them, they pretend that an act of law has no moral implications at all –that decriminalizing certain activities will have no effect on the moral imagination of the populace.

Neither pole, of course, does justice to the complicated relationship between law and morality. The disastrous American experience with Prohibition shows that law cannot always control moral beliefs, and the consequences of liberalizing laws on practices ranging from divorce and same-sex marriage to abortion and assisted suicide reveals that law does in fact exert a significant influence on both mores and morals–no matter what the lawmakers' intention.

We need a more nuanced account of law's pedagogical function in a pluralistic society. In this essay, I make three points, which are treated more fully in my book *Law's Virtues.*[2] First, I lift up for examination key elements of the pedagogical theory of law proffered by Thomas Aquinas, arguing that it is still useful today.[3] Second, I consider why important strands of contemporary legal theory impede consideration of the law's pedagogical function. Third, I briefly discuss the virtues the law might inculcate in pluralistic liberal democracies.

The Pedagogical Function of Law

What is law? In his treatise on law, Aquinas offers a general definition that covers both unwritten law (eternal law, natural law) and positive law (divine law, human law): "it is nothing else than an ordinance of reason for the common good, made by him who has care of the community, and promulgated."[4]

What are the virtues of law? Aquinas shows that we can speak of these virtues in two distinct but related senses. First, he contends that "the purpose of human law is to lead men to virtue"[5] in order to direct their actions toward the common good of the particular community in which they live. This first sense of law's virtues directs our attention to the actions, habits, and character that the law actually fosters in its subjects. Aquinas acknowledges that different communities interpret and understand their common good in different ways; in some cases, the governing ideals may generate laws that deform rather than improve character, as the concepts of a "good Confederate slave owner" or a "good Nazi" suggest.[6]

2 Cathleen Kaveny, *Law's Virtues: Fostering Autonomy and Solidarity in American Society* (Washington, DC: Georgetown University Press, 2012).

3 Let me emphasize that I am drawing on Aquinas's legal arguments here–not his theological authority.

4 Thomas Aquinas, *Summa Theologica*, I–II, q. 90. art. 4.

5 Ibid., I–II q. 96, art. 2, rep.ob.2.

6 Ibid., I–II. q. 92, art. 1, rep.ob.4.

Second, Aquinas reflects on the virtues of good law in general: he wholeheartedly endorses Isidore of Seville's enumeration of the features which positive law ought to exhibit. According to Isidore, "Law shall be virtuous, just, possible to nature, according to the custom of the country, suitable to place and time, necessary, useful; clearly expressed, lest by its obscurity it lead to misunderstanding; framed for no private benefit, but for the common good."[7] Good law–law that actually furthers the common good–not only must inculcate true virtue and promote justice but also must comply with the other, more practical criteria on Isidore's list. These criteria, which comprise the second sense of law's virtues, are themselves interrelated: for example, no law can accord with a country's customs unless it also responds to the specific place and time in which it is enacted. Similarly, without making allowances for the limitations of human nature, no law can be necessary or useful.

There is a relationship between the first and second senses of law's virtues. No teacher can be effective without attending to the capacities and limitations of her students. Some citizens are gifted with good moral habits and an abundance of practical reason, while many others fall short on one or both counts. Aquinas reminds us that the basic requirements of the law are to be framed for ordinary persons, not saints; its lessons are meant to be elementary.[8]

Furthermore, the more coercive aspects of the law's lesson plan concentrate on actions directly relevant to the common good. The law does not require every virtuous act, nor does it prohibit every vicious act; it focuses on the subset of vicious and virtuous actions that impinge directly on the common good. At the same time, the law ought not condone vicious actions or deride virtuous ones, even if it leaves the former unpunished and the latter unrequired for a variety of practical reasons.[9]

Finally, because law is attempting to inculcate virtue, which is a habit, its relationship to custom is complicated, because custom is an entrenched collective habit. Ultimately, Aquinas maintains that "custom has the force of a law, abol-

---

7 Isidore of Seville, *Etymologies*, bk. 5, para. 21, as cited in Thomas Aquinas, *Summa Theologica*, 3 vols., trans. Fathers of the English Dominican Province (New York: Benzinger Bros., 1948), I–II., q. 95, art. 3, ob. 1.

8 "Now human law is framed for a number of human beings, the majority of whom are not perfect in virtue. Wherefore human laws do not forbid all vices, from which the virtuous abstain, but only the more grievous vices, from which it is possible for the majority to abstain; and chiefly those that are to the hurt of others, without the prohibition of which human society could not be maintained: thus human law prohibits murder, theft and such like." Ibid., I–II. q. 96, art. 2.

9 "Human law is said to permit certain things, not as approving of them, but as being unable to direct them. ... It would be different, were human law to sanction what the eternal law condemns." Ibid., I–II, q. 93, art. 3, rep.obj. 3.

ishes law, and is the interpreter of law."[10] Legislating against entrenched customs, even if they are unjust, is a delicate and difficult business, as efforts to outlaw the practice of dueling suggest. A gradualist policy is often the only possibility of being an effective policy in the long run.

One might object that Aquinas's theory is applicable only to a morally and religiously homogeneous medieval community. My response takes the following shape, which I only sketch here. First, even in morally pluralistic liberal democracies, the law communicates moral values and inculcates morally significant habits–those appropriate to living in a pluralistic liberal democracy. Second, identifying those values and habits requires grappling with moral disagreement in a way that medieval communities may not have needed to do. For example, more attention needs to be paid to the purpose and limits of the virtue of tolerance.

In my view, Aquinas's nuanced theory of law as a moral teacher does a better job of accounting for key pieces of American legislation than many other contemporary jurisprudential theories. As my opening example illustrates, the disagreement between Spilka and Lyons is not about whether law conveys a moral message, but about which message is the right one to convey. Yet there are many other examples. Consider America's evolving treatment of persons with disabilities. In 1970, the City of Chicago had on its book an ordinance colloquially known as "The Ugly Law." It provided as follows:

> No person who is diseased, maimed, mutilated or any way deformed so as to be an unsightly or disgusting object or improper person is to be allowed in or on the public ways or other public places in this city, or shall therein or thereon expose himself to public view, under a penalty of not less than one dollar nor more than fifty dollars for each offense.[11]

This ordinance is triply unjust. First, it impedes persons with disabilities from going about their day-to-day business. Second, it encodes morally obnoxious views about who counts as a valuable member of our public life. Third, its dangerous moral message seeps from the public streets to the private sector: how will persons with disabilities be treated in families, churches, and hospitals?

Contrast the moral message of The Ugly Law with that of the Americans with Disabilities Act (ADA), passed in 1990.[12] The ADA's preamble announces its normative convictions:

---

10 Aquinas, *Summa Theologica*, I–II, q. 97, art. 3.

11 Chicago Municipal Code, sec. 36034 (repealed 1974).

12 Americans with Disabilities Act (ADA), Pub.L. No. 101–336, 104 Stat. 328 (1990) (as amended in scattered sections of 42, 47, and 29 U.S.C.). The ADA has parallels with European Law; see Article 26 of the Charter of Fundamental Rights of the European Union and Article 13 of the Treaty of Amsterdam.

> The Nation's proper goals regarding individuals with disabilities are to assure equality of opportunity, full participation, independent living, and economic self-sufficiency for such individuals.[13]

The ADA covers two basic aspects of social existence: employment and accommodation in public facilities. Its legal framework envisions a society that rejects the marginalization of persons with disabilities. Yet, consistent with Aquinas's gradualist account of moral pedagogy, it does not attempt to mandate each aspect of its vision. For example, while the ADA prohibits employment discrimination, it does not require affirmative action. Yet it gestures beyond its requirements to its aspirations. Its purpose is to create a culture where normally abled persons grow accustomed to seeing persons with disabilities in all facets of public and commercial life, and come to value them as equal members of society.

A rich account of the pedagogical function of the law helps us make sense of America's legislative success stories: the Civil Rights Acts, the Americans with Disabilities Act, and the Family and Medical Leave Act. It also sheds light on the fragile nature of moral custom, thereby illuminating contemporary political and legal controversies. For example, progressive Democrats might have done well to let contemporary mores settle for a while after winning groundbreaking constitutional protection for same-sex marriage in *Obergefell v. Hodges* (2015).[14] Instead, they immediately turned to the issue of rights for transgendered persons, which many Americans believed involved a somewhat different set of questions. Similarly, conservative Republicans are now enacting severe restrictions on abortion at the state level, which also conflict with many Americans' complicated views on the question. In both cases, there are good strategic, financial, moral, and political reasons for aggressively pushing the program at hand. At the same time, both aggressive legal strategies risk undermining the relationship between law and a stable moral consensus, thereby fostering a cynical approach to law's moral sway.

Impediments to Thinking about Law's Pedagogy

As Isidore's jurisprudential criteria indicate, grappling with the nature and function of the law as a moral teacher is a multifaceted task–especially in a pluralistic liberal democracy. Yet in the United States, at least, we have not even made a good beginning. Why not? In my view, in part because three legal theories that have dominated the discussion discourage thinking about the law as a moral teacher.

---

13 ADA, sec. 1201(8).

14 Obergefell v. Hodges, 576 U.S. ___, 135 S. Ct. 2584 (2015).

The Hart–Devlin Debate and Liberal Legal Theory

The debate between H. L. A. Hart and Patrick Devlin focused on the narrow question whether the criminal law should target "harmless" sexual acts, such as consensual homosexual encounters.[15] Yet their interchange soon raised the broader issue whether the law as a whole should strive to be morally neutral among competing ways of life and "nonharmful" activities. Joel Feinberg's four-volume series *The Moral Limits of the Criminal Law* is a brilliant articulation and extension of Hart's position.[16] A close examination of Feinberg's theory reveals three features that militate against a nuanced consideration of the pedagogical function of the law.

First, Feinberg's theory incorporates a subjectivist account of value. On his view, human beings do not seek to promote goods, goals, or states of affairs because they are valuable; rather, these goods, goals, and state of affairs are valuable because they are sought after and valued by human beings. Consequently, the idea of law teaching that certain ways of life are more or less morally valuable makes little sense.

Second, like all liberals, Feinberg places a high value on liberty. But his conception of liberty emphasizes negative freedom rather than positive freedom. It also gives more weight to promoting unencumbered future decisions rather than protecting the fruits of past exercises of free decisions. Additionally, it sees freedom as a property that resides in individuals; groups such as families and churches are largely presented as threatening freedom rather than exercising it in their own way. To take one of his own examples, he places more weight on young Farley Fairjoy's right to play rock-and-roll music in his room than on Terrence Trueview's right to protect the community mores he has built over time with others in his planned community.[17]

Third, while Feinberg's defense of freedom explicitly pertains only to the criminal law, its rationale has broader implications. His subjectivist account of value itself suggests that every branch of the law should give the greatest possible scope for individual choice. Moreover, while other branches of law may not have the same severe penalties as the criminal law, they often have a more pervasive impact. Feinberg writes that the threat of criminal prosecution "put the nonconformist in a terror of apprehension, rendering his privacy precarious and his pros-

---

15 See, for example, H. L. A. Hart, *Law, Liberty, and Morality* (Oxford: Oxford University Press, 1963); Patrick Devlin, *The Enforcement of Morals* (Oxford: Oxford University Press, 1965); and Lon Fuller, *The Morality of Law* (New Haven, CT: Yale University Press 1969).

16 Joel Feinberg, *Harm to Others*, vol. 1, *The Moral Limits of the Criminal Law* (New York: Oxford University Press, 1984); vol. 2, *Offense to Others* (1985); vol. 3, *Harm to Self* (1986); and vol. 4, *Harmless Wrongdoing* (1988).

17 Feinberg, *Harmless Wrongdoing*, 57–61.

pects in life uncertain."[18] True enough. But giving tax breaks to some ways of life (for example, home ownership in suburbia) versus other ways (for example, apartment dwelling in the city) is far more likely to exert influence over an ordinary person's life than the remote prospect of being arrested and prosecuted for a private, nonharmful criminal action.

Incentives and Economic Analysis of Law

Economic analysis of law has arguably been the most influential jurisprudential theory in the American legal academy in the past fifty years.[19] While they differ from Feinberg in some respects, many advocates of the law-and-economics approach share his subjectivist account of value. Goods and practices are valuable because people value them. According to many economic theorists of law, the overarching goal of the legal system is to ensure that goods and services find their way to those who value them most, who these theorists believe are those willing to pay the most in a hypothetical market with no transaction costs. Broadly speaking, economic analysis treats law as an incentivizer–not as a teacher of virtue. A legal framework of incentives presupposes that individuals are rational, self-interested utility maximizers. Lawmakers change behavior by changing the costs and benefits of prospective actions, not by shaping the character of the citizenry.

A jurisprudence that highlights the pedagogical function of law will also make use of incentives–but only as a first step. Aquinas recognizes, for example, that one objective of the criminal law is to provide an incentive powerful enough to deter those contemplating vicious acts from their proposed course of action. But the use of incentives must serve the goal of moral pedagogy.[20] Achieving that goal requires helping people internalize the norms embedded in the law, so that they can apply them themselves in exercising their own practical reason. No action performed solely because of a threat or a reward can be considered a virtuous

18 Feinberg, *Harm to Others*, 4.

19 Key texts include Ronald Coase, *The Firm, The Market, and the Law*, rep. ed. (Chicago: University of Chicago Press, 1990); Steven Shavell, *Foundations of Economic Analysis of Law* (Cambridge, MA: Harvard University Press, 2004); and Richard A. Posner, *Economic Analysis of Law*, 8th ed. (New York: Wolters Kluwer Law & Business, 2011).

20 "Since some are found to be depraved, and prone to vice, and not easily amenable to words, it was necessary for such to be restrained from evil by force and fear, in order that, at least, they might desist from evil-doing, and leave others in peace, and that they themselves, by being habituated in this way, might be brought to do willingly what hitherto they did from fear, and thus become virtuous." Aquinas, *Summa Theologiae*, I–II, q. 95, art. 1.

action.[21] Threats and incentives can *train* persons to perform (or refrain from performing) certain acts. But training, in itself, is not teaching, which entails an appeal to the student's reason. Teaching a moral norm gives the student reasons why the required acts make sense in a larger context of her own character, life plan, and the flourishing of her community.

Critical Legal Studies Movements

At its inception in the mid-1970 s, the critical-legal-studies movement sought to undermine the myth that the rule of law is constituted by a network of neutral legal rules that decisively and objectively settle disputes. Highly influenced by Marxist commitments, the movement's adherents exposed how the law served to entrench and enforce social and political power. To this day, critical legal theorists strive to unmask the ways in which legal doctrines and systems serve the interest of the privileged. For example, in his seminal volume, *The Critical Legal Studies Movement*, Roberto Unger explored how the basic presuppositions of contract law, which assumed a bargain between two parties of roughly equal power, ignored the real power disparities between management and workers.[22] In the past decades, critical-legal-studies movements became more diffuse, expanding to consider how the law disadvantages not only the poor but also other oppressed minorities, especially women and persons of color.[23]

Critical legal theorists recognize the normative thrust of the law—they see it can be used to foster or to impede the well-being of the vulnerable. They also tend to adopt a richer conception of personal identity than many liberal legal theorists. They recognize that persons are essentially social, their choices shaped by their families, cultures, education, resources, and experiences. This is a promising anthropological basis for cooperation between a pedagogical account of law whose governing ideals relate the individual and the community through a rich and variegated concept of the common good. At the same time, however, certain aspects of critical legal studies impede full consideration of law's pedagogy.

First, the Marxist commitments of critical legal theory can undermine the concept of the common good. If law is a manifestation of political power, and political power is structured in terms of an endless class struggle between the haves

---

21 Ibid., I–II, q. 6, art. 6.

22 Roberto Mangabeira Unger, *The Critical Legal Studies Movement* (New York: Verso, 2015).

23 See, for example, Richard Delgado and Jean Stefancic, "Critical Race Theory: An Annotated Bibliography," *Virginia Law Review* 79 (1993): 461–516; Adrien Katherine Wing, ed., *Critical Race Feminism: A Reader*, 2nd ed. (New York: NYU Press, 2003); and Fiona Kumari Campbell, *Contours of Ableism: The Production of Disability and Abledness* (New York: Palgrave Macmillan, 2009).

and the have-nots (however these categories are defined), then the idea of law as a moral pedagogy that works with the practical reason of citizens will not ultimately make sense. Whereas liberal legal theory risks overemphasizing an individual's nature as an autonomous chooser free from social constraints and commitments, critical legal theory risks dissolving an individual's powers of practical reason into her social and political position of advantage or disadvantage.

Second, critical-legal-studies movements are not well equipped to deal with the idea of the rule of law, particularly as it shapes the relationship between law and custom. The governing ideal of critical-legal-studies movements is unending political and legal struggle. If law is primarily a tool of oppression wielded by the powerful, then it needs to be quickly overturned and replaced by a legal framework that will favor those who are currently disempowered. After such a revolution, the newly disempowered will work the levers of power in order to overcome their reversal of fortune. Quite ironically, this view of law as a prize in unending political struggle has become dominant in the mainstream American public consciousness, as federal policies on immigration, access to health care, birth-control funding, and religious liberty summarily metamorphose from presidential administration to presidential administration.

Yet the relationship of law, habit, and custom should be of central concern to those interested in reinvigorating a conversation about the pedagogical function of law. As Isidore's criteria indicate, sound and effective legal norms work with the grain of the communities that they purport to govern. On one level, this is a practical necessity. No community, not even a police state, can afford the resources to detect and prosecute every violation of the law. Conformity must become a matter of habit. Moreover, for the rule of law to be stable, most people need to develop a well-honed ability to predict what the law is likely to be in matters affecting day-to-day life.

Attending to the relationship between law and custom allows theorists interested in the pedagogical function of the law to learn from failed lesson plans. Precisely because an act of lawmaking is not an act of magic, changing law will not necessarily change behavior or alter underlying sentiments and commitments. Most Americans are familiar with the civil rights acts of the 1960 s. While those laws certainly were not perfect, or perfectly effective, they constituted major steps toward equality for African-Americans. But fewer Americans realize there was a prior federal attempt to protect civil rights a century earlier. Not only were the civil rights acts of 1864 and 1875 not enforced, they were actively undermined by violent racist groups such as the Ku Klux Klan. Moreover, they precipitated a virulent backlash, as Southern states enacted a sweeping and ruthless regime of Jim Crow laws.[24]

---

24 See Adam Gopnik, "How the South Won the Civil War," *New Yorker*, April 1, 2019, https://www.newyorker.com/magazine/2019/04/08/how-the-south-won-the-civil-war.

Law's Virtues for a Pluralist Liberal Democracy: Razian Autonomy and Solidarity

Any full account of the pedagogical function of the law in a pluralist liberal democracy must give a rich account of the common good, as well as the virtues necessary to equip persons to participate in and contribute to it. In *Law's Virtues*, I suggest two candidates for the governing virtues: autonomy, as understood by the perfectionist liberal Joseph Raz, and solidarity, as understood in the tradition of Catholic social thought.[25]

In any pluralistic liberal democracy, freedom is an important value. The key is to understand it in the right way. In *The Morality of Freedom*, Raz contends that the ultimate point of negative freedom is positive freedom: positively to allow an agent to become a "part author" of his own life.[26] Most importantly, Raz shows that a society can justify the protection of liberty without adopting Feinberg's subjectivist account of value or interest. Rather, according to Raz, freedom deserves social protection because our society has come to recognize that there are mutually incompatible but morally worthwhile ways of living, which deserve protection precisely because they are morally worthwhile.[27]

Raz's approach facilitates a pedagogical approach to the law by recognizing that autonomy is not a fact but rather an individual and social achievement. It is also not a political given; indeed, it is impossible to preserve a political community committed to autonomy unless that commitment is collectively passed down from generation to generation. Doing so requires constant efforts to articulate the moral value of autonomy in new contexts, and to communicate the rationale for giving it political protection even in situations where restrictions on freedom seem to be the most practical and efficient way of organizing civil life.

Moreover, the exercise of autonomy on the part of the individual cannot exist without significant social commitment. Raz argues that individual autonomy has three fundamental requirements: 1) the raw mental capacity to make and carry out choices; 2) freedom from attempts at both manipulation and coercion; and 3) a range of morally worthwhile choices.[28] These requirements will shape law and policy: they will require resources and dedication. A society committed to raising autonomous citizens will ensure that they grow up in a stable and nurturing environment. It will provide children with high-quality education that not only refrains from manipulating them but also gives them tools to recognize manipulation. In addition, a society that values autonomy will develop a range of

---

25 The reflections in this section are taken from my article, "Autonomy, Solidarity, and Law's Pedagogy," *Louvain Studies* 27 (2002): 339–58.

26 Joseph Raz, *The Morality of Freedom* (Oxford: Oxford University Press, 1986), 410.

27 Ibid., 396.

28 Ibid., chap. 14.

morally worthwhile options from which persons may choose the framework to shape their own identities.

Raz's three conditions for the exercise of autonomy point to a socially situated freedom. They envision a person situated within a community and developing an identity that draws equally upon his unique talents and socially constructed opportunities. Two features of Razian autonomy are worth highlighting. First, becoming an autonomous person is an achievement that is realized over many years. Correlatively, acting autonomously is a habit; people need to practice, exercise, and develop Razian autonomy. It is the way that prudence, or right reason with respect to acting, needs to be configured to function in a modern liberal democratic society. Consequently, it is appropriate to use the term "virtue" to speak of autonomy understood in this way.

Second, Raz presses us to move beyond an artificial opposition between individual self-actualization and communal commitments, because he shows us that individuals can develop the virtue of autonomy only in a society dedicated to that virtue. Alternatively, we could say that Raz's understanding of autonomy encourages lawmakers to move beyond individualism to solidarity. Solidarity is, of course, a term with many resonances. It is a term that became prominent in Catholic social teaching under Pope John Paul II,[29] who defined it as "a firm and persevering determination to commit oneself to the common good; that is to say, to the good of all and of each individual, because we are all really responsible for all."[30]

In my view, the virtue of solidarity as understood in contemporary Catholic thought has three fundamental components, which correspond to Raz's conditions for true human autonomy. In essence, the virtue of solidarity asks citizens to be committed to fostering the autonomy of others, as well as their own autonomy. I suggested earlier that Razian autonomy is a configuration of the virtue of prudence suitable for pluralistic liberal democracies. I now suggest that solidarity is an analogous configuration of the virtue of justice.

First, solidarity requires us to meet the basic needs of each person as a being who is an integrated unity of body and soul. Second, solidarity demands attention to the social nature of human beings, preparing each person to function productively within society. Third, solidarity requires us to provide vehicles through which each person can contribute to the community through the expression and

---

29 While many Catholic ethicists use the term "solidarity" in their constructive work, it still merits significantly more analytical reflection. A helpful contribution is Meghan J. Clark, *The Vision of Catholic Social Thought: The Virtue of Solidarity and the Praxis of Human Rights* (Minneapolis, MN: Fortress Press, 2014).

30 Pope John Paul II, *Solicitudo rei socialis* (1987), http://w2.vatican.va/content/john-paul-ii/en/encyclicals/documents/hf_jp-ii_enc_30121987_sollicitudo-rei-socialis.html, para. 38.

development of his own talents and interests. We do not want to reduce the individual to a cog in the collective machine. At the same time, human flourishing generally requires the development of some ultimately positive relationship between individuals and their communities.

A jurisprudential framework that takes account of the pedagogical function of law in a pluralistic liberal democracy will need to be both broad and nuanced. It cannot focus exclusively on the criminal law, which forms just a tiny part of the norms carried by a community's legal system. It must look at tax law, corporate law, family law, and the web of regulations that govern the ordinary details of our lives. All of these legal spheres must be examined with respect to the two senses of laws' virtues: (1) what virtues is the law seeking to inculcate in the populace, and (2) how does the law correspond to the pragmatic criteria laid down by Isidore of Seville? In my view, these criteria for sound law are as valid today as they were fifteen hundred years ago.

The Effects of (Family) Law

Frameworks, Practical Reasoning, Social Norms, Controversy, and Slippage

Brian H. Bix

Introduction

The theme of this book is the impact of law on character formation. My chapter urges significant caution on this gene ral topic, because the impact of law *on anything* is difficult to predict, and law's effects, on careful examination, have frequently been found to be either far less or far different from what lawmakers intended. I will later focus on matters of family law–an area in which I teach and write–sampling some issues of the impact of law on character and virtue.

I must emphasize that this is a work that calls for caution and humility, but not cynicism or despair. I do not claim that law *cannot* (or *should not*) affect character–only that ensuring and measuring its effects are harder than frequently thought, and the results of efforts at forming character are often unexpected and occasionally counterproductive.

In what follows, the first section explores some central and influential views regarding the role and limits of law, while the second section offers examples of the interaction and law and character in the area of family law, before I offer some conclusions.

The Role and Limits of Law

What role should law take in making us better people? In part, this is necessarily a question, first, about what the law *can do*. Here, analytical claims about the limits of what law is able to accomplish inevitably mix with normative claims about what limits should be placed on law (even when still well within the boundaries of what it *can* do); the boundary lines are not always sharp.

What role does law play, or should law play, in general in society? To start at a basic and abstract level, in John Rawls's works about justice and the legal rules of society, he saw the principles of justice as the structure within which people with different comprehensive theories of the good and different objectives could coexist and cooperate.[1] There was then a need for society–through the family and other intermediate institutions–to create and maintain a sense of justice in citizens, but Rawls did not go into great detail as to how this was to be done. However, even if one accepts that the general structure of society is, in a sense, "neutral" between different comprehensive theories of the good, that still leaves open the possibility that legislatures (and other lawmaking institutions) can and should work to create rules that help to form citizens' character.

Another general and abstract observation about law and legal rules: John Finnis and Joseph Raz both argue that legal rules are best seen as a part of practical reasoning generally–that is, reasoning about how individuals should act.[2] Legal rules–either on their own, or through the rewards associated with compliance or the sanctions associated with violation–give citizens reasons for action, to add to whatever moral or religious or prudential reasons they already have. Law is thus seen both as itself a kind of practical reasoning–a working out of ideas through legal science (doctrinal analysis, analogical reasoning, and other forms of legal reasoning)–and a part of every individual's practical reasoning. That role can be direct or indirect. It is direct when someone acts in a particular way, because it is how the law directs behavior (to file taxes on a particular day, to not drive over a certain speed, etc.). It is indirect if someone acts only because of the secondary effects of compliance or noncompliance: a prudential concern about avoiding fines or jail or the reputation of being a criminal and, alternatively, seeking rewards like tax benefits or the reputation of being a good citizen. In general, law is meant to affect behavior and generally does so, but this initial point leaves open the question about what the limits are or should be for such legal efforts.

One suggested limit can be found in the well-known debate between John Stuart Mill and James Fitzjames Stephen.[3] Mill famously asserted: "The only purpose for which power can rightfully be exercised over any member of a civilised community against his will is to prevent harm to others."[4] Mill's argument was that social coercion (through the criminal law or general social pressure) would not be justified if the ground were paternalistic or moral. This has come to be known as "the harm principle." Stephen responded:

---

1 John Rawls, *A Theory of Justice* (Cambridge, MA: Harvard University Press, 1971); John Rawls, *Political Liberalism* (New York: Columbia University Press, 1993).

2 See, for example, Joseph Raz, *Practical Reason and Norms* (Princeton: Princeton University Press, 1990), 149–99; John Finnis, *Natural Law and Natural Rights*, 2nd ed. (Oxford: Oxford University Press, 2011), 314–20.

3 As continued also by later theorists, like Joseph Raz, Michael Moore, Joel Feinberg, and Robert George. See generally the pieces collected in Robert George, *Natural Law, Liberalism, and Morality: Contemporary Essays* (Oxford: Oxford University Press, 1996).

4 J. S. Mill, *On Liberty* (Harmondsworth, Middlesex: Penguin Books, 1974) [originally published, 1859], chap. 1, at 68.

> "How can the State or the public be competent to determine any question whatever if it is not competent to decide that gross vice is a bad thing? ... [T]he object of promoting virtue and preventing vice must be admitted to be both a good one and one sufficiently intelligible for legislative purposes."[5]

While the "harm principle" has remained influential as an argument against certain types of legal regulation (thus raising questions about the project of improving character through the law–at least through law's *coercive* tools), most legal systems have numerous examples of paternalistic or moralistic legal rules.[6]

Another justification for a reluctance to legislate on moral matters can be found in John Finnis's analysis, in which he advocates a position that approximates the concept of subsidiarity. Finnis argues that there are appropriate levels and locations for decisions, and for decisions relating to the leading of a virtuous life the proper locus is the individual, not the state or government. For Finnis, the state still should have a role in *encouraging* virtue–to "encourage, facilitate, and support the truly worthwhile," but he adds that the state should not be required or authorized to "direct people to virtue and deter them from vice" by criminalizing immoral consensual acts between adults.[7]

There is yet another route to this sort of conclusion. As Ronald Dworkin argued, while the state can coerce people into *doing* the correct actions, that is different from making those citizens *good people.* Virtue is about making the right choices, which, Dworkin stated, entails that one has uncoerced choices among alternatives. When the law motivates people to change their lives, their lives are better only if they are in a position *freely and genuinely* to endorse those changes, which cannot occur if the changes are coerced.[8] It takes more than doing the actions a virtuous person would do *to be* a virtuous person. Good moral character is about having the inclinations to do the right thing, and this usually takes something more than, and different from, state coercion.

5 James Fitzjames Stephen, *Liberty, Equality, Fraternity* (Chicago: University of Chicago Press, 1991) [originally published 1874], chap. 4, at 137, 150.

6 Other theorists have offered other principled grounds for creating significant constraints on the reach of the criminal law (not least in matters relating to recreational drugs). See, for example, Douglas Husak, *Overcriminalization: The Limits of the Criminal Law* (Oxford: Oxford University Press, 2008).

7 John Finnis, "Liberalism and Natural Law Theory," *Mercer Law Review* 45 (1994): 687–704, at 697–98. Finnis's examples of immoral acts that the state should not prohibit are the use of contraceptives and homosexual acts. Obviously, not everyone would consider those to be immoral acts, but the point Finnis is making is a general one.

8 Ronald Dworkin, "Liberal Community," *California Law Review* 77 (1989): 479–504, at 484–87.

Moving from what law should (and should not) do, to what law can (and cannot) do, Karl Llewellyn reminds us of a common error of thinking about the law–believing that because a legal rule prescribes something (a) this must describe how citizens actually act, and (b) this rule actually guides judges' decision-making (and does not merely get mentioned in judicial opinions without having actually influenced the court's reasoning).[9] Llewellyn's point is, of course, that one should not be too quick to equate the standard set by the law with the behavior of either citizens or judges. Altering behavior is neither immediate nor easy, and even state guidance and state coercion can misfire. In a way, this is (at least today) an obvious point, but it remains a stubborn habit of thought that all one needs to do to effect change in a certain direction is to pass a law.

On reflection, we all know that law often does not do what we want it to do. Sometimes the law has little discernible effect on behavior because of strong resistance to the changes intended. In the area of civil rights, Gerald Rosenberg has used social-science evidence to question the influence of the United States Supreme Court and other courts in furthering social change.[10] This is in contrast to the idealized picture, common in some circles, that lawyers and courts were central (and effectual) in ridding our society of grave injustices. Another version of this critique argues that social change seems only to happen when the legislatures (also) get involved. In that view, law is still important, but only so long as new laws come from the right sources and in the right way.

In general, there are numerous examples of law having limited effect when it attempts to work against entrenched practices, preferences, and values: not just issues of race in the United States, but also the U.S. attempt to legislate against the consumption of alcohol during the era of Prohibition; and, in India, the difficulties in making inroads against practices regarding caste, dowry, etc. In general, scholars have written at length about the relationship between legal norms and social norms, and what needs to happen if the law is to help alter social norms and practices, and not just wait to follow social norms that have already changed.[11]

---

9 Karl N. Llewellyn, "A Realistic Jurisprudence–The Next Step," *Columbia Law Review* 30 (1930): 431–65, at 441–53.

10 See Gerald N. Rosenberg, *The Hollow Hope: Can Courts Bring About Social Change?* 2nd ed. (Chicago: University of Chicago Press, 2008). Derrick Bell's "interest convergence theory" offers a different skeptical view about law and civil rights, arguing that courts and legislatures will move to protect the rights of minorities only when doing so also serves the interests of the powerful. See Derrick Bell "*Brown v. Board of Education* and the Interest-Convergence Dilemma," *Harvard Law Review* 93 (1980): 518–33. However, this goes more to the motivation of law than to its effectiveness.

11 For example, Cass R. Sunstein, "Social Norms and Social Roles," *Columbia Law Review* 96 (1996): 903–68.

Where the law tries to discourage certain behavior, or encourage certain behavior, through the use of significant penalties or significant rewards, frequently what results is behavior that meets the letter of the law while being contrary to its spirit: what Leo Katz calls "avoision" (a hybrid of "avoidance" and "evasion").[12] Such attempts to get around the law may occur most frequently in areas like tax law and criminal law, but one sees it in family law as well.

Scholars in the field of law and economics have pointed out that "rational" responses to legal rules can similarly undermine their purposes. Antidiscrimination laws can hurt the groups they mean to help, by effectively making hiring members of that group more expensive. The protected class actually becomes, in practice, the burdened class, because potential employers know that any decision to fire, demote, or refuse to promote a member of the class might invite expensive litigation, where similar decisions for employees outside the class would not.[13] In a similar way, rent control and housing-code enforcement can lessen, not increase, the availability of housing to the poor: rent control, by putting a cap on allowable rents at levels that might make housing (or housing improvements) unprofitable for landlords, and thus discouraging the creation of new rental housing; housing-code enforcement by potentially requiring expensive features that increase rent prices beyond what some renters can afford.[14] Similarly, antipollution requirements on automobiles can increase pollution by increasing the costs of new cars that meet the requirement, causing people to keep their (more polluting) older vehicles; and so on.[15]

It was also law-and-economics scholars who reminded us that when the law tries to regulate the interactions of parties through entitlements and civil liability, parties may still contract around those initial legal rights, so that entitlements generally end up with whichever party values them the most.[16] Thus, parties can agree to waive their rights or to send all disputes to a forum (like arbitration without the option of class actions) which is unlikely to lead to rights being fully enforced.[17] Whatever effect law may hope to have on character by granting certain

---

12 Leo Katz, *Ill-Gotten Gains* (Chicago: University of Chicago Press, 1996), 52.

13 See, for example, Richard Posner, *Economic Analysis of Law*, 9th ed. (New York: Wolters Kluwer, 2014), 451.

14 Ibid., 655–56.

15 Ibid., 511.

16 This is the basic insight of Ronald H. Coase in "The Problem of Social Cost," *Journal of Law and Economics* 3 (1960): 1–44. Matters can be complicated by transaction costs, but the basic insight remains.

17 See, for example, Judith Resnik, "Diffusing Disputes: The Public in the Private of Arbitration, the Private in Courts, and the Erasure of Rights," *Yale Law Journal* 124 (2015): 2808–943.

rights to consumers, employees, and tenants may amount to little if those rights can—and will—be waived in contracts of purchase, employment, and tenancy.

Moving from traditional (neoclassical) law and economics to behavioral law and economics[18] does not change the analysis significantly. Studies in behavioral law and economics present empirical research to question the model of human behavior underlying traditional approaches. Based on these empirically grounded changes to the model, behavioral law and economics offers different prescriptions for legal rules intended to alter behavior. The analysis thus incorporates knowledge of cognitive biases in creating incentives and disincentives for action. However, the basic approach has not changed, in that the question is how to change behavior through rules: a focus on actions, rather than character. There is one additional wrinkle to consider here. The traditional law-and-economics approach treats individuals' preferences as exogenous, not subject to alteration through the operation of legal rules. By contrast, some behavioral law-and-economics theorists argue that empirical work shows that legal rules can change our preferences.[19] We can be manipulated into eating healthier foods, putting money aside for retirement, and recycling our garbage. However, as discussed above, in connection with ideas from John Finnis and Ronald Dworkin, I think that there is a difference between the law getting us to do the right things (by force or by trick) and our having a (more) moral character.

Sometimes the disconnect between legal directive and citizen response is subtle and indirect (and hard to predict). This is one of the conclusions advocated by the approach known as the cultural study of law.[20] This school of thought speaks about the "slippage" between intended effects and actual consequences. For example, attempts to prohibit an activity—whether owning guns, wearing a

---

18 On behavioral law and economics, see, for example, Eyal Zamir and Doron Teichman, *Behavioral Law and Economics* (Oxford: Oxford University Press, 2018). On behavioral economics generally (of which behavioral law and economics can be understood as a subset, or an application), see, for example, Daniel Kahneman, *Thinking, Fast and Slow* (New York: Farrar, Straus and Giroux, 2011); Richard H. Thaler, *Misbehaving: The Making of Behavioral Economics* (New York: W. W. Norton & Co., 2015).

19 For example, Ariel Porat, "Changing People's Preferences by the State and the Law," forthcoming in *Theoretical Inquiries in Law* (2020), also at https://papers.ssrn.com/sol3/papers.cfm?abstract_id=3444963. To be sure, at some point the line between preferences and values can become thin, as can the line between collective preferences, collective dispositions, and character.

20 For example, Paul W. Kahn, *The Cultural Study of Law: Reconstructing Legal Scholarship* (Chicago: University of Chicago Press, 1999); Naomi Mezey, "Law as Culture," *Yale Journal of Law & the Humanities* 13 (2001): 35–67; and Naomi Mezey, "Mapping a Cultural Studies of Law," in *The Handbook of Law and Society*, ed. Austin Sarat and Patricia Ewick (Chichester: Wiley Blackwell, 2015), 39–55.

hijab, or drinking alcohol–may actually encourage, rather than discourage, that activity, at least among some groups, as the legal prohibitions unintentionally change the meaning of such actions. Some people may take up a prohibited action not from intrinsic interest but to appear rebellious or dangerous.[21] A less subtle form of legal rules having the opposite of their intended effects is exemplified by the idea of backlash: how the judicial and legislative recognition of a right contrary to the strong views held by many (for example, on abortion, same-sex marriage, the death penalty, or prayer in schools) can lead to a significant countervailing political or cultural response: anything from state legislation meant to circumscribe access to abortions to support for religious exemptions from certain laws to political campaigns supporting candidates who promise to appoint judges with values more consistent with an aggrieved group.[22] The idea of backlash is cousin to the psychological idea of repression: that attempts to suppress a powerful force or drive will rarely succeed entirely, but will only result in its reappearance in some other form and location.

Family Law and Character

This section takes some of the general points already made and applies them to legal rules in the area of family law. Regarding social norms, Naomi Cahn and June Carbone have shown how family practices and family law both diverge sharply between "blue" (culturally liberal) and "red" (culturally conservative) states and communities in the United States.[23] This divergence includes different attitudes regarding what counts as good character in the areas of contraception, abortion, marriage age, nonmarital births, and women's workplace participation. In this comparative story, it is almost certainly a case of legal norms reflecting the social norms of the location, rather than any sense of divergent legal norms *creating* the varying practices and attitudes.

In family law, as elsewhere, the law has tended more often to reinforce changes in social norms that were already under way rather than to lead the

---

[21] Cultural study of law also emphasizes the way that certain ideals–like the rule of law or legal objectivity–are, at best, fictions, but are worthy of study for the way they are used and the role they play in the legal system and in society generally. For example, Kahn, *The Cultural Study of* Law, 31–90 (chap. 2, "Imagining the Rule of Law").

[22] See, for example, Robert Post and Reva B. Siegel, "*Roe* Rage: Democratic Constitutionalism and Backlash," *Harvard Civil Rights-Civil Liberties Law Review* 42 (2007): 373–433; Linda Greenhouse and and Reva B. Siegel, "Before (and After) *Roe v. Wade:* New Questions About Backlash," *Yale Law Journ*al 120 (2011): 2028–87.

[23] Naomi Cahn and June Carbone, *Red Families v. Blue Families* (Oxford: Oxford University Press, 2010).

movement for change. Arguably, this has occurred on topics as diverse as child abuse and neglect, domestic violence and abuse, sexual harassment, and no-fault divorce.[24] Regarding child abuse and neglect and domestic violence, the background change in social norms included a growing consensus that mistreatment of family members was a public concern, not a private matter.[25] Feminist activists and others changed the view of sexual harassment from an accepted part of the workplace (that female employees simply had to live with) to an unacceptable form of workplace sex discrimination.[26] And no-fault divorce was made available after a long period when, in many states, lawyers, judges, and clients had quietly colluded to replace fault with agreement between parties as the practical grounds for many divorces.[27] At least for the examples of child abuse, domestic violence, and sexual harassment, one might argue that the law encourages good character and virtue (the case of no-fault divorce is complicated, and its proper characterization remains controversial), but many would see the role of law itself to be modest compared to other social forces.

Sometimes the resistance to legal rules comes not from the general public but from other officials; we have seen this frequently in the great civil rights struggles, but one also sees it in more mundane family law situations. For example, there are cases where the legislature might instruct courts to remove all gender presumptions, but a maternal preference in custody matters may remain the implicit norm that governs custody for many of the jurisdiction's judges. Another sort of example from family law: statutory and case law may not authorize prenatal orders in surrogacy cases, or stepparent adoptions by same-sex couples,[28] but lawyers know that certain judges will authorize such options–unless and until an appellate court has occasion to order them to stop.

When we think about law's impact on character, one obvious complication is that there is frequently no consensus as to what counts as good character or virtue, at least once one moves from the most general terminology (for example, altruism and honesty) to more specific virtues, attitudes, and attributes. Does a le-

---

24 Catharine MacKinnon was an activist in a number of such areas. Some of her recent reflections on the possibility and limits of legal and social change can be found in MacKinnon, *Butterfly Politics* (Cambridge, MA: Harvard University Press, 2017), 1–33, 325–31.

25 See Barbara Nelson, *Making an Issue of Child Abuse* (Chicago: University of Chicago Press, 1984).

26 See, for example, Catharein MacKinnon, *Sexual Harassment of Working Women: A Case of Sex Discrimination* (New Haven: Yale University Press, 1979).

27 See Lawrence M. Friedman, "Rights of Passage: Divorce Law in Historical Perspective," *Oregon Law Review* 63 (1984): 649–69.

28 This was an important issue before American law changed, allowing same-sex couples to marry.

gal rule (or, more likely, a *set* of legal rules) encouraging marriage increase or decrease virtue and good character? On one hand, the law in such cases encourages parties to make long-term commitments–commitments that seem beneficial to the parties, to any children born to the marriage, and to society generally. On the other hand, some would say that such laws reinforce an institution that critics argue is still deeply sexist, while punishing those who need or prefer alternative family forms (and their children).[29]

For long-term unmarried but cohabiting couples, if the legal standard allows stay-at-home partners some property or alimony rights after the relationship ends, this may effectively discourage marriage for others, but if no remedy is allowed, this will cause suffering for vulnerable and innocent parties who have been in such relationships. Which is the path of greater virtue? Some have argued that a comparable choice–between creating the right incentives for future couples and doing justice for the parties before the court–is present in deciding whether to give substantial and long-term alimony for stay-at-home spouses after a marriage has ended.[30] Similarly, others have pointed out how legal rules meant to create a realistic and appropriate set of entitlements to unwed parents regarding their children (in the United States, often giving greater rights to unwed mothers than to unwed fathers) may also work to reinforce stereotypes and discourage men from taking on the (virtuous) responsibilities of parenthood.[31]

Does allowing gestational surrogacy and enforcing surrogacy agreements increase virtue by allowing infertile couples to have children with the assistance of other (competent and often altruistic) adults? Or would such rules decrease virtue by encouraging the exploitation (through surrogacy) of women in desperate circumstances?[32] And, of course, similar questions can be raised about laws authorizing (or forbidding) the use or sale of donor eggs and sperm, and even the enforcement of contact agreements in the adoption process (so-called open adoptions).

More than thirty years ago, Carl Schneider wrote a well-known article lamenting an apparently diminished willingness of U.S. family law to speak in moral terms.[33] In general, he asserted that "[American] family law has become ever

29 See, for example, Vivian Hamilton, "Mistaking Marriage for Social Policy," *Virginia Journal of Social Policy and the Law* 11 (2004): 307–71.

30 June Carbone, "Economics, Feminism, and the Reinvention of Alimony," *Vanderbilt Law Review* 43 (1990): 1463-501.

31 See Sylvia A. Law, "Rethinking Sex and the Constitution," *University of Pennsylvania Law Review* 132 (1984): 955–1040, at 988–98.

32 For a generally critical view of legal surrogacy, see Martha A. Field, "Compensated Surrogacy," *Washington Law Review* 89 (2014): 1155–84.

33 Carl E. Schneider, "Moral Discourse and the Transformation of American Family Law," *Michigan Law Review* 82 (1985): 1803–80.

more reluctant to discuss and resolve moral problems."[34] He ascribed the perceived change to many factors, including the tradition of government noninterference in the family and "the ideology of liberal individualism." As has been emphasized in this chapter, discussing moral problems and resolving them are two quite different tasks, and one should not too quickly assume that the first will lead to the second. Writing a decade later, Naomi Cahn argued that any perceived "decline in morality in family law" was in fact just a shift in the values being promoted, from sexual fidelity and commitment to "caring, commitment, and equity."[35]

The move from fault divorce to no-fault divorce in the United States may be a good example of the difficulty of speaking about the impact of family law on character or virtue. For a very long time, most American states allowed divorce only on fault grounds; currently, all states have a no-fault option.[36] Part of the idea of fault-only divorce was that divorce should be a remedy or reward given *only* to an innocent and harmed spouse, and there was something unseemly about allowing (for instance) adulterous spouses out of a marriage without hindrance or sanction.[37] It is easy to understand the criticism that the move to no-fault divorce is a move *away from* morality, a move away from encouraging virtue and good character. Even at a more nuanced level, no-fault divorce seems to discourage spouses from investing time and energy into the family ("investments" which would yield no "return" if one's spouse decided to end the marriage and could do so without cause or sanction), while encouraging egoistic investments in self and career (investments that would bring value even in case of divorce).[38]

However, a large part of the original motivation and current justification for no-fault divorce rejects the view that fault-only divorce laws build character or encourage virtue. One concern was that courts are not in a good position to adjudicate actual marital fault; human interactions are complicated, and a recent faulty act may be a response to other faulty acts (which may themselves be less salient and less easy to prove).[39] What fault-based divorce did encourage (along

---

34 Ibid., 1879.

35 Naomi Cahn, "The Moral Complexities of Family Law," "*Stanford Law Review* 50 (1997): 225–71.

36 Some states have a fault alternative as well, and the extent to which states allow "unilateral divorce" still varies state to state.

37 Some states still allow fault to be taken into account in decisions regarding property division or alimony, but this is only a small number of states, and the level of fault generally has to be extreme.

38 See, for example, Martha Minow, "Consider the Consequences," *Michigan Law Review* 84 (1986): 900–18, at 915 (summarizing an argument by Lenore Weitzman).

39 Cf. Elizabeth S. Scott and Robert E. Scott, "A Contract Theory of Marriage," in *The Fall and Rise of Freedom of Contract*, ed. F. H. Buckley, 201–44 (Durham, NC: Duke University Press, 19992), at 41–43.

with some good behavior), the critics say, was massive fraud in many courts (collusive divorce, pretending fault)[40] and litigation trying to prove fault, litigation which tended to be both costly and harmful (especially for couples who need to continue coparenting minor children after the divorce). So it is far from obvious which set of legal rules would best work to encourage character and virtue.

Conclusion

The effect of law on life is unpredictable at best, negligible at worst. (Depending on one's views and one's attitude toward the current government, or governments in general, negligible effects may be exactly what one prefers). Yet it is, of course, *too* pessimistic to think that law has no effect at all on behavior and character. Certainly, criminal sanctions–at least, if effectively, predictably, and fairly applied, and *not* made to go against strong social norms or strong biological impulses–can lead to some measure of outward compliance, if not inward goodness. And law likely can operate to support virtuous social norms, though one should be careful not to overstate the likely force and effect of that support.[41]

In general, the effect of law on character or virtue is a complicated topic. As discussed in this chapter, there are grounds for wondering to what extent law *should* concern itself with such matters (inward virtue, rather than mere prevention of harm to others), with reasonable views on both sides of the question. When these complexities are added to the controversies regarding which side of issues (for example, relating to divorce, abortion, surrogacy, open adoption, etc.) is the side of good character, and to the concern about unintended consequences, the need for caution on these matters is clear. Additionally, there are ways in which legal rules–even laws that fall far short of being "evil"–can work *against* good character. Law can make "self-help, personal involvement and teamwork less enticing,"[42] or make us less inclined to keep our promises.[43] Finally, as empha-

40 See, for example, Friedman, "Rights of Passage."

41 And, of course, there is always the danger that the "elite signaling" (to use John Zaller's phrase) that law provides can just as easily move in the direction of vice as virtue. See, for example, Paul Waldman, "Why Republicans Are Growing More Willing to Embrace Discrimination," *Washington Post*, June 25, 2019, on how support for allowing businesses to discriminate against certain groups on religious grounds can lead to a general increase in discriminatory views and actions among the general population.

42 Saul Levmore, "Addictive Law." SSRN (August 24, 2019), https://papers.ssrn.com/sol3/papers.cfm?abstract_id=3441870, 10.

43 Seana Valentine Shiffrin, "The Divergence of Contract and Promise," *Harvard Law Review* 120 (2007): 708-05.

sized throughout this chapter, there are many ways in which legal rules can have effects far different from what the lawmakers intended.

"There Oughta be a Law About this—Not Necessarily"

The Limits of Law as a Teacher of Value and Virtues

Jean Bethke Elshtain[1]

One of the most eloquent defenses of law in the dramatic theater is put into the mouth of Saint Thomas More by the playwright Robert Bolt.[2] Realizing that his life may well be in jeopardy, given the latest moves by King Henry VIII against the church for not granting the king a divorce, More speaks to his daughter, Meg, and his hot-headed son-in-law, Roper.

> *More:* What would you do? Cut a great road through the law to get to the Devil?
> *Roper:* I'd cut down every law in England to do that!
> *More:* (*Roused and excited*) Oh? (*Advances on* Roper) And when the last law was down, and the Devil turned round on you–where would you hide, Roper, the laws all being flat? This country's planted thick with laws from coast to coast–man's laws, not God's –and if you cut them down ... d'you really think you would stand upright in the winds that would blow then? (*Quietly*) Yes, I'd give the Devil himself benefit of law, for my own safety's sake.[3]

This is stirring stuff. And to those of us from law-governed societies, such as the United States, a society that does political philosophy primarily in the form of constitutional law, it is often all, or nearly all, that needs to be said. "Yes," we cheer. "The rule of law, not of men." It follows that we are often loath to take up the possibility that the law or, perhaps better put, an excess of legalities, may not so much

---

1 This chapter was first presented on October 26, 2007, as the Overton and Lavona Currie Lecture at the Center for the Study of Law and Religion, Emory University, and published as Jean Bethke Elshtain, "'There Oughta be a Law'–Not Necessarily," *Emory Law Journal* 58 (2008): 71-86. It is reprinted here with permission of the Center and the *Journal.* See further Jean Bethke Elshtain, "The Perils of Legal Moralism," *Journal of Law and Politics* 20 (2004): 549.

2 See Robert Bolt, *A Man for All Seasons: A Play in Two Acts* (New York: Vintage Books 1962).

3 Ibid., 38.

protect us against tyranny as itself constitute a tyrannical structure of sorts. This is not a new observation or concern but, rather, a very old one that I hope to illustrate in this chapter. I then go on to contrast legalistic overreaching with the "freedom of the Christian" tethered, as it is, to responsibility. Initially, I will be painting in broad strokes to sketch out some differences between traditions within Christian thought.

The "Inner" and the "Outer": Old Worries, New Concerns

There are intimations of concern in Saint Thomas Aquinas's *Summa Theologica* lest law overreach.[4] Saint Thomas, fretting about legal pride, worries that the law should pretend that it can reach into the human heart, govern interiority, create a kind of moralistic omniscience.[5] Saint Thomas no doubt mentions this because many Christians may be tempted in that very direction. Did not Jesus himself talk about the grave sin of "lusting in the heart" and not just doing a sinful deed? That is so.[6] But Saint Thomas reminds us that only God can see into, pry into human hearts.[7] When human law aims to do so, it is deeply problematic at best, tyrannical at worst. Consider, once again, the words of Thomas More at his trial: "What you have hunted me for is not my actions, but the thoughts of my heart. It is a long road you have opened."[8]

Chastening legal overreach that turns law into a tyranny over human beings requires that law acknowledge that it cannot eliminate or prohibit every human action, because in "seeking to eliminate all evils, one would thereby also take away many goods and not benefit the common good necessary for human companionship."[9] Tyrannical law is no real law at all—no matter how well-intentioned it may be. Given Saint Thomas's high view of law and of law's normative function, his wariness about legal overreach should give us pause. Law is an ordination of reason for the common good. Law helps to habituate human beings to virtue. But, again, there are limits. Not every sin is a crime, and not every sin can or should be punished by the civil law. Law, yes; legalistic overreach, no.

---

4 Saint Thomas Aquinas, *Summa Theologica,* 5 vols., English trans. (London: Fathers of the English Dominican Province, 1947) vol. 1, Q. 91, art. 4, at 998–99.

5 Ibid.

6 Matthew 5:28.

7 Aquinas, Q. 91, art. 4, at 998–99.

8 Again, a line from Bolt's wonderful play and the film by the same title. See *A Man for All Seasons,* 91.

9 Aquinas, Q. 91, art. 4, at 998.

Surely part of what is going on here implicates Saint Thomas's general Aristotelian approach, including the assumption that one's inner world can be transformed as one conforms or habituates to worthy norms. That is, the outer can help to reconfigure the inner. From the point of view of law, behavior counts more than intention, again because the law cannot probe into human hearts–only God can do that. With the coming of Protestantism, one found more stress on interiority–a response and, at times no doubt, an overreaction to Catholic emphasis on "doing," on ritual, on sacraments, on being with others within that strong ecclesiological body, *mater ecclesia.* Protestants–again painting in very broad strokes–invited praying in secret and private devotion, together with participation in church. The dialogic sociality of personal confession was eliminated. Interior transformation precedes exterior behavior. That I finally come to see the light will, in turn, prompt an alteration of how I act in the world.

Law could not help but be affected by these broad changes in orientation. For Saint Thomas, law aimed at a public or common good[10]–always with the proviso that earthly dominion was a good, but never the *summum bonum.*[11] The aim of the law was, in the first instance, regulative, to make regular our social relations and to guarantee, if you will, that society not fall below a level of minimal decency. Law could not make perfect. But how high could it aspire? For Saint Thomas, higher than it could for Saint Augustine, who reckoned that we could reach higher than a den of robbers but perhaps not that much higher most of the time.[12] Saint Thomas put a stronger stress on the *res publica,* so law aims higher–not for ultimacy or perfection, but higher.[13] If, however, law becomes totalistic, it threatens to turn us into spies and informers who try to pry into our neighbors' hearts, look into their windows, and pay less attention to the mote in our own eyes.

The upshot? A golden mean of sorts couched as a warning: do not too readily conflate sins and crimes. A looser social order than what came later is clearly what Saint Thomas works with and knows. This view will no doubt surprise many who see the Middle Ages as an authoritarian time, not least on matters of sex and marriage. But bear in mind that life and work were not yet tied to the clock; the work force was not yet disciplined in the way it later came to be disciplined. This was before the era of identification cards, personal income tax, Social Security numbers, medical records, and all the other insignia of modern identity. Mind

10 Ibid., Q. 96, art. 1, at 1017–18.

11 Ibid., Q. 91, art. 4, at 998–99.

12 See John Mark Mattox, *Saint Augustine and the Theory of Just War* (London: Continuum, 2006), 27.

13 Aquinas, Q. 96, art. 1, at 1017–18.

you, I am not lamenting modernity–just observing a major distinction between then and now.[14]

If anything, the law acquires an even higher normative status with Protestantism.[15] The secular vocations, including housewifery and husbandry, were lifted up. The distance between the spiritual and temporal was reduced. Charles Taylor has called this the "affirmation of ordinary life."[16] I called it "the redemption of everyday life"[17] in my 1981 book, *Public Man, Private Woman: Women in Social and Political Thought*, and certainly part of that redemption or affirmation is the greater expectation that high standards, embodied in law, could be attained and sustained.

Where is the problem? It comes into focus as one recognizes that it is but a few short steps from granting the law a high moral and normative purpose to legal moralism and a quest for perfectionism. We say, concerning nearly every problem and issue, "there oughta be a law," and before you know it, there is another and then another and then another. And sometimes these laws go way too far.

Let me give you an example from my own experience of thirty-five years in the American academy as a teacher. The example is sexual harassment codes. There was a problem, absolutely. How to remedy it? The solution was, frequently, a stifling overreach based on the presumption that all men were rapists *ipso facto.* This was the radical feminist orthodoxy of the 1970 s and 1980 s. Women had been treated to the bitter truth in text after text that all men harbored a desire to rape and ravish. This was provided by Susan Brownmiller, Andrea Dworkin, Catharine A. MacKinnon, Mary Daly, and other legalistic authoritarians. You could not just regulate behavior and punish egregious infractions. You had to try to arrest every possible bad thought, because there was a direct conduit between a

---

14 See Natalie Zemon Davis, *The Return of Martin Guerre* (Cambridge, MA: Harvard University Press, 1983), 82 (alerting us to the old, loosely structured medieval world that is passing and the newer, more Protestant and ordered world that is coming into being.)

15 I think it is fair to say that no one has done more to recuperate this often-glorious history than John Witte Jr. Greater attention was paid to human hearts and inner motivation, not just with the aim of getting people to behave in certain ways but, as well, in holding up a higher set of expectations for the honor and virtue of ordinary folks. See John Witte Jr., *Law and Protestantism: The Legal Teachings of the Lutheran Reformation* (Cambridge: Cambridge University Press, 2002); John Witte Jr. and Robert M. Kingdon, *Sex, Marriage and Family in John Calvin's Geneva* (Grand Rapids, MI: Eerdmans, 2005); and John Witte Jr., *The Reformation of Rights: Law, Religion, and Human Rights in Early Modern Calvinism* (Cambridge: Cambridge University Press, 2007).

16 Charles Taylor, *Sources of the Self: The Making of the Modern Identity* (Cambridge, MA: Harvard University Press, 1989), 13–15.

17 Jean Bethke Elshtain, *Public Man, Private Woman: Women in Social and Political Thought* (Princeton, NJ: Princeton University Press, 1981), 335.

bad thought and an ugly deed, given the ontological taint borne by male human beings.

Do you think I exaggerate? Think again. Go back and reread those texts and tracts and the *remedies* proposed to fight back against the male threat. Thus Brownmiller: "all men" carry a lust to power that comes out as an ideology of rape.[18] Actual rapists are the "shock troops" doing the dirty work on behalf of all men.[19] The man who overtly repudiates rape covertly approves of and benefits from the practice.[20] Thus Mary Daly: men are "demons" sucking the life blood of women. "Like Dracula, the he-male has lived on women's blood."[21] Women who do not share her view are "mutilated, muted, moronized ... docile tokens mouthing male texts."[22] Thus Shulamith Firestone: all women are oppressed because of biology itself. Even the female cocker spaniel is oppressed because she is female.[23] The sexual division itself creates a biological tyranny, and law must be severe to counter this tyranny.[24]

---

18 Susan Brownmiller, *Against Our Will: Men, Women and Rape* (New York: Bantam Books 1976), 4–5.

19 Ibid., 209.

20 Brownmiller comes perilously close to justifying the murder of young Emmett Till. Ibid., at 270–74. She claims to abhor Till's death but insists that the overwhelming thrust of her "evidence" in the case loads the discussion against him, since she knew the Southern white man's "property code." Yet this young teenager, in a macho display of male will-to-power, whistled at a married white woman who happened to be brandishing a gun in his direction at the time. Till's whistle–and not just the woman's gun waving–was, Brownmiller states, a "deliberate insult just short of a physical assault, a last reminder to Carolyn Bryant that this black Boy, Till *had in mind to possess her.*" Ibid., 273 (emphasis added). Here Brownmiller claims to know what is in Till's mind–his intent–and that is germane to her insistence that the whistle is, in her words, an act "just short of physical assault." This is very, very dangerous stuff based on the assumption of the inner state of a fourteen-year-old boy.

21 Mary Daly, *Beyond God the Father: Toward a Philosophy of Women's Liberation* (Boston: Beacon Press, 1985), 172.

22 Mary Daly, *Gyn/Ecology: The Metaethics Of Radical Feminism* (Boston: Beacon Press, 1990), 5.

23 Shulamith Firestone, *The Dialectic of Sex: The Case for Feminist Revolution* (New York: Bantam Books, 1970), 1–15.

24 Again, for those who think I am replowing old ground, I suggest checking out Paul Nathanson and Katherine K. Young, *Legalizing Misandry: From Public Shame to Systematic Discrimination against Men* (Montreal: McGill/Queens University Press, 2006). In this 650-page tome–the second in a promised three-volume series–the authors meticulously document the ways in which a legal double-standard has emerged in Canada and the United States that accepts as fact the most dismal accounts of male-female interactions, whether in marriage, work-life, education, or other fields of human endeavor. This double

Just as radical feminist ideology declared an identity between public and private, so law must eschew altogether any distinction between the intimate and the public and must breach any barrier of inhibition, shame, or taboo. There was, after all, proclaimed Dworkin, a "Dachau in the heterosexual bedroom," so law had to reach into its interstices.[25] Let me be absolutely clear. This went well beyond any level of punishment of physical abuse and violence to become an absolute catechism in which every sin becomes a crime–although the category of sin is, of course, eliminated because God is a patriarchal tyrant who supports female oppression. But you get my point, I trust.

The law reaches into the human heart, for men must be turned inside out, and even then, they could not be trusted unless there was a klieg light shining on every deed, so that any untoward thought could not usher into an action. All men were guilty as charged. It was a small step from that to punishing–as did a sexual harassment code at a university where I was then teaching–"unsolicited ogling." There were also proposals–hence my klieg light reference–to cut down all the trees and bushes on this beautiful campus, because rapists might be lurking there at all times. This natural greenery was to be replaced by klieg lights so that all darkness was repelled.[26]

Every interaction between male and female was to be policed. A sexual code of behavior at one liberal arts college indicated that any touch, any gesture–"May I put my arms around you?" and the like (you can imagine how that might go in a romantic scene)–had to be confirmed by a loud "Yes." Were I a young man in such a situation, I would insist on taping the entire encounter. This fundamental mistrust of people, this loathing of the messily human, was a perverse mirror image of the uplifting of the ordinary that I characterized as one feature of the rise of

---

standard is the work of what the authors call "ideological feminism," in contrast to the "egalitarian feminism" they endorse. Ibid., 269–308, 325. The long list of legislative initiatives alone offers compelling evidence of an urge not to right the balance, but to criminalize maleness itself in many instances. I should note that the book is published by a respectable university press and is written by two liberals. One has to say these things, or books of this nature, tackling a subject most prefer to avoid, are discounted before anyone has even cracked them open.

25 Andrea Dworkin, *Pornography: Men Possessing Women* (New York: Perigee Books, 1981), 68–69.

26 This suggestion put me in mind of an excellent film portraying National Socialist Germany by following an actor, devoted to his craft, as he continues to act under Nazi conditions. At the film's terrifying denouement, the protagonist is suddenly trapped as klieg lights–a horrible parody of the stage lights that he, an actor, loves–come on, the sirens blare, and he is a captive of the totalitarian state. Everything is always illuminated; there is no place to evade the klieg lights of the omnipresent state.

Protestantism. It turns out that we trusted people too much. Now we've got to clamp down.

The upshot was that all of this made young women not stronger but weaker. How were they to feel, up against what they were told was such a relentless, implacable foe–and this is what the law, certainly the campus law, told her, too. All must be regulated; human sociality, or at least male being, is so thoroughly corrupted that nothing else is possible.[27] Legal overreach makes people weak; removes responsibility and an appropriate level of culpability; puts everything in the hands of tort lawyers and gives to judges in excess, and all the rest we know way too much about.

Each one of us can produce examples. One wonders: what sort of person does not know coffee is hot?[28] As I worked on this chapter, there came a report that a six-year-old boy was suspended from school for drawing two smiling stick figures –he and his school chum.[29] The suspended artist is depicted shooting at his school chum as little circles come out of his gun. Turns out, the boy was representing a water pistol that he and his best friend were using while at play. But the child was declared a threat under the school's new draconian code, so it was suspension time.[30]

This is one small example of the sort of thing I am talking about–criminalizing normal, innocent forms of child behavior. It bespeaks a desire for a legally sanitized world with no slack in the order, with little boys being suspended for drawing stick figures, and for sandbox sexual harassment. In this scheme of things, all must be construed though the lens of the legal or illegal, the permitted or forbidden. And, *pace* Saint Thomas, we do think we can pry into human hearts. Alas, legal moralism does *not* guarantee a decent order. It can, in fact, constitute a great disorder.

I realize it is too easy to draw examples from National Socialist Germany–a very legalistic society with new laws being promulgated nearly every day to cov-

---

27 I recall one student telling me that the fact that *Playboy* magazine was sold in a news-and-magazine shop in the town in which the university was located–just the fact that it was there, albeit in brown wrapper and behind a counter–was so emotionally draining that she could scarcely crawl out of bed in the morning. Clearly, this young woman needed professional help, but instead, she was constantly fed a diet of intense rage and fear that worsened her condition.

28 The reference here is to the infamous case involving take-out coffee from a fast-food chain that spilled, apparently, when the customer opened it. The customer suffered a burn, going on to sue for millions.

29 See Associated Press, "7-Year-Old Suspended over Stick-Figure Drawing," MSNBC, Oct. 21, 2007, http://www.nbcnews.com/id/21397455/ns/us_news-education/t/-year-old-suspended-over-stick-figure-drawing/#.Xz2AIkl7mRs.

30 Ibid.

er nearly every vice, including the vice of secretly harboring antiregime notions, even though one had said or done nothing–a habit some in Europe got into with the French Revolution.[31] I do not intend to do an *ad Hitlerum* here. But there are aspects to Nazi law that should concern us and compel us to focus on grave matters. We all know about and deplore the race laws and the eugenics madness. But I am going to report on something else: the expansive public-health laws of the Third Reich. Because German doctors had articulated the link between smoking and lung cancer in the 1920 s, the Third Reich prohibited all public smoking, even by soldiers; pushed nonsmoking for pregnant women, who were, after all, mothers of the master race (or at least some mothers were); pushed herbal and homeopathic medicine and alternative treatments against the "Jewish science" of much of modern medicine; forced prisoners at Dachau to tend to the largest herbal gardens in Europe; and pushed vegetarianism. All this while they were murdering Down syndrome children and other persons with mental or physical handicaps.[32]

Why mention all this? Because the rush to become legally virtuous–in a totalizing way–does not mean a society is, in fact, virtuous. It may be anything but virtuous. The fact that we get on a moralistic high horse about something, like smoking, does not necessarily signal how advanced we are or have become. In fact, pettiness may reign rather than virtue. For example, our own censorious totalists now want to go back into the classics of cinema and air brush out cigarettes –Bogie without a cigarette in *Casablanca* as he sits at the table at Rick's Cafe. Once you start mucking about with film classics, you are going a statute too far. We lose a sense of history and place in this manner, even as we pat ourselves on the back about just how advanced we have become.

The way things used to work was by means of a moral object lesson–to wit, when I was an eighth grader, we signed a pledge never to allow demon rum to pass over our lips; this followed a dramatic display of the dangers of drink when an earthworm was dropped into a glass of gin and appropriately, and predictably, shriveled up and died. Of course, water would have invited the same outcome, although it might have taken a bit longer, but one was not supposed to point that out. The enforcer of that pledge, however, was one's own conscience. One of my eleven-year-old grandsons this year had to sign a pledge at his school never to bully anyone, a document that has the force of law in the school. Bullying is left tantalizingly vague. Is sticking up for yourself bullying? If, in our political culture,

---

31 The result was forty thousand people guillotined, 70 percent of them working-class. Hannah Arendtmarks the distinction between the French Revolution and its prying into human hearts and the very different approach to law, politics, and inner life in the American Revolution. Arendt insists that the entry of "the heart" into politics is in general dangerous and often pernicious. Hannah Arendt, *On Revolution* (New York: Viking Press, 1966).

32 The complete, sad story is found in Robert Proctor's award-winning book, *The Nazi War on Cancer* (Princeton, NJ: Princeton University Press, 1954).

those who take to the airwaves to proclaim that they are being censored and marginalized–because someone has the audacity to disagree with them–are then thought to have been bullied, it does not take much of an imagination to see an overzealous "manager" construing a vigorous disagreement as an instance of someone, probably the boy, bullying someone else. And it is not one's conscience that is the enforcer now–it is the lopsided legalistic structure that we have invented and secured in our schools and universities and nearly everywhere else.

Consider another example from our recent legislation and the culture that fueled it. I refer to the category of the hate crime. When hate-crime legislation was first debated, I recalled in my study of early medieval legal codes–in the Frankish clans and tribes–a system called the *wergeld*, whereby lopping off the arm of the lord was a far more serious offense than lopping off the arm of the peasant or serf. Arms are missing in each instance, but the one was a more punishable crime than the other. So, too, is the case with hate crimes. A person has been murdered. But we rank the victim morally and legally higher in our estimation if he is black, homosexual, or from some other category against whom hate crimes are most likely to occur in the view of those who formulate such legislation. We do this by assessing murder a more egregious offense in the case of a hate crime than a plain, old-fashioned murder. Is this not a disparate valuing of human beings when the focus should be on the dreadful equality of violent death?

On what does the determination of a hate crime turn? Once again, we pry into the human heart. Does it not suffice that a precious human life has been taken, for there is an objective offense here, a rending of the fabric of the moral universe? Punish the crime of murder. If the victim is the white, male CEO of an international global conglomerate, does his life count for less than that of the gay man attacked on his way home from a gay bar on a Saturday night?[33] A human life is a human life.

We can never adequately plumb motive. Who can really figure out the mass murderers–the Stalins, the Hitlers, or the Ted Bundys? Many have tried, and all such efforts come up short–often because those who try nowadays have expunged their terms of discourse of any reference to evil or sin. Be that as it may, surely the important question is, *What* did they do? Severely punish the deeds. God will deal with the human heart. As the saying goes, if the law could look into our hearts, none would escape whipping. Our lives are structured through and

---

33 There are ideological claims that, if taken seriously, create a situation in which a member of "the oppressor class"–white and male–is always culpable for a hate-crime possibility, whereas members of the "oppressed classes"–women, blacks, gays, etc.–cannot *by definition* be guilty of hate crimes. The law, of course, does not state this. But there is an underlying assumption that runs along these lines, making it far more likely–depending to some extent on jurisdictions–that the leap to hate crime will come more readily if the alleged perpetrator is male and white.

through with certain saving graces, tissues that make life bearable–hypocrisies some would say.[34] I speak here of saving graces and the moral equality of persons, something hate-crime legislation violates in believing that motivation in and of itself is a punishable offense, an add-on to the crime of homicide.

I recognize that the above claims concerning hate crimes are highly controversial and quite easy to misconstrue. I by no means wish to minimize racially (or any other) prejudicial form of hate that may goad someone to violence. This is a very tough issue in a society with a long history of racial tension. But there is, once again, a real danger in the aspiration toward comprehensiveness here; trying to find a covering law for everything, including adding hate as an additional punishable offense. In a loaded racial context, this is understandable, but it often stokes the fires of racial suspicion and hatred. It is widely assumed that motive is relevant to the degree of punishment. But there is a fundamental difference when hate-crime law lifts the relevance of motive from judicial judgment about punishment to a statutory categorization.[35]

We can never satisfactorily separate intention, motivation, and other "inner" drives as directly causal to "the deed," although good police work often helps to discern whether a murder is one of highly personal rage or a more impersonal desire to kill just anyone who happens to pass by. Again, such information is entirely appropriate and quite important to take into account in a judicial proceeding. We also assess situations by whether a victim was entirely helpless or whether the victim was killed during a mutual altercation, and so on. The law discriminates in many essential ways. But to lay on a global, generic category like "hate crime" opens the way to legalistic overreaching and the differential valuation of persons. That is what I oppose.

Finally, I will turn to one architect of lofty legalism, Immanuel Kant. The anti-Nazi German theologian Dietrich Bonhoeffer characterized Kant, the great philosopher, as a tormenter of humanity.[36] I will not provide a complete discussion, but I want to say enough to put into place portions of Bonhoeffer's critique of Kant, and then go on to offer a real-world example from current international relations that shows how problematic a hard Kantianism can be in practice. Bonhoeffer, in

---

34 A homey example: We say "Thanks, Aunt Mildred, for this ... er ... embroidered thingy." In the interest of full transparency, we *should* say: "I don't want this dreadful thing. Here, take it back." Truth, and nothing but the truth, can be an exceedingly cruel taskmaster. There are saving graces in telling innocent untruths, if that is the best way to put it. Our relationship with Aunt Mildred, our basic God-given human sociality, is far more important than whether we really dislike the embroidered thingy.

35 I thank Kent Greenawalt for pushing me to clarify this issue and for offering challenging suggestions.

36 See Dietrich Bonhoeffer, *Ethics* [1955], ed. Eberhard Bethge, trans. Neville H. Smith (New York: Macmillan, 1968), 365–69, 369n1.

the name of Christian freedom, takes Kant to task in his book *Ethics*, in a chapter titled "What Is Meant by 'Telling the Truth'?"[37]—which some have mistakenly construed as a piece of situationist ethics. It is not. Rather, it is a preliminary foray into the area of legalistic-moralistic overreach in the name of truth, an approach Bonhoeffer links to Kant's severe deontology.[38]

Bonhoeffer reminds us that it is Kant who insisted one must give an honest answer to the query put by a would-be murderer as to whether his intended victim, and one's friend, is hidden on the premises.[39] If the friend is indeed hidden, then one has no choice—for the prohibition against lying is absolute—but to reveal this fact and to give one's friend over, thereby, to the murderer. This Kantian answer invites the comment I alerted us to earlier, when Bonhoeffer calls Kant a tormenter of humanity. Kantian severity breaks sociality, breaks friendship, splits us off from the responsibilities of *caritas*, of tending to the bleeding brothers and sisters of Jesus Christ.[40] Certainly, Christians did face the prospect that the scenario was none too hypothetical —at least those who put themselves on the line as rescuers did. Suppose the Gestapo knocks on the door and asks, "Is your Jewish neighbor hidden within?" Well, if you are a Kantian deontologist you must say yes.[41] We are familiar with the severity of categorical imperatives: they cannot be modified and cannot conflict with one another. One lives in a rigid and overly simple moral universe in Kant's world. There is insufficient nuance, a lack of awareness of the fact that the raggedy ends of lived life do not conform to a deontological grid. So the Jewish neighbor is given over to his *depradator*. I do not exaggerate. This is the outcome. Kant, quite unconvincingly, said, in response to criticism, "After you have honestly answered the murderer's question as to whether his intended victim is at home, it may be that he has slipped out so that he does not come in the way of the murderer, and thus that the murder may not be committed.[42] But the die was cast.

In the name of responsibility, in the name of *caritas*, in the name of Christian freedom, Bonhoeffer insists: do not break the bonds of sociality; do not deny the neighbor.[43] Bonhoeffer argues that a school child speaks more "truth" in denying a teacher's accusation that the child's father is a drunk—even though the father is a drunk—because the child speaks to the truth of fundamental human social-

---

37 Ibid., 363–72.

38 Ibid.

39 Ibid., 369n1.

40 Ibid., 365–66.

41 See Immanuel Kant, "On a Supposed Right to Lie from Altruistic Motives," in Immanuel Kant, *Absolutism and Its Consequentialist Critics* [1797], ed. Joram Graf Haber (Lanham, MD: Rowman & Littlefield, 1994), 15.

42 Ibid., 17.

43 Bonhoeffer, *Ethics*, 365–66.

familial relations, which the teacher ought not to be in the business of assaulting publicly.[44] If you follow the deontological line and add to it some of the histrionic overreach I alerted us to earlier with the eradication of any public or private distinction, you may wind up in a legalistic nightmare where, as Bonhoeffer says, everything has a placard posted on with either the word "permitted" or "forbidden."[45]

Another area one might probe at present with legalism, including its deontological form, is the fraught matter of torture and contemporary warfare (at least the American version). Some of the legalists have argued that interrogators should go before a judge and seek "torture warrants" to permit them to legally torture a terrorist suspect who likely has–with a very high degree of probability–information that, if revealed, would save many human lives.[46] Such warrants seem to me a stunningly bad idea.[47] Nowadays we are making warfare, as waged by the United States, more and more a legalistic matter. Soldiers are hemmed about with a slew of legalisms. I am *not* referring to rock-bottom, fundamental *jus in bello* rules of engagement dictating that you do not target civilians. Instead, I have in mind taking some account of the anxiety and fear in ordinary soldiers that they might commit a legal infraction based on a split-second decision made under the stress of battle, in the realm of harsh necessity.

Imagine the soldier who, upon seeing a mortally wounded enemy with a hideous head wound–someone who cannot possibly survive–and, to be merciful, administers a *coup de grâce*–then finds himself hauled up on charges. Once again, we see the inverse of the uplifting of the capacity of ordinary people for making decent judgments, even under conditions of horrible stress. We need the laws of war, and we have had them for hundreds of years now. But these must be tempered by the realities of war and the imperfections of human judgment under such stress. Soldiering is a rule-governed activity in the just war tradition, which is by no means identical to being legalistically overdetermined. For every soldier in the field nowadays, someone estimated that there are seven civilian lawyers making determinations about everything from mission to uniforms to diet. Is this proliferation of legalistic codes making warfare more humane? No, legalisms do not do that. Training in the norms of *jus in bello* do, however, together with new generations of weapons with less destructive collateral damage.

In fact, excessive legalism can also become an easy way out for soldiers in particular circumstances. Arguably, this happened during the bombing of Serbia

---

44 Ibid., 367–68.

45 Ibid., 24.

46 See, for example, Alan Dershowitz, "Tortured Reasoning," in *Torture: A Collection*, ed. Sanford Levinson (New York: Oxford University Press, 2004), 257–80.

47 Jean Bethke Elshtain, "Reflections on the Problem of 'Dirty Hands,'" in Levinson, *Torture*, 77, 83.

at the height of the Kosovo campaign by NATO. Lawyers and ethicists legitimated targets and soon ran out of those targets. Secretary of State Madeleine Albright had insisted that the Serbian leader, Slobodon Milosevic, would capitulate in seven days, but he did not. It became more difficult to find appropriate targets. Legalistically driven, hair-splitting calculations were entered into that were very troubling to someone working within the ethical framework of the just war tradition. Again, the onus of responsibility was taken off the soldiers–the military trained in the laws of war, which are infused with *jus in bello* restraints–and put in the hands of lawyers: if it is legal, it is okay. This does not seem to me the way war ought to be conducted.[48]

I turn to a final example, also drawn from current international relations. As I have already indicated, once you get into the realm of laws, norms, and rules, categorical imperatives are ready at hand. In the stronger deontological versions, one finds a tight combination of teleological certainty ushering into "perpetual peace"–from the title of Kant's famous essay–and in this world one law governs all.[49] The will to war is no more. Observe that you must go in and extirpate a "will," an "intent." As for Kant, what matters is a good will. Kant offers a hard teleology whereby nature has dictated this and so there is a kind of inevitability. Nature herself wills that something should follow.

The British international relations scholar Martin Wight warned that followers of Kantian ideals "could be merciless and unrestrained .... They could see themselves as righteous agents of historic necessity bringing about a better world."[50] For this reason, Wight concludes that "if you are apt to think the moral problems of international politics are simple, you are a natural, instinctive Kantian."[51] And, as we all know, those who are in possession of a Grand Telos very commonly look askance at those of us who are more inclined to agree with Max Weber that politics is, most of the time, the "slow boring of hard boards."[52]

---

48 For a more complete detailing of this story, see Jean Bethke Elshtain, "Humanitarian Intervention and Just War: The Grotius Lecture," *American Society of International Law Proceedings Annual Meeting* (2001): 1.

49 Immanuel Kant, *Perpetual Peace and Other Essays on Politics, History, and Morals,* trans. Ted Humphrey (Indianapolis, IN: Hackett Publishing 1983) 107–44.

50 Martin Wight, *Four Seminal Thinkers in International Theory: Machiavelli, Grotius, Kant, and Mazzini,* ed. Gabriele Wight and Brian Porter (New York: Oxford University Press, 2005), xli. For the work that prompted Wight's response, see Robert Latta, *Preface to Immanuel Kant, Perpetual Peace: A Philosophical Essay,* trans. M. Campbell Smith (London: George Allen & Unwin, Ltd., 1917).

51 Wight, *Four Seminal Thinkers,* 33.

52 Max Weber, *From Max Weber: Essays in Sociology* [1946], trans. H. H. Gerth and C. Wright Mills (New York: Oxford University Press, 2001), 238.

An additional instance of the severity of Kantian international politics is present in the realm of humanitarian intervention. Humanitarian intervention is not a new thing–it has been talked about in one way or another for centuries. For Augustine, sparing the innocent from certain harm is a legitimate *casus belli* for an outside party to bring military force to bear.[53] Current discussions of humanitarian intervention stress "right intention," a criterion, of course, of just war doctrine. It follows, according to such advocates of humanitarian intervention, that humanitarian intervention must be entirely disinterested. How so? Disinterestedness is not entailed in the classic just war notion of right intention–nothing so severe as that; no probing to be certain one's motives are entirely pure, if you will. If humanitarian intervention requires an a priori right intention criterion construed as disinterestedness, we will never see humanitarian intervention. Augustinian Christianity teaches that all human motives are mixed; we are limited, finite creatures who will and nill simultaneously. Absolute purity of intention we are not going to find–not on this earth. An antiperfectionist Augustinian perspective insists that one cannot eradicate *superbia* (pride) or the *libido dominandi* (the lust to dominate), in human affairs on any and every level. You can attempt to deflect or mute these effects, but the law should be modest in this regard, as human action can never be entirely sanitized.

Advocates of humanitarian intervention, operating within a Kantian-infused peace politics, push disinterestedness with scant regard to the very *raison d'être* of the state, which is "to protect its own citizens and to defend the national interest: an absolute disinterestedness would be, by definition, a grave failure of the state's responsibility."[54] Do mixed motives disqualify humanitarian intervention? Kant would say yes, because there can be no consequentialist consideration of any kind; all must be transparent, nothing held in reserve. If we accept that all human motives are a complex admixture, a humanitarian intervention is not perforce invalidated if it overlaps other political motives.

How, indeed, could one possibly disentangle them? When the hard-core legalists get hold of this, however, they add to disinterestedness a requirement that humanitarian intervention must be approved by the United Nations, which pretty much guarantees that little or nothing will be done to save lives.

There is much, much more to be said on this, but let us conclude with Kant in this way: "[I]t is as naïve to believe that a purely humanitarian intervention is possible in the reality of international relations as to believe that an intervention that is not at first motivated by humanitarian goals cannot have, in fact, a human-

53 See Jean Bethke Elshtain, *Just War Against Terror: The Burden of American Power in a Violent World* (New York: Basic Books, 2003), 57.

54 Jean-Baptiste Jeangène Vilmer, "Humanitarian Intervention and Disinterestedness," *Peace Review: A Journal of Social Justice* 19 (2007): 207, 208.

itarian effect."[55] Remember, "By their fruits ye shall know them," scripture tells us. By their fruits.

We would do well to recall the words of Dr. Martin Luther King Jr., who, at one point, at the height of the civil rights struggle, cried: "We're not asking you to love us, just get off our backs."[56] Just behave. There is no need to convert, however, because in behaving one might just convert along the way. King imagines the possibility of what Saint Thomas hearkened to: altered behavior over time may bring about inner change.

Let me acknowledge a danger in the position I am staking out here–or the bits and pieces of what would be a position, were I to get more systematic. I want to recall a famous exchange between Sigmund Freud and Albert Einstein on the question, "Why War?"[57] For Freud, war happened because people had not sufficiently rearranged their interior furniture[58]–they were still driven by what Augustine would call the *libido dominandi.*[59] In peaceful times, matters of such inner transformation–or not–are rarely put to the test. The law restrains reckless and violent behavior. But when the barriers are down, one learns who has truly been reconstituted internally and cannot find it in his or her heart to hate sufficiently to kill–for Freud assumed, wrongly, I believe, that wartime killing was always accompanied by hate.[60] Freud's assumption here is a very Protestant enterprise, one might say. He even opined in an essay that we must take moral responsibility for our dreams.[61] Freud thought he was offering a secular substitute for Catholic confession, but in the interiorizing of the subject he is surely more Protestant, even Puritan.

Be that as it may, I submit that the democratic wager is such that we cannot base our law, our politics, and our social relations on worst-case scenarios: all men are rapists; all human beings are beasts underneath; the patina of civilization is shockingly thin, and the like. We simply must make the wager: most human beings most of the time are capable of minimally decent behavior, even if, from time to time, they harbor murderous thoughts. The law cannot get into those thoughts,

---

55 Ibid., 212.

56 Jeff Weintraub and Krishan Kumar, *Public and Private in Thought and Practice: Perspectives on a Grand Dichotomy* (Chicago: University of Chicago Press, 1997), 178.

57 For the fascinating exchange, prompted by a short query from Einstein, see "Why War?," in *The Standard Edition of the Complete Psychological Works of Sigmund Freud: New Introductory Lectures on Psycho-Analysis and Other Works,* ed. and trans. James Strachey (London: Vintage, 1968), 22:199–215.

58 Ibid., 209.

59 See Lucy Beckett, *In the Light of Christ* (San Francisco: Ignatius Press, 2006), 111.

60 See Freud, *Standard Edition*, 22:209.

61 See Sigmund Freud, *Moral Responsibility for the Content of Dreams,* in Freud *Standard Edition,* 19:131.

and the law will run amok if it tries. We will all be suffocated and, ironically, because we think law covers everything, we may, in fact, let down our guard in how we form minimally decent societies. I end on a note of Christian freedom, here putting together Augustine, Saint Thomas, and Luther in a salutary way. A full treatment of these fraught issues awaits another day.

The Law as Educator?

Rüdiger Bittner

Introduction

"Law" is going to refer here, not to the body of laws valid in some society, whether written statutes or rules of adjudication established by custom, or even principles deemed to hold independently of human institution. The term will refer instead to the set of legal practices comprising the production, interpretation, application, and enforcement of laws as well as the training and selection of those who carry out these practices. Thus, law is here going to be a set of things people do, and so it can itself be called a practice, a big one. Individual laws–that is, statutes, rules, principles, etc.–function in this practice like props on a stage: they are employed in the legal practices. Think of the usage where people are said to be "in the law," meaning that they do some sort of legal work: that in which they are then said to be is what is here meant by "the law." (In German one might speak of *das Rechtswesen* in contrast to *das Recht.*)

The question before us is this: can the law, so understood, serve as a moral landmark, that is, as something by reference to which individuals who differ in their thinking and acting and upbringing, in their aims, attitudes, and commitments can, as by the spire of the village church, determine the right path for them to take? The question is especially relevant with regard to education: can the law, important as this practice is for life in present societies, guide us in bringing up a new generation? My answer is going to be that the law cannot so serve. It cannot be our guide in general or regarding education in particular. In what follows I shall first give two arguments to make this negative answer plausible and then try to show that its truth is no reason for concern.

The Law Is Not Unified

The reason for denying the law the function of moral landmark is not that law is a practice of human institution and varies with time and place. Moral orientation does not need to be provided by something we were given or something that we found, like the laws handed down from Mount Sinai or some basic feature of human nature. It may well be based merely on human practices and what emerges from them. Nor need we search for a guidance invariable over time and place. There is moral learning, not just for individuals but for cultures, too, and we can come to know better in moral matters. To leave room for that growth in knowledge, we should aspire to no more than moral orientation "for the time being," not to an orientation that is protected from being superseded by better insight. The law as it exists today, the result of a vast number of things various people did,[1] and differing widely in different places, is not thereby, then, disqualified from serving as a moral landmark.

Rather, the law is disqualified from so serving by the fact that it is not one but a lot of things, namely, a lot of things people do. Note the difference: what disqualifies the law is not that the law here is other than the law there, or that today it is other than it was yesterday. What disqualifies it is the fact that the law here and today is diverse in itself. A mere bunch of things people do will not give moral orientation. The result is the same if by "law" we should understand (other than proposed here) the set of laws valid somewhere: a collection of texts or established rules does not give moral orientation any more than varied practices do. True, they might: if the things people do, or the laws which make up the law could be assumed to be all pulling together, then that common undertaking could serve as the moral center by reference to which to understand, judge, and adjust our steps. Yet given pluralism, which is and will remain the condition under which we are living together, there is no reason to think that people's doings which make up the law, or the texts and rules they use, are pulling together, they are pulling hither and thither. Thus, they cannot serve as a moral assembly point. They are as disconcerted as we ourselves are.

This is to raise doubts about the very terms in which the question before us is cast, namely, as a question about the realities and potentials of law as one of the "powerful social systems" which have their own "internal value systems, institutionalized rationalities, and normative expectations that together help to shape each individual's morality and character." While we cannot examine here what the conception of law as a social system in general amounts to and how useful it is for understanding the role of law in current societies, all the particular assumptions implied in the expressions just quoted are contestable. No, law does not come with an internal value system (more on this in the following section), it does not have a rationality of its own (there are no different rationalities, just rationality), and while those in the law may harbor certain expectations, the law

---

1 See Friedrich Nietzsche, *Zur Genealogie der Moral* (1887), in Nietzsche, *Sämtliche Werke*, Kritische Studienausgabe, ed. G. Colli and M. Montinarieds (Berlin: de Gruyter, 1980), 2:12–13.

itself does not. Most importantly, we should give up thinking of law as a "powerful social system."

It is not the law, a collection of what people do, that has power; it is the people themselves who, partly thanks to their position within the institutions of law, hold various powers and, thus empowered, do various things to people. In doing them, however, they pursue a wide variety of aims. It is an unwarranted simplification, indeed a kind of modern mythology, to suppose that in whatever they do they are basically pursuing one thing, or two, like justice and order. The alleged unity of the law, as an agent of its own, which can be said to be valuing, expecting, pursuing things, and the like, is in fact merely nominal. It is we who, guided by a number of similarities, cut out from the mass of what people do a certain subset and call it the law. We should not fall into the conceptualist trap and endue what we so demarcate with substantiality or even with agency.

The Law Cannot Be Trusted

This is the first reason for saying that the law cannot serve as a moral landmark: it lacks the required unity, it does not speak with one voice. Assume now that all this is wrong. The law *is* a powerful social system, it *is* an agent of its own, giving individuals determinate directions for action. Here, then, is the second reason for saying that the law cannot serve as a moral landmark: even if it is supposed to be capable of guiding us, it cannot be trusted to guide us right.

It cannot be trusted because it does not have so much as a moral commission; it is not in the moral business at all. Even assuming that the set of practices called the law is unified enough to be aiming at one thing, that aim need not have any moral significance. To be sure, it may, but then as well it may not, or it may even have negative moral significance. Moral distinctions just cut across the law's purpose, assuming there is one. The law with more or less success tries to regulate what people do. The moral merit or demerit of the regulations is irrelevant to this endeavor.

That used to be different, or it used to be supposed to be different. The law, that is, used to be seen as in principle trustworthy in guiding people to doing what is right to do. Socrates is reported by Xenophon as saying that acting rightly is the same as acting in accordance with the laws of the city,[2] and as late as 1821 Hegel quotes with approval a certain Xenophilos's remark, reported by Diogenes Laërtius,[3] that the best way to educate people is to make them citizens of a city

[2] Xenophon, *Memorabilia* IV, 4, 12.

[3] Diogenes Laërtius, *Vitae* VIII, 16.

with good laws.[4] This trusting attitude came to grief most prominently with the Nazis' seizure of the law in 1933. The Weimar Republic could claim to be a state with reasonably good laws, so by that criterion it should have been advisable to let that state morally guide people, and in particular to leave the moral education of the young to their life in that state. Actually, that was not advisable. After 1933 it was right to educate people in Germany in opposition to, not in accordance with, what they were taught by the laws of the state.

So Socrates and Xenophilos are wrong. The laws cannot be trusted. Acting in accordance with them is not always right, and the education of the young cannot always safely be left to them. Sure enough, it is a child once burnt who is speaking here. That does not weaken the point, though; on the contrary. However, once you shed all basic trust in the laws, you need to find out on your own whether the situation confronting you is one for following the law, for quietly disregarding, or for positively defying it. The law will not serve as a moral landmark. It will be just one of the uncounted voices that have been addressing you since childhood, pretending to tell you which path to take. It is one of the uncounted voices about whose trustworthiness you will have formed your own more or less definite judgment.

In fact, it did not take the political experiences of the twentieth century to teach us that the law cannot be trusted. Sophocles's *Antigone,* first performed around 442 BCE, makes the point quite effectively. Creon's decree that Polynices be left unburied is valid law in Thebes, and neither Antigone nor anyone else in the play denies that it is. She just thinks it is a law which, while valid, it is still wrong to obey, and the play invites us to agree with her. So here already we learn that the law cannot be trusted, and that you need to determine yourself what to do about a law's command.

It will be countered that the law does have a moral commission, that it is essentially linked to justice. Thus Augustine made justice a condition for something's being a law,[5] and many authors followed him in insisting that laws, merely to be laws, need to be just. With regard to the present issue, however, this insistence does not advance matters. We want to know whether the existing practices which we call law can be trusted to guide us morally, and Augustine's and his followers' refusal to call them law unless they are just does not speak to this question; it is only a verbal maneuver. Indeed, implying that what he calls law is a subset of what is commonly called law, Augustine suggests a negative answer to our question: no, the practices actually existing in some society which we, though not he, call law, cannot be entrusted our moral guidance, because they are morally unreliable.

---

4 G. W. F. Hegel, *Grundlinien der Philosophie des Rechts*, ed. J. Hoffmeister, 4th ed. (Berlin: Meiner, 1955), § 153, at p. 143.

5 Augustine, *De libero arbitrio* I 11, 33.

More promising here may appear the position of Gustav Radbruch, who served in the Weimar Republic as minister of justice, and whose writings later had a formative influence on constitutional jurisdiction in the Federal Republic. Radbruch held that "law is the reality whose sense it is to serve the idea of law," and that idea is justice.[6] Having the sense to serve justice, however, is compatible for Radbruch with actually not serving it, with being unjust. Thus he explicitly admits that there are laws which are not as they ought to be.[7] Still, they are law for him only because, while unjust, they are still directed toward justice.[8] This distinction between the character of the law itself and the idea of law to which it is directed allowed him to develop in 1946[9] the formula that was later adopted by the German constitutional court for dealing with the legal problems arising after the end of Nazi rule,[10] and later after the end of the German Democratic Republic (DDR).[11] The formula essentially says that, in principle, unjust law is still law and must be applied by the courts regardless of being unjust, but that sometimes the conflict between law and justice becomes so sharp as to be intolerable, and then the alleged law can no longer be considered law by the courts.[12]

In fact, Radbruch's line is once again open to doubt. For what can it even mean to say that some act within the law, a piece of legislation or a verdict, say, has the sense to serve justice while it actually is unjust? It could mean that the agents of the act intended it to be just but failed to achieve what they intended. That certainly is a common fate, but generally to explain law's directedness toward justice in this way requires supposing that everyone acting within the law strives to bring about justice, and that is implausible. As argued earlier, people act within the law with all sorts of intentions, to further their career, to support their political party, to enhance their reputation, and to aim for such things they do not need to be exceptionally bad people, they only need to be like the rest of us. If, instead, law's directedness toward justice is taken to be independent of what those acting within the law actually intend, then it becomes obscure what that directedness could be. A sense inherent in a practice which is nonetheless given the lie by what the practitioners have in mind to do seems to be a fiction, merely invented to have an ideal dome above the motley collection of what people actually intend.

---

6 Gustav Radbruch, *Rechtsphilosophie*, ed. E. Wolfc, 7th ed. (Stuttgart: Köhler, 1970), 123 f., 127.

7 Ibid., 209.

8 Ibid., 123 f.

9 Gustav Radbruch, *Gesetzliches Unrecht und übergesetzliches Recht* (1946), in Radbruch, *Rechtsphilosophie*, 347–57.

10 See *Entscheidungen des Bundesverfassungsgerichts* [Decisions of the Federal Constitutional Court] (= BVerfGE) 23, 98.

11 See BVerfGE 95, 96.

12 Radbruch, *Gesetzliches Unrecht und übergesetzliches Recht*, 353.

Given such doubts about law's being directed toward justice, one wonders why people hold on to the idea nonetheless. Here is a suggestion. In many people's minds, the laws have still not shed their divine origin, and this is what makes it appear mandatory to think of them as by their nature directed to the good, which in their case is justice. The idea is that the god standing behind the laws does not allow a merely technical conception of them as simply devices, more or less satisfying, for regulating and coordinating behavior. The god wants things to be heading for the good, and that is why the laws, which are understood as depending on him, need to aim at justice.

That the laws are understood to depend on god is evident in the Judeo-Christian tradition. For old Israel, law *is* god's word, and while Christianity recognizes human lawgiving, human laws have the power to subject agents to obligations only if they derive from god's eternal law, "derive" being the word both Augustine and Thomas Aquinas use.[13] The image is different, the matter the same in the Greek tradition: Heraclitus of Ephesus wrote around 480 BCE that "all human laws are nourished by the one divine law, for that is lord over whatever it wants, suffices for all, and still is not exhausted."[14] Here the nourishment of the human laws presumably consists once again in their getting their strength, that is their obligatory force, from their accord with the divine law;[15] and via Stoicism this thought became part of our heritage in which Christian and Greek sources merge. Not that everybody read Heraclitus or Augustine. They did not have to. These authors gave expression to a thought that became part of our tradition, and it is the presence of this thought in our tradition, even after the divine or natural law had been replaced in modernity by a law founded in reason, which explains the persistent idea that laws aim for justice. Note, this is not an argument against this idea, as if its origin in certain traditional views would make it doubtful. It is only to show why the idea hangs on. What speaks against the idea that laws aim for justice is simply the fact that there is no reason to think it is true.

As for the Radbruch formula itself, it allows judges to cease applying existing law by appealing to the putative fact that the law in question is no longer covered by that ideal dome, in contrast to ordinary unjust laws which still are. Yet how to tell ordinary from intolerable injustice the formula does not say, and Radbruch admits this defect when he says "that it is impossible to draw a sharper line" here.[16] Without a sharper line, however, he opens the door for judges to decide cases according to political opportunity or personal conviction rather than to law,

---

13 Augustine, *De libero arbitrio* I 6, 15; Thomas Aquinas, *Summa theologiae* I/II 96, 4.

14 Heraclitus B 114.

15 This reading of the fragment is controversial. I am following here Jonathan Barnes, *The Presocratic Philosophers*, rev. ed. (London: Routledge, 1982), 133.

16 Radbruch, *Gesetzliches Unrecht und übergesetzliches Recht*, 353.

contrary to a fundamental principle of the rule of law or of *Rechtsstaat*, which requires that judges decide cases according to law.

Radbruch's intermediate proposal failing, then, we should rather go for the anti-Augustinian extreme represented by Hans Kelsen, who insisted on "severing the links that were always claimed to hold between law and morals" and denied "that law, as law, is in any sense and any degree a moral matter."[17] Admittedly, Kelsen's own reason for taking this line is not convincing. He claims that justice, being an absolute value, is inaccessible to rational cognition, as is shown in his view by the history of failed attempts to give an account of it.[18] In fact, no history of failures, however long, can show that a theory of justice cannot now succeed. What does support Kelsen's separation thesis is the fact that law, the collection of things people do and the texts and traditions they use in what they do, can be fully understood without any recourse to justice or to other moral concerns. Justice is not what is on the minds of people in the law, but hosts of other things are, and to claim that the practice in itself, regardless of what the people involved have on their minds, is headed toward justice is to be talking mysteries. Practices, in contrast to people carrying on the practices, are not aiming for anything, they just exist and are what they are.

It is true, the German constitutional court held that the Federal Republic's basic law had, in establishing a number of basic rights of citizens, "also erected an objective order of values,"[19] and in many subsequent cases the court invoked that opinion of 1958 to support its decisions.[20] First, however, it is hard to see what basis the court had for its claim. The text of the basic law speaks consistently merely of citizens' rights, in line with the tradition going back to the 1789 Declaration of the Rights of Man and of the Citizen, with the court itself referring to that tradition.[21] Yet the text provides no support for the assumption that an objective order of values has been set up by the list of basic rights, nor does the court offer any argument for this assumption. Second, it is hard to see what it could even mean to erect an objective order of values. If there is such a thing as an objective order of values, then it does not need erecting, it just exists, independently of what the constitution might say about the matter. After all, you neither erect an objective order of numbers. If, on the other hand, the erecting is meant to amount to a command addressed to citizens that they value things according to the order implicit in the constitution's list of basic rights, then the constitution's own commitment to liberty, in particular to liberty of opinion,[22] would be in jeopardy. A liberal

17 Hans Kelsen, *Reine Rechtslehre*, 1st ed. (Leipzig: Deuticke, 1934), 12.

18 Ibid., 13 f.

19 BVerfGE 7, 198, paragraph 27.

20 See Ute Mager, "The Constitution as Value System," in this volume.

21 BVerfGE 7, 198, paragraph 25.

22 Grundgesetz Art. 2 I, 5 I.

state may regulate to some extent what people do, but what they value must be left to them.[23] And what an objective order of values could be other than either something's *being* more valuable than another thing or something's being *valued* by people more highly than another thing is not clear. Both for legal and for philosophical reasons, then, the court's claim would appear untenable.

The Law Is Not Needed as a Moral Educator

The law cannot serve as a moral landmark, first, because it pulls in different directions; second, because it cannot be trusted to lead us right. This result, however, is no cause for concern: we do not need a moral landmark. We do not need such a thing, not merely in the sense that we can at a pinch make do without it, but in the sense that, really, we would not know what to do with it.

There is a widespread worry that we in the developed Western countries (and only of these can I speak with some confidence) have lost our moral orientation. It is generally agreed that religion, for reasons not to be investigated here, no longer provides that orientation, and this leads many to ask what will take its place. Indeed, the present volume can be understood as convened under just this question. It is devoted to law in particular, and other volumes will take up other spheres of our common life today, but all with the intention of bringing to light resources of moral orientation which, it is said, we badly need.

We do not need them. The demise of religion did not leave behind the empty pulpit, ready to be taken over by other providers. It demoted the pulpit itself. Moral landmarks, that is to say, institutions, professions, or even people to which, if not all, then at least many of us look up with reverence and trust in their guidance are not in sight, not because our time is too weak or too corrupt to produce, or too skeptical to admit, such towering figures. We just have no use for them. Ours is a village without a spire.

We manage without them by piecing together our moral convictions from the odds and ends we collect on our way, from what we pick up from parents, classmates, colleagues, from stories heard and movies watched, from institutions of which we became members, and doctrines of which we became adherents, and so also, but only among so many other things, from the law. Nor do we just take in these lessons, we also check how we fare in following them. A moral outlook so put together is each person's in particular, but because our experiences are broadly similar, they resemble each other, more or less, depending on how far apart temporally, spatially, or socially we grew up. Our moral outlook need not have

23 See Immanuel Kant, *Beantwortung der Frage: Was ist Aufklärung?* (1784), in: *Kants gesammelte Schriften*, Königlich preußische Akademie der Wissenschaften (Berlin: Reimer), 8:36–38.

a center, like one institution, one experience, one principle founding the various attitudes that make up one's moral view, but that lack of a center precisely gives it some stability: in a boat thus patched together you can exchange a rotten plank and still stay afloat. Nor should we look down on or pity those who "have no principles." Finding one's way just by attending to the merits of the case in question may well be more sensible for those who know so little and whose circumstances are changing fast. It is true, there are those among us who live a life under the guidance of one idea or institution. Their doing so is a private thing, though, in marked contrast to the universal claims often raised on behalf of the ideas or institutions. Still, in general lives are not like this. They are patchwork, and no worse for it.

The stew that we thus cook up for our purposes we then pass on to the next generation to use it the way we used what we received. They will take into account, some way or other, what we propose–propose not only by telling them how to do things but also, more importantly, by how we actually go through our own lives. More wisdom than that we do not have to offer, but then more wisdom is not needed. It does not take a set of undisputed principles or a set of institutions we can trust to educate the young. We may just help them to find paths in the world, in view of the paths we figured out for ourselves.

To conclude, the law not only cannot serve as a moral landmark, being neither unified nor trustworthy; there is no need for it to do so. We are no worse off without that service. This does not exclude, indeed it opens the door for, appreciating what the law contributes in particular countries under particular circumstances, but especially today and in this country, to the protection of liberties that many of us care about and to an ordering of political processes that provides a useful framework for peaceful cooperation. We do not need the law as educator. We do need the law.

Part Two: How Does Law Teach Values? Public, Private, and Penal Law Examples

Are Constitutional Courts Civic Educative Institutions? If So, What Do They Teach?

James E. Fleming

Introduction

I am delighted to contribute to this ambitious volume on law and character formation in modern pluralistic societies. In *Ordered Liberty: Rights, Responsibilities, and Virtues*, Linda C. McClain and I put forward our main views on law and character formation in such societies. We defended a "formative project" of government and civil society working together to inculcate civic virtues, encourage responsible exercise of rights, and develop the capacities of citizens for self-government in a morally pluralistic constitutional democracy such as the United States.[1] We hope over the next few years to write a sequel on civic education in the Trump era, taking into account the increase in polarization, attacks on basic institutions, breakdown of civility, fraying of civic bonds along with mutual respect and trust, and emergence of intractable conflicts of rights.

In this chapter, I focus on conflicts between gay and lesbian rights (protected through antidiscrimination laws together with judicial decisions like *Obergefell v. Hodges* safeguarding the right of same-sex couples to marry[2]) and religious liberty. *Ordered Liberty* defends a role for government in inculcating civic virtues like tolerance and respect for gays and lesbians and promoting public values like securing the status of equal citizenship for all. Recent developments have dramatically posed the question whether laws recognizing same-sex marriage and protecting against discrimination on the basis of sexual orientation (including in the marketplace) should grant exemptions to business people who disapprove of such rights on religious grounds. The four justices who dissented in *Obergefell* have warned that protecting the right of same-sex couples to marry threatens the reli-

1 James E. Fleming and Linda C. McClain, *Ordered Liberty: Rights, Responsibilities, and Virtues* (Cambridge, MA: Harvard University Press, 2013) (drawing idea of a "formative project" from Michael J. Sandel, *Democracy's Discontent: America in Search of a Public Philosophy* [Cambridge, MA: Harvard University Press, 1996]).

2 135 S. Ct. 2584 (2015).

gious liberty of those who oppose same-sex marriage.[3] Yet Chief Justice Roberts, in dissent, acknowledged that every state that had recognized same-sex marriage had created religious exemptions.[4] Nothing in *Obergefell* implies that the state statutes already granting such exemptions were unconstitutional, nor would it prohibit legislatures prospectively from creating them as long as they do not impose a substantial burden on the rights of others. *Obergefell* leaves room for the democratic processes to continue to operate as before in creating religious exemptions. To be sure, exemptions will not satisfy those who oppose same-sex marriage altogether. Nor will they satisfy many supporters of equal rights. Yet such exemptions seem to be a reasonable approach to ameliorating clashes between gay and lesbian rights and religious liberty as well as other basic liberties.

In *Ordered Liberty*, McClain and I argued for conceiving religious exemptions concerning same-sex marriage as a prudential remedy, rooted in recognition of religious and moral objections to extending marriage to same-sex couples. These exemptions stop just short of affording full, equal citizenship to gays and lesbians, for the time being, out of respect for and deference to those religious objections. We acknowledged that there may be prudential or pragmatic reasons for creating such religious exemptions during periods of rapid cultural and constitutional change. Doing so, we observed, might help to minimize backlash against gay and lesbian rights. But we tendered the hope that the prudential, mutual adjustment by granting religious exemptions concerning same-sex marriage will follow the path of same-sex civil unions in Vermont: that religious exemptions will prove to be a ladder to full, equal citizenship through acceptance of same-sex marriage. Thus, we hope that the need for such exemptions will wither away along with religious objections to such marriage.[5] After all, in a morally pluralistic constitutional democracy such as that of the United States, the aspiration is to social cooperation on the basis of mutual respect and trust, not the absolutist vindication of the rights claims of one group over those of another. At the same time, we should recognize that religious exemptions undermine the government's formative project of inculcating civic virtues like tolerance and promoting the public value of securing the status of equal citizenship for all, including gays and lesbians. Religious exemptions are sites of resistance.[6]

In a perceptive article, Christopher L. Eisgruber asked: "Is the Supreme Court an Educative Institution?" He argued that the Court teaches by offering lessons

---

3 Ibid., 2625 (Roberts, C. J., dissenting), 2638 (Thomas, J., dissenting), and 2642–43 (Alito, J., dissenting). Justice Scalia had made such a warning in dissent in *Romer v. Evans*, 520 U.S. 620, 636, 646 (Scalia, J., dissenting).

4 Ibid., 2615, 2625 (Roberts, C. J., dissenting).

5 Fleming and McClain, *Ordered Liberty*, 174–75.

6 Ibid., 92, 146–47.

capable of inspiring Americans to honor their values.[7] Despite the implications of the title of this chapter, I do not fully explore here the question whether constitutional courts (such as the U.S. Supreme Court) are "civic educative institutions." Instead, I sketch several senses in which a supreme court might be such an institution, and I illustrate one sense by discussing two recent cases involving conflicts between gay and lesbian rights and religious liberty.

First, a supreme court opinion might exhort the government and the people themselves to live up to their constitutional commitments in cases where it holds that the government has violated those commitments. Think of *West Virginia v. Barnette*, which struck down a compulsory flag salute on the ground that "no official ... can prescribe what shall be orthodox in politics."[8] Second, an opinion might also be hortatory while upholding governmental actions. Consider Justice Brandeis's concurrence in *Whitney v. California*, upholding a restriction on advocacy of radical change while proclaiming, "Those who won our independence by revolution were not cowards. They did not fear political change. They did not exalt order at the cost of liberty."[9]

Third, a supreme court opinion might bring out the civic dimension of constitutional commitments, perhaps highlighting their role in a civic educative project or emphasizing their significance for performing civic duties. For example, in interpreting the First Amendment's guarantee of freedom of speech, the opinion might emphasize protecting speech that is essential to democratic self-government and elaborate the responsibilities of citizens in self-government. Consider again Brandeis's concurrence in *Whitney:* "[F]reedom to think as you will and to speak as you think are means indispensable to the discovery and spread of political truth; ... the greatest menace to freedom is an inert people; public discussion is a political duty."[10] This civic dimension is largely absent in recent freedom-of-speech decisions, which appear to be grounded in distrust of government and a deregulatory rather than civic conception of the First Amendment.[11]

Fourth, a supreme court opinion might underscore each governmental institution's roles and responsibilities in maintaining the successful functioning of the constitutional order. For example, the court might articulate its own responsibil-

---

7 Christopher L. Eisgruber, "Is the Supreme Court an Educative Institution?" *New York University Law Review* 67 (1992): 961.

8 319 U.S. 624, 642 (1943).

9 274 U.S. 357, 375 (1927) (Brandeis, J., concurring).

10 Ibid., 377.

11 See, for example, *United States v. Alvarez*, 567 U.S. 709 (2012) (holding that government may not forbid people to lie about military honors); *National Institute of Family and Life Advocates v. Becerra*, 138 S.Ct. 2361 (2018) (ruling that government may not regulate "crisis pregnancy centers" by requiring them to post factual information about government-provided reproductive health care services).

ities, such as safeguarding the rule of law during the "war on terror" (*Boumediene v. Bush*[12]); upholding the perception that courts decide cases as a matter of principle and build out lines of decisions with coherence and integrity, rather than overruling precedents simply because of a change in personnel (*Planned Parenthood v. Casey*[13]); and, on the basis of moral progress and new insights, extending our constitutional commitments to fulfill the Constitution's promise of liberty to all (*Obergefell*[14]). Furthermore, as against arguments by dissenters that democratic majorities should be free to decide matters such as how to inculcate patriotism, regulate abortion, or define marriage, a supreme court opinion might seek to educate concerning the form of self-government embodied in the Constitution: it is not a majoritarian democracy but a constitutional democracy, with certain fundamental rights limiting what majorities may do (*Barnette*, *Casey*, and *Obergefell*).

In this chapter I focus on a fifth sense of civic educative institution: that supreme court opinions, in attempting to resolve conflicts between rights in "culture wars"–in particular, between gay and lesbian rights and religious liberty–might teach lessons to citizens concerning how to accommodate such conflicts. Court opinions might model how to secure the central range of application of each conflicting right rather than vindicating one right absolutely to the exclusion of the other, with one side winning it all. They also might teach how to speak with respect concerning both gay and lesbian rights and religious liberty.

I focus on the U.S. Supreme Court's decision in *Masterpiece Cakeshop, Ltd. v. Colorado Civil Rights Commission*[15] but also discuss the decision of the New Mexico Supreme Court in *Elane Photography, LLC v. Willock.*[16] Such cases teach (1) that antidiscrimination laws properly exact a commitment to nondiscrimination in the marketplace as "the price of citizenship" (to invoke a phrase from *Elane Photography*) and (2) the importance of government affording equal respect to both gays and lesbians and religious opponents of gay and lesbian rights.

At first glance, *Masterpiece Cakeshop* and *Elane Photography* seem quite different. *Elane Photography* holds for the same-sex couple and against the photographers (the Huguenins), who declined to photograph a same-sex ceremony on the basis of religious objections. *Masterpiece Cakeshop*, by contrast, holds for the baker (Jack Phillips), who refused to bake a wedding cake to celebrate a same-sex couple's marriage (that of Charlie Craig and David Mullins). Justice Anthony Kennedy's majority opinion chastises a Colorado civil rights commissioner's "hostility" toward Phillips's religious beliefs, holding that it "was inconsistent with the

---

12 553 U.S. 723 (2008) (holding that the President and Congress had unconstitutionally suspended the writ of habeas corpus).

13 505 U.S. 833 (1992) (reaffirming the right to decide whether to terminate a pregnancy).

14 135 S.Ct. 2584 (2015) (extending to same-sex couples the right to marry).

15 138 S.Ct. 1719 (2018).

16 309 P.3d 53 (N.M. 2013).

First Amendment's guarantee that our laws be applied in a manner that is neutral toward religion."[17] On closer examination, these cases prove to be quite similar.

Two Cases Teaching Lessons Concerning Respect and "The Price of Citizenship"

Elane Photography[18]

In his concurring opinion in *Elane Photography,* Justice Richard C. Bosson stressed that the New Mexico antidiscrimination law is broader than Title II of the Civil Rights Act of 1964, which prohibited discrimination in public accommodations (hotels, restaurants, gas stations, and entertainment venues) on the basis of race, color, religion, or national origin. New Mexico's law has expanded to "preclude invidious discrimination in most every public business" (including photography businesses). It also has extended the "prohibited classifications" from "the historical classes"–those in Title II, as well as sex (or gender)–to include sexual orientation. Bosson interpreted this expansion of New Mexico's law in terms of evolving understanding of what forms of discrimination are "intolerable." "The Huguenins today can no more turn away customers on the basis of sexual orientation ... than they could refuse to photograph African-Americans or Muslims."[19] He treated racial, religious, and sexual-orientation discrimination as intolerable, without saying that the Huguenins are bigots for the sincere beliefs they hold. To the contrary, Bosson stated: "[T]heir religious convictions deserve our respect."[20]

But are the Huguenins, as conservative critics charge, being unjustly driven from the public square? Bosson acknowledged that they are "compelled by law to compromise the very religious beliefs that inspire their lives"–a "sobering result." Nonetheless, he would tell the Huguenins, "with the utmost respect," that this is part of the "price of citizenship" that we all have to pay in "our civic life."[21] Civic life in a "multicultural, pluralistic society" requires some "compromise" with and accommodation of the "contrasting values of others." The Huguenins retain the constitutional protection "to think, to say, to believe, as they wish," and to "follow [their God's] commandments in their personal lives," but in "the smaller, more focused world of the marketplace of commerce, of public accommodation," they

---

17 *Masterpiece Cakeshop,* 1723.

18 In this section, I have drawn extensively upon the analysis of my sometime coauthor Linda C. McClain in her book, *Who's the Bigot: Learning From Conflicts over Marriage and Civil Rights Law* (New York: Oxford University Press, 2020), 186–91.

19 *Elane Photography,* 79.

20 Ibid., 83.

21 Ibid., 79–80.

"have to channel their conduct ... to leave space for other Americans who believe something different." Notably, Bosson concluded that such compromise "is part of the glue that holds us together as a nation, the tolerance that lubricates the varied moving parts of us as a people."[22] This concurrence exemplifies a civic educative function of a supreme court opinion.

Masterpiece Cakeshop

Masterpiece Cakeshop teaches similar lessons. Many contend that *Masterpiece Cakeshop* was a narrow holding. Maybe so, in the sense that the Supreme Court did not accept the baker's broad arguments regarding religious liberty and freedom from compelled expression:[23] arguments which, if accepted, would have imperiled the structure of antidiscrimination laws. The Court only set aside the Colorado Civil Rights Commission's (CCRC) order against Phillips, postponing to "later cases" how best to resolve the many "difficult" and "delicate" questions the case raised. It stated that "the Commission's consideration of Phillips's case was neither tolerant nor respectful of Phillips's religious beliefs."[24] Basically, the Court held that the baker was entitled to a hearing before the CCRC that was neutral and free from hostility toward his religious views.

But it is important to appreciate that in reaching that narrow holding, the Supreme Court taught some broad lessons concerning antidiscrimination laws with profound implications concerning clashes of rights and the price of citizenship. The best way to appreciate these lessons is to quote the passages from Justice Kennedy's majority opinion, with which Justice Ruth Bader Ginsburg opened her vigorous dissent. Ginsburg began: "There is much in the Court's opinion with which I agree." (1) "[I]t is a general rule that [religious and philosophical] objections do not allow business owners and other actors in the economy and in society to deny protected persons equal access to goods and services under a neutral and generally applicable public accommodations law." (2) "Colorado law can protect gay persons, just as it can protect other classes of individuals, in acquiring whatever products and services they choose on the same terms and conditions as are offered to other members of the public." (3) "[P]urveyors of goods and services who object to gay marriages for moral and religious reasons [may not] put up signs saying, 'no goods or services will be sold if they will be used for gay marriages.'" Gay persons may be spared from "indignities when they seek goods and services in an open market." (4) Ginsburg concluded: "I strongly disagree, however, with the Court's conclusion that Craig and Mullins should lose this case. All of the

22 Ibid., 80.

23 *Masterpiece Cakeshop*, 1723–24.

24 Ibid., 1731–32.

above-quoted statements point in the opposite direction."[25] In a nutshell, the Court made broad pronouncements about the legitimacy of antidiscrimination laws in seeking to secure the status of equal citizenship for gays and lesbians by promoting nondiscrimination and even equal dignity and respect for them in the marketplace.

Another way to bring out how narrow (and broad) the ruling was is to focus on how the Supreme Court conceived the baker's right to free exercise of religion. Let us notice several available conceptions of religious liberty articulated in the U.S. culture wars which the Court did not embrace or presuppose.

(1) Some religious opponents of same-sex marriage assert or presuppose that respecting their religious liberty requires that the state must define marriage, in accordance with their religious beliefs, as the union of one man and one woman. Put another way, they assert or presuppose a right that same-sex marriage not be recognized. You may think no one argues this. Yet the dissents in the Supreme Court's own gay and lesbian rights decisions from *Romer* through *Obergefell* make clear that Justices Antonin Scalia, Clarence Thomas, and Samuel Alito believe that recognition of gay and lesbian rights as such imperils religious liberty. And I have heard Ryan Anderson argue that antidiscrimination laws prohibiting discrimination on the basis of sexual orientation as such deny religious liberty.[26]

(2) Some religious opponents of same-sex marriage assert or presuppose a less ambitious right not to be compelled to be complicit in same-sex marriage: for example, a right not to be compelled, by antidiscrimination laws, to bake a cake for a same-sex wedding ceremony. Perhaps this formulation is synonymous with the next.

(3) A right to religious exemptions from laws protecting gay and lesbian rights. That is, if a state prohibits discrimination on the basis of sexual orientation or extends to same-sex couples the right to marry (as it must under *Obergefell*), religious opponents have a right to religious exemptions from such laws. Note that the assertion of a right to religious exemptions is a second-best solution. One argues for religious exemptions only when one has lost the larger battle against gay and lesbian rights under antidiscrimination laws or marriage-equality laws. The religious opponents' ideal would be to "win it all" in these larger battles, as I have heard Matthew J. Franck of the Witherspoon Institute say, insisting that "a house divided against itself cannot stand."[27]

---

25 Ibid., 1748 (Ginsburg, J., dissenting).

26 "Religious Liberty or a License to Discriminate?" Debate between Ryan T. Anderson and Linda C. McClain, sponsored by *Princeton Tory*, Princeton University, April 12, 2017. See also Ryan T. Anderson, *Truth Overruled: The Future of Marriage and Religious Freedom* (Washington, DC: Regnery Publishing, 2015).

27 "Marriage and the Law," Murphy Lecture Roundtable Discussion, Princeton University Program in Law and Public Affairs, May 4, 2012. Colloquy between Matthew J. Franck

(4) We come finally to a weaker formulation: a right that government, in any proceeding under a constitutionally permitted antidiscrimination law prohibiting discrimination on the basis of sexual orientation, not express hostility toward religious objections to gay and lesbian rights. Put another way, a right that government be neutral toward religion in such a proceeding.

Which of these available formulations of rights to religious liberty did *Masterpiece Cakeshop* assert or presuppose? Clearly the last.

In closing, Kennedy offered the following guidance to courts considering future cases: "[T]hese disputes must be resolved with tolerance, without undue disrespect to sincere religious beliefs, and without subjecting gay persons to indignities when they seek goods and services in an open market."[28] Arguably, the *Elane* concurrence is a model of respectful rhetoric and of "resolv[ing] with tolerance," since it explicitly says the Huguenins' beliefs "deserve our respect," even as it says they must follow New Mexico's law.

Jack Phillips, the baker, argued that the CCRC showed hostility toward his religion; he cited a comment by an individual commissioner during a hearing on his case: "Freedom of religion and religion have been used to justify all kinds of discrimination throughout history, whether it be slavery, whether it be the [H]olocaust .... And to me it is one of the most despicable pieces of rhetoric that people ... use their religion to hurt others."[29] This comment troubled Justice Kennedy, who concluded that it expressed hostility toward the baker's religious opposition to baking the wedding cake.

First, to compare Phillips's religious beliefs about marriage to religious defenses of slavery and the Holocaust, Kennedy thought, was a "sentiment ... inappropriate" for someone charged with "neutral enforcement" of the Colorado Antidiscrimination Act (CADA), which protects "on *the basis of religion* as well as sexual orientation." Second, the commissioner's "despicable piece of rhetoric" comment "disparaged" Phillips's religion, Kennedy found, in "at least two distinct ways": (1) by calling the appeal to religious beliefs "despicable" and (2) by "characterizing it as merely rhetorical–something insubstantial and even insincere." Another factor showing hostility, Kennedy said, was the disparity in how the Commission ruled in a different case, when it affirmed the right of three other bakers–on the basis of "conscience-based objections"–to decline to bake cakes

---

and Linda C. McClain concerning religious exemptions, drawing an analogy to Abraham-Lincoln's famous argument against slavery. See Matthew J. Franck, "Can Religious Freedom Survive Same-Sex Marriage?," *First Things*, August 26, 2013, https://www.firstthings.com/blogs/firstthoughts/2013/08/can-religious-freedom-survive-same-sex-marriage.

28 *Masterpiece Cakeshop*, 1732.

29 Ibid., 1729 (quoting the transcript).

bearing anti-same-sex marriage imagery and text requested by a customer named William Jack.[30]

Let us break down the commissioner's statement into two propositions. The first part: "Freedom of religion and religion have been used to justify all kinds of discrimination throughout history, whether it be slavery, whether it be the [H]olocaust." But this proposition is undeniably true as a matter of historical fact,[31] even if religious people today do not wish to be reminded of it. In concluding that this statement expressed hostility toward Phillips's religious beliefs, the Court in effect seemed to be imposing a religious political correctness upon the commissioner by forbidding him to say what is indisputably true because it offends religious sensibilities.

The second part: "And to me it is one of the most despicable pieces of rhetoric that people ... use their religion to hurt others." Here Kennedy was nearer the mark in his interpretation that this remark expressed hostility toward Phillips's religious convictions. But Justice Ginsburg made good arguments that the Court was flawed in attributing the attitudes of this one commissioner to the entire CCRC and in turn to the Colorado Court of Appeals decision upholding the Commission.[32]

Is the majority in *Masterpiece Cakeshop* right that the Commission showed hostility toward Phillips's religious beliefs? In a process free from hostility, could the Commission still have ruled against Phillips and in favor of the three bakers who declined to make cakes requested by William Jack? The justices disagreed with each other concerning whether these cases could be distinguished. Let us consider the following hypotheticals to test the majority's conception of hostility to religion.

(1) Suppose that a baker refused to bake a cake for an interracial wedding, citing the Bible in support of segregation and religious objections to such marriage. (Recall that in *Loving v. Virginia*, the trial judge had cited the Bible in opposition to interracial marriage.[33]) Suppose that a civil rights commissioner quoted the Supreme Court's statement in *Newman v. Piggie Park Industries, Inc.*, that such religious arguments were "patently frivolous,"[34] and the Commission rejected the baker's claim. Does the majority in *Masterpiece Cakeshop* imply that such a statement would express unconstitutional hostility toward the baker's religious convictions?

(2) Suppose that a baker refused to bake a cake for a same-sex wedding, citing the Bible in support of religious objections. Suppose that a commissioner quoted the Court's statements in *Romer v. Evans* that traditional religious objections to

30 Ibid., 1729–30.

31 For an instructive account of the Christian "theology of segregation" to justify slavery and segregation, see McClain, *Who's the Bigot?*, 80–86.

32 *Masterpiece Cakeshop*, 1751–52 (Ginsburg, J., dissenting).

33 388 U.S. 1, 3 (1967).

34 390 U.S. 400, 402n5 (1968).

gay and lesbian rights amounted to "animus against, and a bare desire to harm, a politically unpopular group."[35] Does the majority in *Masterpiece Cakeshop* imply that such a statement would express hostility toward the baker's religious convictions? (Bear in mind that Justice Scalia, in dissent in *Romer*, accused the majority of tarring the "seemingly tolerant Coloradans" with the brush of bigotry–that is, he accused the majority of expressing hostility toward their religious convictions.[36])

(3) Suppose that a baker refused to bake a cake for an interfaith wedding between a Christian and a Muslim, citing religious objections. Suppose further that a commissioner argued the following in support of the baker (quoting President Trump's statements which these same five conservative justices, who were in the majority in *Masterpiece Cakeshop*, concluded did not express unconstitutional hostility toward Muslims in *Trump v. Hawaii*, the travel ban case[37]): "Islam hates us," Muslims "do not respect us at all," we need a "total and complete shutdown of Muslims entering the United States." Does the majority in *Masterpiece Cakeshop* imply that those statements would express hostility toward the Muslim's religion (notwithstanding the majority's decision in *Trump*)?

(4) What if, in the previous three hypotheticals, the commissioner in question had simply observed, as a matter of historical fact, that people have asserted religious beliefs as a reason to discriminate on various bases, including race, religion, and sexual orientation, and that there is no absolute protection to act on religious beliefs in the marketplace? Does the majority in *Masterpiece Cakeshop* imply that even that factual observation would signal hostility toward religion?

As suggested above, my initial reaction to the majority opinion's finding of hostility toward Phillips's religious beliefs was to fear that the Court was in effect imposing a conservative or religious political correctness upon civil rights commissioners by forbidding them to recognize undeniable facts that religion has been used to justify the Holocaust and slavery, not to mention denial of civil rights in the United States, because those facts offend contemporary religious sensibilities. I feared that Scalia had bludgeoned Kennedy into this finding over the years with his pugnacious, overwrought culture-warrior dissents in all the gay and lesbian rights cases from *Romer* through *Obergefell*.

The students in my seminar, "Jurisprudence: Contemporary Controversies over Law and Morality," however, argued that even if what the commissioner said was undeniably true historically, bringing up these general facts in the context of the baker's particular hearing might imply hostility toward his particular religious convictions. From this perspective, it might have been perfectly appropriate to say these very same things in a legislative proceeding concerning whether to

---

35 517 U.S. 620, 632, 634 (1996).

36 Ibid., 636, 646 (Scalia, J., dissenting).

37 138 S.Ct. 2392, 2435–40 (2018) (Sotomayor, J., dissenting).

establish religious exemptions from antidiscrimination laws prohibiting discrimination on the basis of sexual orientation. But it would not be appropriate to do so in an administrative proceeding concerning whether a particular religious person, here the baker, had discriminated on the basis of sexual orientation in violation of the CADA. On this view, the case is teaching an important civics lesson about respect for religious liberty in a particular case, together with respect for gays' and lesbians' rights in general to be secure in the status of equal citizenship through acknowledging the legitimacy of antidiscrimination laws prohibiting discrimination on the basis of sexual orientation.

Seen in this light, Justice Kennedy, in *Masterpiece Cakeshop*, implicitly acknowledges what Justice Bosson in *Elane Photography* called "the price of citizenship." Government must respect religious convictions: it must be neutral and may not express hostility toward a particular person's religious convictions when determining whether that person has violated an antidiscrimination law. But when one operates a business, a public accommodation, engaging in commerce, one likewise must tolerate or even respect gays and lesbians. Recall the passages from Kennedy's opinion emphasized in Ginsburg's dissent.

Furthermore, it is important to grasp that *Masterpiece Cakeshop* does not entail that, after a neutral proceeding, Jack Phillips may not be held to have violated the CADA. Nor does the Court entail that he has any right to a religious exemption from the act's prohibition of discrimination on the basis of sexual orientation. This is the import of Justice Kagan's concurrence, joined by Justice Breyer. She offered a blueprint to guide civil rights commissioners in future controversies, showing how it could have been possible to apply Colorado's law against Phillips "untainted by any bias against a religious belief."[38]

To recapitulate: Kennedy's majority opinion in *Masterpiece Cakeshop* models how to resolve conflicts between gay and lesbian rights and religious liberty in a manner respectful to both sides in the culture war. One, accept the structure and aspirations of antidiscrimination laws. Two, make clear that antidiscrimination laws may protect gays and lesbians from discrimination that denies their equal dignity and undermines their status as equal citizens. Yet, three, also make clear that government in applying antidiscrimination laws must be respectful toward, and not express hostility against, religious convictions that are critical of antidiscrimination laws' aspirations. Through it all, do not imperil antidiscrimination laws with broad holdings regarding rights to religious exemptions or rights not to be compelled to express antidiscrimination laws' message of equality for gays and lesbians.

38 *Masterpiece Cakeshop*, 1733 (Kagan, J., concurring).

Religious Exemptions and the Moralization of Commerce in a Large Commercial Republic

Stepping back from these judicial opinions, I want to reflect on antidiscrimination laws and arguments for religious exemptions more generally. In *Ordered Liberty*, McClain and I defend government's role in a formative project of inculcating civic virtues, developing the capacities of citizens for self-government in a morally pluralistic constitutional democracy, and promoting public values like securing the status of equal citizenship for all, including gays and lesbians. We view antidiscrimination laws as playing a vital role in such a formative project, as mechanisms for promoting the public value of equality.[39] Public accommodations laws, for example, are not just about protecting the right to procure a hamburger or a hotel room when traveling in interstate commerce. More importantly, they are about securing equal dignity for all, whatever one's race, religion, gender, or sexual orientation.

Antidiscrimination laws are not simply negative: protecting minorities against denials of equal dignity. They also are affirmative: part of a formative project of government promoting the public value of equal citizenship for all. As we see it, through antidiscrimination laws, government is implicitly aspiring to change the attitudes of the discriminators themselves: it is aspiring to teach the discriminators that their discrimination is intolerable. I believe it is this recognition that drives the discriminators to object, invoking *West Virginia v. Barnette*, that government through antidiscrimination laws is "prescrib[ing] what shall be orthodox"[40] or compelling them to express a message with which they disagree. This is also what fuels Justice Thomas's and Justice Gorsuch's acceptance of the "compelled expression" argument in concurrence in *Masterpiece Cakeshop.*[41]

Elsewhere, I and my coauthors elaborate a conception of the U.S. constitutional democracy as a "large commercial republic."[42] The large commercial republic is religiously and morally diverse. In such a diverse society, the hope is that even though people disagree about religion and morality, they may be able to engage in commerce with one another. The further hope is that people's getting together and trading with one another may moderate their religious and moral differences. Perhaps people will see that, despite their religious and moral disagreements, they

39 *Masterpiece Cakeshop*, 1733 (Kagan, J., concurring).

40 319 U.S. 624, 642 (1943).

41 *Masterpiece Cakeshop*, 1740–48 (Thomas, J., with whom J. Gorsuch joins, concurring in part and concurring in the judgment).

42 See James E. Fleming et al., *Gay Rights and the Constitution* (St. Paul, MN: Foundation Press, 2016), 78–82, 419, 426; Sotirios A. Barber and James E. Fleming, *Constitutional Interpretation: The Basic Questions* (New York: Oxford University Press, 2007), 41–45.

can trade with, get along with, and maybe even come to appreciate other, different people.

We portray the large commercial republic as a mechanism of the formative project of inculcating civic virtues like tolerance and promoting public values like equal citizenship for all, including gays and lesbians. Again, the aspiration is that trade will moderate religious and moral disagreements and differences and will promote social cooperation on the basis of mutual respect and trust. For trade facilitates contact with people who are different from us and promotes at least toleration if not appreciation and respect. For this mechanism to work, people have to trade, come to see and even appreciate their commonalities and their differences, and come to accept, even to respect, others with whom they disagree on religious and moral grounds.[43]

From this standpoint, religious exemptions for businesses–including wedding photographers and bakers–undercut the significant, moderating influences of trade in the large commercial republic. They undermine the salutary civic function of such a republic in moderating difference, promoting tolerance, and securing the status of equal citizenship for all. They balkanize trade and, in doing so, balkanize the polity. And so, if we are to keep in view this larger formative project of promoting social cooperation on the basis of mutual respect and trust, we should be cautious about creating broad exemptions. From this vantage point, it may be that Justice Bosson in *Elane Photography* and Justice Kennedy in *Masterpiece Cakeshop* model a better course: according respect both to gay and lesbian rights and to religious beliefs in opposition to such rights, while yet acknowledging that antidiscrimination laws exact the price of citizenship.

What is more, we should acknowledge forthrightly that the moralized commerce that comes with religious exemptions is a double-edged sword. Religious exemptions from antidiscrimination laws moralize commerce in a divisive way and in doing so undercut the aspirations and operation of the large commercial republic to promote the moral objective of securing the status of equal citizenship for all. In a culture war, both sides can moralize commerce in divisive ways. For example, when a state declines to prohibit discrimination on the basis of sexual orientation, or creates broad religious exemptions for businesses with religious objections to marriage equality, corporations sympathetic to gay and lesbian rights can take their business to other states. In turn, customers who support such rights can boycott businesses asserting or exercising religious exemptions. For example, you can be sure that many opposite-sex couples in Colorado who are committed to gay and lesbian rights are not going to order wedding cakes from

43 To avoid misunderstanding, I wish to make clear that I do not conceive commerce itself as a moral or civic virtue, nor do I celebrate the morality of trade or capitalism. I simply view the large commercial republic as a mechanism that promotes social contact and, one hopes, moderates differences.

Masterpiece Cakeshop. They probably will not buy cookies or cupcakes there either (even though Phillips offered to sell such baked goods to gays and lesbians). Moralizing commerce will be easy in the era of Twitter, Facebook, Yelp, Google reviews, TripAdvisor, and other sources of reputational information and sanction.

Recognizing all of this, I hope, might give us pause before we head down this road of moralizing and balkanizing trade in these divisive ways. In other words, proponents of religious exemptions should be careful about what they wish for. Proponents of religious exemptions (and thus moralized commerce) commonly cry foul when supporters of gay and lesbian rights engage in such boycotts (and thus moralized commerce) against businesses with religious opposition to gay and lesbian rights. But this is exactly what is to be expected when we moralize commerce in divisive ways.

As mentioned above, in *Ordered Liberty*, McClain and I adopted a prudential attitude toward granting religious accommodations, at least in periods of rapid cultural and constitutional change. We tendered the hope that the need for them would wither away.[44] We must acknowledge, though, that prudence also might counsel against granting broad or longstanding exemptions in a large commercial republic that aspires to secure the status of equal citizenship for all.

Recapitulation

Thus, Justice Kennedy's opinion in *Masterpiece Cakeshop* and Justice Bosson's concurrence in *Elane Photography* serve a valuable civic educative function: they model how to resolve conflicts between gay and lesbian rights and religious liberty. These opinions teach valuable civics lessons concerning the price of citizenship. They recognize the importance of respect on both sides. Fortunately, *Masterpiece Cakeshop* did not accept the compelled-expression argument (the argument accepted by the culture warriors Thomas and Gorsuch.) That would have been a winner-take-all victory in the culture wars. That would have imperiled antidiscrimination laws and the quest for securing the status of equal citizenship for all. That would have imperiled law and character formation in the morally pluralistic U.S. constitutional democracy.

44 Fleming and McClain, *Ordered Liberty*, 174–75.

Bigotry, Civility, and Reinvigorating Civic Education

Government's Formative Task amid Polarization

Linda C. McClain

Bigotry, Incivility, and Challenges to *E Pluribus Unum*

"Calling out" bigotry and arguing over whether a public figure is or is not a bigot are visible and contentious features of daily public life in the United Sates. Charges, denials, and countercharges of bigotry seem increasingly frequent, as do claims that one is being unfairly branded a bigot. People turn to the language of bigotry in so-called culture-war issues around marriage, LGBTQ rights, and religious liberty, as well as in controversies over race, immigration, and borders. Images of climate change and the endangered "atmosphere of public life" vividly capture the worry that bigotry and a "climate of hate" damage "the protective layer of civility, which makes political discourse possible."[1] Charges of bigotry meet countercharges that political correctness is a form of bigotry or ideological intolerance. Indeed, one provocative claim is that, in the present environment, "the most pervasive form of bigotry" is *political* bigotry: intolerance toward people with different political opinions.[2]

In my recent book, *Who's the Bigot? Learning from Conflicts over Marriage and Civil Rights Law*, I explore why there is so much controversy in the United States over bigotry when renouncing–and denouncing–it seems to be a shared political and constitutional value with a long history.[3] On one hand, there appears to be strong bipartisan agreement that bigotry in all its forms is un-American and contrary to American ideals; on the other, there is often sharp, partisan disagreement over bigotry's forms and over who has the moral authority to call it out. During the 2016 presidential campaign, the Republican and Democratic Party platforms both

---

1 Robert Darnton, "Voltaire Versus Trump," *New York Times*, Jan. 2, 2019, A19.

2 Joey Clark, "The Most Pervasive Bigotry Isn't What You Think," *Foundation for Economic Education*, Aug. 22, 2017, https://fee.org/articles/the-most-pervasive-bigotry-isnt-what-you-think/.

3 Linda C. McClain, *Who's the Bigot? Learning from Conflicts over Marriage and Civil Rights Law* (New York: Oxford University Press, 2020).

denounced bigotry and various forms of intolerance, but their lists of those forms differed strikingly. Further, the Democratic platform explicitly condemned the Republican nominee, Donald Trump, for creating a "climate of bigotry."[4] During Trump's campaign and continuing into his presidency, bipartisan warnings sounded that "bigotry seems emboldened" and "normalized."[5] Civil rights groups asserted that Trump's statements and his administration's policies "tapped into a seam of bigotry and hate that resulted in the targeting of American Muslims and other minority groups."[6] Trump's critics argued that such bigotry included racism, anti-Semitism, nativism, populism, xenophobia, homophobia, misogyny, and sexism.[7] On the other hand, some conservative commentators countered that critics of Trump and his supporters are "anti-Trump bigots" and that their "political correctness" is a form of bigotry.[8]

The 2018 midterm elections intensified concern over polarization and brought fresh battles over bigotry. In one preelection poll, 61 percent of Democrats and those leaning Democratic would use the terms "racist/bigoted/sexist" to "describe Republicans today;" 54 percent chose "ignorant," and 44 percent "spiteful." Among Republicans and those leaning Republican, only 31 percent

4 Republican Party Platform 2016, at 9, http://www.presidency.ucsb.edu/ws/index.php?pid'117718; Democratic Platform 2016, at 18, http://www.presidency.ucsb.edu/ws/index.php?pid'117717.

5 Maegan Vazquez, "George W. Bush: Bigotry and White Supremacy Are 'Blasphemy' against the American Creed," CNN, Oct. 19, 2017, https://www.cnn.com/2017/10/19/politics/bush-freedom-event/index.html ("emboldened"); Sasha Abramsky, "How Trump Has Normalized the Unspeakable," *Nation*, Sept. 20, 2017, https://www.thenation.com/article/how-trump-has-normalized-the-unspeakable; Michael Gerson, "Trump Deepens the Moral Damage to the GOP," *Washington Post*, Aug. 28, 2017, https://www.washingtonpost.com/opinions/trump-abuses-his-power-in-the-cause-of-bigotry/2017/08/28/1f473e3c-8c22-11e7-84c0-02cc069f2c37_story.html.

6 "CAIR Report Shows 2017 on Track to Becoming One of the Worst Years Ever for Anti-Muslim Hate Crimes," *Council on American Islamic Relations*, July 17, 2017, https://www.cair.com/press-center/press-releases/14476-cair-report-shows-2017-on-track-to-becoming-one-of-worst-years-ever-for-anti-muslim-hate-crimes.html.

7 Mythili Sampathkumar, "Trump Impeachment Vote to Happen Next Week, Congressman Promises," *The Independent*, Nov. 30, 2017 (quoting Representative Al Green); Charles M. Blow, "Trump Is a Racist. Period," *New York Times*, Jan. 15, 2018, A19.

8 See "Sean Hannity Show," *Fox News Today*, Dec. 26, 2017 (guest Todd Starnes calls CNN "a dog whistle for race baiting anti-Trump bigots" and argues that those who oppose Trump are bigoted), LEXIS News Transcripts 122601cb.253; Shelby Steele, "The Soft Bigotry of Political Correctness," *Hoover Institution*, April 24, 2017, https://www.hoover.org/research/soft-bigotry-political-correctness.

chose the terms "racist/bigoted/sexist" to "describe Democrats today," while 49 percent chose "ignorant," and 54 percent "spiteful."[9]

Commentators diagnose a new tribalism in the United States, in which the left believes that the bigotry and racism of "right-wing tribalism" is "tearing the country apart," while the right believes the "identity politics" and "political correctness" of "left-wing tribalism" are doing so.[10] Americans, some argue, have growing contempt for their political opponents.[11] Prominent political scientists warn of the possible death of democracy in the United States and elsewhere if core norms of "mutual toleration" erode, allowing "extremist demagogues" to go unchecked.[12]

Concerns over a decline in civility and tolerance–and a surge in bigotry–are not confined to the United States. Around the world, shocking incidents of lethal extremist violence motivated by hatred of religious and racial groups make condemning–and preventing–bigotry seem urgent. The role of social media on the internet in fostering hate that spills into violent action is a particular concern. It has spurred local and international demands, such as the Christchurch Call, that social media be more accountable for their content.[13] In the report *Pluralism in Peril: Challenges to An American Ideal* (2018), J. M. Berger explains the amplifying effect of social media. "Extremism has existed for thousands of years," takes many forms, and is "part of the human experience and not exclusive to any one group." However, "thanks to a brave new world of instant global connectivity, the problem is perhaps more diverse than before. Extremism is a socially transmitted disease, and there are more vectors for infection than at any time in history."[14]

---

9 Kim Hart, "Exclusive Poll: Most Democrats See Republicans as Racist, Sexist," *Axios*, Nov. 12, 2018, https://www.axios.com/poll-democrats-and-republicans-hate-each-other-racist-ignorant-evil-99ae7afc-5a51-42be-8ee2-3959e43ce320.html (citing Survey Monkey online poll conducted Oct. 30 to Nov. 2 among 3,215 adults).

10 David Blankenhorn, "The Top 14 Causes of Political Polarization," *The American Interest*, May 26, 2016, https://www.the-american-interest.com/2018/05/16/the-top-14-causes-of-political-polarization/ (quoting Amy Chua, *Political Tribes* (New York: Penguin, 2018)).

11 Arthur C. Brooks, *Love Your Enemies: How Decent People Can Save America from the Culture of Contempt* (New York: Broadside Books, 2019); see also Karen Stohr, "Our New Age of Contempt," *New York Times*, Jan. 23, 2017, https://www.nytimes.com/2017/01/23/opinion/our-new-age-of-contempt.html.

12 Steven Levitsky and Daniel Ziblatt, *How Democracies Die* (New York: Penguin, 2018), 168.

13 See "Christchurch Call to Eliminate Terrorist and Extremist Content Online," christchurchcall.com; Damien Cave, "The Global Push to Make Social Media Accountable for Its Content," *New York Times*, April 1, 2019, A5.

14 J.M. Berger, "Out of Many One: Defining the Opposite of Extremism," in *Pluralism in Peril: Challenges to an American Ideal: Report of the Inclusive America Project* (Aspen Institute, Justice Society Program, Jan. 2018), 89, 91.

If, as Berger persuasively argues, extremism poses a stark challenge to a healthy pluralism and is the opposite of the ideal of "out of many one" (*e pluribus unum*),[15] then what concrete measures can counter extremism? What meaning can the ideal of *e pluribus unum* have in this fraught and polarized environment? What concrete steps might tackle the alarming brew of hate and "otherization" that social media sites facilitate? Turning from virtual space to the shared real spaces of people's daily interactions, what tools does government have to restore civility and to decrease contempt and prejudice (or even "political bigotry")? What does the virtue of civility require, and how can government inculcate it? Is there a way forward from the bigotry-versus-political-correctness divide?

A Way Forward? The Civic Roles of Schools

This chapter argues that civic education in public schools is one concrete method that government may employ to address these vexing challenges by teaching people how to coexist peacefully and cooperatively in a multiethnic and multireligious polity and to engage respectfully across difference. At a time of "heightened concern about the state of U.S. politics and democracy," attention has understandably turned to the role of K-12 education in America and whether schools are "equipping students with the tools to become engaged, informed, and compassionate citizens."[16]

Civic education bears on this volume's topic of the role of law in forming character, educating about ethics, and expressing values in pluralistic and polarized societies. Such education could help to reduce dangerous forms of contempt and hate. Further, one possible component of a reinvigorated civic education should be religious literacy—nonsectarian education about religion—since "religious *illiteracy* is often a contributing factor in fostering a climate whereby certain forms of bigotry and misrepresentation can emerge unchallenged and thus serve as one form of justification for violence and marginalization."[17] Such education might help change a climate of bigotry and prepare students for respectful engagement and cooperation across difference in an increasingly pluralistic constitutional democracy.

---

15 Berger, 89.

16 Michael Hansen et al., "The 2018 Brown Center Report on American Education: How Well are American Students Learning?" (Brown Center on Education Policy at Brookings, June 2018), 1.

17 Diane L. Moore, "High Stakes Ignorance: Religion, Education, and the Unwitting Reproduction of Bigotry," in *Civility, Religious Pluralism, and Education*, ed. Vincent F. Biondo III and Andrew Fiala (New York: Routledge, 2014), 112, 114.

As James Fleming and I argue elsewhere, "[e]ducation of children is one of government's most significant formative responsibilities."[18] We defend an account of constitutional liberalism in which government has a responsibility to carry out a formative project of fostering deliberative democracy (political self-government) and deliberative autonomy (personal self-government). In the U.S. constitutional and political order, schools (ideally) prepare children not only for "success in life" (to quote *Brown v. Board of Education*), but also provide "education for democracy"–they inculcate core political values and equip children with the knowledge, skills, and habits (or dispositions) for responsible and meaningful participation in civic life.

A few examples of those prerequisites for participation are the capacity for critical thinking and reflection and for empathy and reciprocity (allowing for perspective-taking).[19] "Civility" typically refers to skills that citizens need to interact with one another: how to be "responsive to one's fellow citizens," "to question, to answer, and to deliberate with civility," and "to build coalitions and to manage conflict in a fair, peaceful manner."[20] An important caveat: calling out bigotry is not necessarily uncivil or antithetical to civility. During the civil rights movement, critics of civil rights activists who challenged white supremacy and an unjust status quo accused them of incivility.[21] Those who call out bigotry today might argue that, far from being uncivil, they seek to vindicate civic ideals by demanding that the polity and its political leaders live up to them.

The term "civic education" typically refers to the task of preparing youth for responsible citizenship and is, proponents argue, "essential to the preservation and improvements of American constitutional democracy."[22] Because the literature on civic education typically uses the rhetoric of "responsible citizenship" or of developing "competent and responsible citizens,"[23] I use these terms here, while acknowledging that aims of civic education also apply to persons within U.S. bor-

---

18 James E. Fleming and Linda C. McClain, *Ordered Liberty: Rights, Responsibilities, and Virtues* (Cambridge, MA: Harvard University Press, 2013), 118. I have also advanced a liberal feminist account of the dual authority of families and schools to educate children and foster civic virtue. See Linda C. McClain, *The Place of Families: Fostering Capacity, Equality, and Responsibility* (Cambridge, MA: Harvard University Press, 2006), 50–84.

19 McClain, *Place of Families*, 68–73.

20 Campaign to Promote Civic Education, *The Role of Civil Education: An Education Policy Task Force Position Paper with Policy Recommendations* (Sept. 1998), 4.

21 Randall Kennedy, "State of the Debate: The Case Against 'Civility,'" *American Prospect*, Dec. 19, 2001, https://prospect.org/culture/state-debate-case-civility/.

22 Fleming and McClain, *Ordered Liberty*, 118 (quoting Center for Civic Education, *National Standards for Civics and Government* [1994], Introduction).

23 Fleming and McClain, 119 (sources omitted).

ders who are not citizens but are members of communities and participants in local and national politics.

The Civic Role of Schools and Challenges in Carrying out Such Roles

Civic education faces challenge in the current political climate in the United States. How do schools carry out their civic role in times of "democratic discord," in "an increasingly polarized and partisan political climate"?[24] As education scholars Meira Levinson and Jacob Fay explain, in *Democratic Discord in Schools: Cases and Commentaries in Educational Ethics:* "It should not be at all surprising that democratic discord finds its way into schools, since ... schools 'are, and ought to be, political sites.'" Schools are political in "complicated ways": they "function simultaneously as institutions *in* a democracy and as institutions that prepare students *for* democracy."[25]

Levinson and Fay identify three "distinct civic roles" that schools play in educating both in and for democracy. Their account provides a helpful foundation for appreciating the connection between law and civic education and for considering what form a "reboot," or reinvigoration, of civic education might take to meet current challenges. First, "public schools have responsibilities in democracies as legal agents of the state, responsible for implementing democratically enacted public policies and laws."[26] For example, many states have laws requiring schools to adopt bullying-prevention policies. Such policies impose responsibilities and duties on teachers and administrators, such as "protecting students from cyberbullying and inappropriate digital content."[27] Such laws may also require the development of an appropriate bullying-prevention curriculum, which shapes what teachers teach in schools.[28]

---

24 See Jacob Fay and Meira Levinson, "Schools of, by, and for the People: Both Impossible and Necessary," in *Democratic Discord in Schools: Cases and Commentaries in Educational Ethics*, ed. Meira Levinson and Jacob Fay (Cambridge, MA: Harvard Education Press, 2019), 3.

25 Levinson and Fay, 4.

26 Meira Levinson and Jacob Fay, "Educating for Civic Renewal," in Levinson and Fay, *Democratic Discord*, 272.

27 Ibid., 273.

28 For example, after the Massachusetts legislature passed the Bullying Prevention and Intervention Law (2010), school officials developed guides for how to integrate bullying prevention into the curriculum. See Dr. Carol R. Johnson (Superintendent, Boston Public Schools), "Embedding Bullying Prevention in Core Curriculum: A Teacher's Guide K–12" (Focus on Children, Boston Public Schools).

A second civic role is that "schools exist in democracies as *objects* of adults' and students' ongoing democratic expression and engagement." For example, students may engage in "walkouts and other forms of protest to transform their schools ... into objects of democratic expression."[29] More than fifty years ago, the U.S. Supreme Court, in *Tinker v. Des Moines Independent School District* (1969), declared that neither students nor teachers "shed their constitutional rights to freedom of speech and expression at the schoolhouse gate"; the court upheld students' right to wear armbands in silent protest of the Vietnam War. The high-water mark of protecting students' First Amendment rights in school, *Tinker* illustrates the place of schools as sites of democratic expression, with an important proviso: such expression must not impinge on the rights of other students or "substantially interfere" with the operation of the school.[30]

A third civic role of school is that "schools are sites of civic preparation for future democratic citizens." [31] Undertaking civic education, I argue, is one form of such civic preparation.

Levinson and Fay caution that "in times of partisan contestation and civic upheaval," it is challenging for schools to fulfill "any one of the roles." Challenges multiply when "the roles themselves come into conflict"–for example, when "young people's civic vision and activism clash with school and district policies."[32]

This chapter considers some of the challenges of carrying out civic education in the present political climate. I begin with a brief articulation of civic education as one way that law shapes character. I introduce the "why" and the "what" of civic education, that is, its aims and content. The chapter also addresses the "how," that is, how to carry out civic education.

The Why, What, and How of Civic Education—and Civic Gaps

As to the "why" and "how" of civic education, consider the admonition of Benjamin Rush, signer of the Declaration of Independence. He asserted that the legislature must play an indispensable role in aiding with the "one method" of "rendering a republican form of government durable": "disseminating the seeds of virtue and knowledge through every part of the state, by means of proper places

---

29 Levinson and Fay, "Educating for Civic Renewal," 273 (emphasis in original).

30 393 U.S. 503, 506, 508–09 (1969).

31 Levinson and Fay, "Educating for Civic Renewal," 273.

32 Ibid.

and modes of education."[33] Such a premise is part of a long history of admonitions that inculcating seedbeds of virtue–or seedbeds of *civic* virtue–is necessary to sustain the American experiment in constitutional democracy. As expressed by former U.S. Supreme Court Justice Sandra Day O'Connor (a strong proponent of civic education), another premise is that "the practice of democracy" must be "taught and learned anew by each generation of citizens."[34] This chapter focuses on the role of government–in the form of schools–to do such teaching, but readers should bear in mind that another important (although not unproblematic) premise about civic virtue is that the family, religious institutions, and other parts of civil society are also important seedbeds of such virtue.[35]

Conversations within the United States and in Europe suggest notable parallels with respect to challenges concerning the what and how of civic education. As Per Mouritsen and Astrid Jaeger explain, introducing a survey of civic education in several European countries: "At its heart, civic education is designed to produce 'good citizens'–though ideas about what constitutes such an individual vary from country to country."[36] Within the United States, that idea varies state-to-state (and even within states), as do specifics about how best to inculcate that idea and how much to invest in doing so.

This regional diversity might seem surprising, since robust civic education is a perennial concern of various *national* commissions and summits. The title of a report from one such summit captures this concern: "The Republic is (Still) at Risk –and Civics is Part of the Solution."[37] Civic education, however, has not been part of federal testing mandates, such as the bipartisan No Child Left Behind Act of 2002, or the more recent Common Core State Standards Initiative, launched by a bipartisan group of governors and focused on mathematics and "English language arts and literacy."[38]

---

33 Peter Levine and Kei Kawashima-Ginsberg, "The Republic Is (Still) at Risk–and Civics is Part of the Solution" (Briefing Paper for the Democracy at a Crossroads National Summit, Sept. 21, 2017), 19, quoting Rush.

34 Ibid., 19.

35 See McClain, *Place of Families*, 50–84 (critiquing inattention to problems of sex inequality in the family in accounts of families as seedbeds of civic virtue); Fleming and McClain, *Ordered Liberty*, 81–111 (critically evaluating calls for renewal of civil society).

36 Per Mouritsen with Astrid Jaeger, *Designing Civic Education for Diverse Societies: Models, Tradeoffs, and Outcomes* (Integration Futures Working Group, Migration Policy Institute Europe, Feb. 2018), 1. The report "examines the diversity of national models that have emerged in Europe, focusing on Denmark, France, Germany, Sweden, and the United Kingdom": Mouritsen and Jaeger, 3.

37 Levine and Kawashima-Ginsberg, "The Republic Is (Still) at Risk."

38 Dana Goldstein, "Common Core After 10 Years: Pass? Or Fail?," *New York Times*, Dec. 7, 2019, A1. The Common Core standards concern (1) English language arts/literacy and

In the United States, "all 50 states have standards for social studies, which is a broad category that includes civics, American government, American history, and other subjects considered especially relevant to learning to be an effective and responsible citizens."[39] States vary considerably, however, on how much civics they teach and how they teach it.[40] One national measure of young people's civic knowledge is discouraging: only 23 percent of eighth graders taking the National Assessment of Education Progress (NAEP) civics exam performed at or above the proficient level, and "achievement levels have virtually stagnated since 1998."[41] Also troubling is that there are "profound disparities in civic knowledge and participation" among young people: those "flat and low results" mask "substantial gaps" in scores, with more affluent children and children with college-educated parents "more than five times more likely to score 'proficient'" on the NAEP than those eighth graders who qualified for free or reduced-price lunch and whose parents lacked a high school diploma.[42]

Contours of an Improved Model—or Reboot—of Civic Education

The current environment, including the displacement by social media of print newspapers and the ever-growing diversity of the U.S. population, requires new thinking about effective forms of civic education. If, as educators propose, civic education "must be different in the 21st century"[43] to be effective, then what form should that reboot take? In the confines of this chapter, I can offer only a sketch.

A helpful starting place is the briefing paper "The Republic Is (Still) at Risk– and Civics is Part of the Solution," written by Peter Levine and Kei Kawashima-Ginsberg for the Democracy at a Crossroads National Summit, held in 2017. This report begins with the problem of Americans' loss of trust in each other, in whether their fellow citizens are capable of governing the republic, and in political institutions. The problem of polarization, the report observes, is not simply one of political disagreement, but that an "increasing proportion of Americans 'dislike, even loathe' people of a different political party of their own." Young people are

(2) mathematics. See Common Core State Standards Initiative, http://www.corestandards.org/.

39 Levine and Kawashima-Ginsberg, "The Republic Is (Still) at Risk," 17.

40 Sarah Shapiro and Catherine Brown, "The State of Civics Education," Center for American Progress, Feb. 21, 2018, https://www.americanprogress.org/issues/education-k-12/reports/2018/02/21/446857/state-civics-education/.

41 Ibid., 1.

42 Levine and Kawashima-Ginsberg, "The Republic is (Still) at Risk," 7.

43 Ibid., 10.

coming of age as citizens in a “caustic environment,” which may be an explanatory factor in low youth turnout in elections and declining faith in democracy as a form of government.[44]

“Civic learning,” properly carried out by schools, is “an essential part of the solution” to this caustic environment, the briefing paper contends, and the “best vehicle” for training young people to “sustain our democracy”:

> In a society characterized by weak civic institutions, balkanized public discourse, and profoundly unequal civic engagement, schools can offer all young people opportunities to learn fundamental facts and skills, engage with each other and with their communities, and develop dispositions and values supportive of a republican form of government.[45]

Civic education matters both for the individual and for society: individuals lacking “the levels of skills, literacy, and training essential” to the new era will be “effectively disenfranchised”; further, a high level of “shared education” is critical for “a free, democratic society and to the fostering of a common culture, especially in a country that prides itself on pluralism and individual freedom.” Moreover, as noted earlier, the decline in associational life in the United States is “felt unequally”: low-income youth are “widely disconnected from civic life,” and “30 % of urban and suburban residents see themselves living in civic deserts.” Thus, civic education must acknowledge and address inequalities (economic and race-based) both in opportunities for civic engagement and in learning outcomes about civics.[46]

What “works” in civic education? Fortunately, the briefing paper reports, there is useful knowledge from the field of civic learning about “promising practices”–or “proven practices”–that are “effective when done well.” The report describes six such practices: (1) courses on civics, government, law, and related topics; (2) deliberations about current, controversial issues; (3) service-learning; (4) student-led voluntary associations; (5) student voice in schools; and (6) simulations of adult civic roles. Some of these practices occur within the classroom. For example, with respect to the second practice, deliberation: “a large body of research finds that facilitated, planned discussions teach deliberative skills and increase students’ knowledge and interest.” Teaching such skills and habits would

44 Ibid., 1–3.

45 Ibid., 3.

46 Ibid., 3, 8–9. Recognizing these issues, one recent report calls for a model of civics that attends to the “interests, identities, and life experiences of young people of color.” Cathy Cohen, Joseph Kahne, and Jessica Marshall, “Let’s Go There: Making a Case for Race, Ethnicity and a Lived Civics Approach to Civics Education,” GenForward at the University of Chicago, Chicago, IL, 2018, https://www.civicsurvey.org/publications/292.

be a valuable corrective: "perhaps the most evident deficit in American civic life today is the lack of discussion across political and social differences."[47]

Other proven practices might take place inside and outside of the classroom, such as simulations of adult civic roles. Traditional simulations include mock trials and Model UN programs; newer forms include the widely used iCivics learning program, which engages students in online role-playing games to "simulate how government works" and to participate in processes like national elections.[48]

Some proven practices take place outside of the classroom, such as student-led voluntary associations, in which students learn Alexis de Tocqueville's famous "arts and sciences of association." Levine and Kawashima-Ginsberg explain that when such groups work on "shared projects over time," members develop "habits of participation that persist for decades." Fostering "student voice in schools" so that students feel that they are influencing the "climate and policies of their schools" and that their voices are "respected and valued," helps young people develop into "more effective, skilled, and knowledgeable citizens." Finally, service-learning combines in-class and out-of-class experience, as students engage in community service as well as "academic study of the issues addressed by the students' service," where students might discuss "underlying causes of social problems." Positive outcomes from such service-learning include habits and values of engagement.[49]

The briefing paper recommends these proven practices. It offers examples of a few states successfully passing and implementing legislation that makes civics a priority and incorporates some of the practices.[50] It also calls for innovation because "civics must be different in the 21st century" to meet challenges of polarization, growing diversity, and growing inequality. It must, in the words of the report:

- Prepare students for a world of social media instead of printed local newspapers.
- Equip them to navigate a polarized society that faces complex and environmental challenges.
- Engage a generation that is far more diverse in terms of race, religion, ethnicity, national origin, and economic circumstances than any since World War II [and recognize that] [t]his rich diversity of cultural backgrounds is an asset that requires responsive teaching.

---

47 Levine and Kawashima-Ginsberg, 4.

48 Ibid.

49 Ibid.

50 Ibid., 12–16.

- Empower all students for effective civic engagement, countering the unequal resources and opportunities in their schools and communities.
- Start early and be a priority from grades K to 12.[51]

The first item on the list, teaching students "news media literacy education," seems an obvious component of effective twenty-first-century civic education, as people turn to social media instead of printed local newspapers for information. This turn brings benefits and costs. As social media platforms "give access to an enormous variety of sources and perspectives," young people "are increasingly empowered to influence the topics and stories that are widely shared." On the other hand, they are "deluged with unreliable information and actual propaganda, and research shows that most young people perform poorly at distinguishing fake news from reliable news." The briefing paper expresses confidence that schools *can* teach young people such discernment skills and to be "effective producers of news."[52] Such media literacy seems crucial after the 2016 U.S. presidential election drew attention to "the susceptibility of American voters' beliefs to false or misleading information."[53]

Some Challenges about "Engaging" Diverse Students and Teaching Controversies

"The Republic Is (Still) at Risk" proposes a new practice of engaging a more diverse generation of students but does not explicitly discuss how civic education could engage students who identify as LGBTQ. Doing so is important since, surveys find, such students are significantly more likely than their heterosexual or cisgender peers to experience bullying, harassment, or negative self-image, and to miss school because they feel unsafe or experience discrimination based on their sexual orientation or gender expression.[54] A Human Rights Campaign survey found that "only 13 % of LGBTQ youth report hearing positive messages about being LGBTQ in school," and some students hear about the LGBTQ community only in the context of conversations about HIV/AIDS.[55] These images can have

---

51 Ibid., 10.

52 Ibid., 5.

53 Hansen et al., "Brown Center Report," 1.

54 I use the term "cisgender" here to refer to a person whose sense of gender corresponds to the sex identified to them at birth–for example, male or female. For recent surveys, see Joseph G. Kosciw et al., *The 2017 National School Climate Survey: The Experiences of Lesbian, Gay, Bisexual, Transgender, and Queer Youth in Our Nation's Schools* (New York: GLSEN, 2018); Human Rights Campaign (HRC), *2018 LGBTQ Youth Report* (2018).

55 HRC, *2018 LGBTQ Youth Report*, 8.

a powerful impact on students' feelings of self-worth. As Sarah Schmidt observes, in "Queering Social Studies: The Role of Social Studies in Normalizing Citizens and Sexuality in the Common Good": "Gay must be bad if the only images and discussions we can find are negative."[56] When students are unable to see positive reflections of themselves in school materials, they will have difficulty seeing their worth in other areas of their lives.

In writing about the role of schools in fostering resilience in LGBTQ youth, legal scholar Martha Albertson Fineman contends that "[m]ost schools ... do not effectively educate around concepts and practices of what used to be called 'civic virtue'–the idea that diversity, civility, tolerance, compromise, and commitment to nonviolent dispute resolution are essential life-skills in a diverse democracy."[57] If students are not taught these skills in school, and are not given the opportunity to practice them with their peers, the consequences can be negative and immense, particularly for LGBTQ students. By comparison, when civic education focuses on teaching tolerance and explicitly teaches about LGBTQ issues, it can be extremely beneficial for students who identify as LGBTQ and have a positive impact on their feelings of safety in school and their likelihood to attend school.[58] Similar positive effects can follow when staff members are supportive of LGBTQ students and of in-school clubs and organizations, such as gay-straight alliances (GSAs).[59] Schmidt argues that civic education should "explore the discourse of sexuality and citizenship" to understand how LGBTQ issues are "part of the common good." Students should be taught to think critically about the common good so that the concept includes "advanc[ing] equality and justice for all," rather than simply reifying the status quo.[60]

Teaching students to think critically and to deliberate respectfully across difference is no easy task, as the case studies and commentaries presented by Levinson and Fay in *Democratic Discord in Schools* make vividly clear. Educators may share a commitment to "teaching the controversies," or helping students learn how to research and critically evaluate and discuss controversial issues but may disagree over whether certain matters should be subject to debate. For example, in one study presented in the volume, Northern High School uses a tenth-grade social studies curriculum, "Power of Persuasion" (PoP), to challenge students "to research and critically evaluate a controversial issue, take a position, and present

---

56 Sandra J. Schmidt, "Queering Social Studies: The Role of Social Studies in Normalizing Citizens and Sexuality in the Common Good," *Theory & Research in Social Education* 38, no. 3 (Summer 2010): 314.

57 Martha Albertson Fineman, "Vulnerability, Resilience, and LGBT Youth," *Temple Political & Civil Rights Law Review* 23 (2014): 307, 323–24.

58 GLSEN, *2017 National School Climate Survey*, 56.

59 Ibid., 109–10.

60 Schmidt, "Queering Social Studies," 319.

their arguments to classmates." After the class presentation, each social studies class selects the strongest pro and con position papers for a schoolwide "Pop-Off" during the morning assembly. Before the assembly, students complete "an anonymous poll about where they stood on the issue," and then the winning representatives from each class have ninety seconds to present their "Pop-Talk to convince their peers about the desirability of their position." At the conclusion, another poll is taken, and the declared winner, or "PoP-Off Powerhouse," for that topic is whichever team converted the largest number of people to its position.

This was a popular program, but much depended on "teachers' selecting the right controversial issue to focus on each time."[61] For example, sharp disagreement arose among the teachers when one teacher, Jack, hesitantly proposed the topic of "the debate about transgender students' access to bathrooms," since it was "big in the news right now." Jack's hesitation stemmed from a concern over whether "we should be treating transgender bathroom rights as a controversial question." Even though Jack recognized that it *was* being debated in various statehouses as controversial, he asked: "How can we treat gender discrimination as something that is controversial, not just wrong?" Other teachers expressed surprise that Jack, who normally did not shy away from discussing controversial issues, would advocate taking this issue off the table. They countered that they must prepare students to be "informed and engaged citizens" and to think about the questions critically, especially since the school had already received "two different sets of federal guidelines about who should use which bathroom." Some teachers argued that, while caution is needed, given the present "polarized and partisan" political debate, it was important to facilitate the conversation among students. Jack countered that while "inquiry, critical thinking, and persuasive writing and speaking are incredibly important," he did not think that "debating what are effectively human rights questions is ethically responsible," since the school should be upholding "basic democratic principles like tolerance, equality, and human rights." Indeed, he did not think that "as a school we should be encouraging students to treat this as having multiple reasonable perspectives." Colleagues expressed concern about teachers taking sides or engaging in "censorship of mainstream political issues;" they stressed the need to create a safe space for students to discuss the arguments and counterarguments they would need when discussing the issue in the world. The case study ends without resolution, as one of the teachers asks, "How should we be preparing our students for democratic citizenship in what feels like an increasingly uncivil world?"[62] The several commentaries on this case study address this and other questions as they

---

61 See Ellis Reid, Heather Johnson, and Meira Levinson, "Politics, Partisanship, and Pedagogy: What Should be Controversial in K-12 Classrooms," in Levinson and Fay, *Democratic Discord in Schools*, 177–78.

62 Ibid., 179–81.

point out the numerous challenges educators face in engaging students in encountering and understanding different perspectives on controversial issues, but also in creating the conditions so that students may do so in a safe and respectful environment.[63]

Religious Literacy as a Component of Civic Education

One promising feature of a twenty-first-century reinvigorated civic education *not* mentioned in "The Republic (Still) at Risk," but one that arguably could foster civility and combat bigotry, is religious literacy–nonsectarian education about religion. I will briefly sketch the case for including religious literacy as among the best practices for effective civic education.

The basic case for religious literacy is well put by Diane L. Moore, founding director of the Religious Literacy Project at Harvard Divinity School. In her essay "High Stakes Ignorance: Religion, Education, and the Unwitting Reproduction of Bigotry," Moore argues:

> First, there exists a widespread illiteracy about religion that spans the globe; second, one of the most troubling and urgent consequences of this illiteracy is that it often fuels prejudice and antagonism, thereby hindering efforts aimed at promoting respect for pluralism, peaceful coexistence, and cooperative endeavors in local, national, and global arenas; and third, it is possible to diminish religious illiteracy by teaching about religion from a nonsectarian perspective in primary, middle, and secondary schools.[64]

The report *Pluralism in Peril* similarly diagnoses a widespread and dangerous religious illiteracy and recommends that "teaching about religion and engaging youth in religious literacy programs in public and private schools and youth service organizations can diminish that illiteracy and the prejudice that attends it, so long as it is done using the non-devotional, academic perspective called religious studies."[65]

Both of these arguments for teaching religious literacy in public schools draw on 2010 guidelines offered by an American Academy of Religion (AAR) task force on religion in the public schools, chaired by Moore. The guidelines cautioned that "illiteracy regarding religion is widespread" and that the "prejudice and antago-

---

63 See, for example, Neema Avashia, "Moving Beyond the Echo Chamber," in Levinson and Fay, *Democratic Discord in Schools,* at 183–86.

64 Moore, "High Stakes Ignorance," 112

65 Allison K. Ralph and Seán Rose, "Religious Literacy and Inclusion in Education Settings and Youth-Serving Organizations: Opportunities to Grow the Field," in *Pluralism in Peril,* 17, 18.

nism" such illiteracy fueled was a great threat to the United States.[66] The guidelines explained how K-12 public schools could teach about religion in a constitutional manner.[67]

Moore argues that while "[l]earning about religion is no guarantee that religious bigotry and chauvinism will cease," it "will make it more difficult for such bigotry and chauvinism to be unwittingly reproduced and promoted."[68] Effective education about religions and religious pluralism will, she contends, increase understanding of different religions and make it likely that students will be more conscious and less judgmental of the religious values of their peers.

Readers may ask: why schools, rather than parents and religious communities? After all, the First Amendment prohibits governmental establishment of religion and protects the free exercise of religion, and under the Fourteenth Amendment, parents have a fundamental liberty concerning the care, control, and education of their children. Moore argues that schools have a proper role and responsibility to provide nonsectarian education *about* religion, which has the pedagogical purpose of creating a more tolerant and stable society.[69] "Religious illiteracy has moral and civic consequences that are often dire."[70] Thus, it is vital to teach about religion in a way that is responsible, conscientious, and clearly aligned with other educational values in order to increase tolerance and combat bigotry in society. Educators therefore "need to be clear" about why teaching about religion is "a valid and, indeed, important focus for inquiry in relation to the broader educational goals that a given teacher, school, district, or nation affirms and intentionally tries to promote."[71] Such clarity not only will help students better learn about religion by aligning it with other educational values, but also will allay parental fears about religious education in schools.

Moore describes two different types of parental fears that will be familiar to anyone who has studied controversies between parents and schools over curriculum. On one hand, "[c]onservative religious practitioners from many faith traditions often oppose learning about religion in schools for they feel that it is the role of faith communities and families to teach about religion from their own theological perspectives." Thus, "learning about religion from an academic lens presumes the legitimacy of multiple religious worldviews, which is theologically problematic in some circles." On the other hand, areligious parents are likely to "fear that if religion is introduced in the schools some teachers will inevitably

---

66 American Academy of Religion, "Guidelines for Teaching about Religion in K-12 Public Schools in the United States" (April, 2010), 4-7.

67 AAR, "Guidelines," 7-9.

68 Moore, "High Stakes Ignorance," 115.

69 Ibid., 116.

70 Ibid., 125.

71 Ibid., 120.

proselytize either by intention or default due to a lack of adequate training and clear understanding of the distinction between an academic and devotional approach."[72] While religious parents may fear that their children will begin to question their faith in relation to other, purportedly equally legitimate religions, areligious parents may worry that religious education in schools will bring their children into a specific religion.

To quell fears on both sides, Moore argues, it is important that there be "a difference between religion understood through the lens of personal devotional practice and the academic study of religion."[73] Parents and students alike must understand that the academic purpose of religious education is to increase understanding of different perspectives, rather than force any particular perspective onto students. "Training in religious literacy," Moore argues, "provides citizens with the tools to better understand religion as a complex and sophisticated social/cultural phenomenon and individual religious traditions themselves as internally diverse and constantly evolving as opposed to uniform, absolute, and ahistorical." In contrast to the way that religion is currently taught, Moore argues that students must learn to see the nuance in religion and learn about the historical contexts in which religions formed and evolved, so that they can better understand religion as something that is living and changing rather than fixed.[74]

Many public-school teachers, however, do not have the training needed to effectively teach religious education to a diverse population of students. Thus, it is necessary "to give teachers the training they need to do so more responsibly than they are often currently able to do."[75] Encouragingly, there are a number of resources for doing so in addition to the AAR guidelines. For example, after a pilot study in Hartford, Connecticut, Moore's Religious Literacy Project has developed a "continuing-education program" for teachers with "webinars, in-person seminars, and hybrid online/in-person opportunities."[76]

In *Pluralism in Peril,* contributors Allison K. Ralph and Seán Rose argue that teaching students to "engage intentionally with religious pluralism and diversity" can help to "build strong and resilient communities and a functioning democratic process." They further argue that, in addition to public schools, a vital resource for such engagement is youth-serving organizations (such as Boys and Girls Clubs of America, the YMCA, and others), which "have almost unparalleled reach in diverse communities throughout the United States."[77]

---

72 Ibid., 115–16.

73 Ibid., 113.

74 Ibid., 115.

75 Ibid., 116.

76 Ralph and Rose, "Religious Literacy and Inclusion," 20–24. For more examples, see The Religious Literacy Project, https://rlp.hds.harvard.edu/.

77 Ralph and Rose, 18, 24.

To be sure, teaching religious literacy in public schools presents various challenges, of which addressing competing types of parental objections is but one example.[78] One common and important premise that justifies such education, however, is that "what most undermines a pluralistic society is ignorance–both an ignorance of civic knowledge and an ignorance of religious knowledge."[79] Such education might help change such a climate and prepare students for respectful engagement and cooperation across difference in an increasingly pluralistic constitutional democracy.

Grounds for Optimism?

Let us assume, then, that a "high-quality civics education" would combine the six proven practices with some of the additional ones recommended in the briefing paper "The Republic Is (Still) at Risk," such as media literacy.[80] How well are states doing if measured against that checklist? One recent fifty-state inventory that added media literacy found that "some–but certainly not all–[proven practices] are widespread throughout the country." The briefing paper concludes by offering some "grounds for optimism," based on such indicators as more young people interested in iCivics games and more states considering strengthening their civic-learning standards.[81] Innovation and experimentation, the authors conclude, are critical to carrying forward "the American experiment in republican self-government."[82]

Contemporary discourse about civic education offers considerable insight about those "proper places and modes of education" to which Benjamin Rush refers, and how legislatures may promote them. Might we hope that a renewed commitment to civic education, transformed in the ways discussed earlier, could help to bring about a healthier, less-toxic climate with a more responsible, virtuous citizenry in which calling out bigotry is less frequent and necessary?

---

78 For examples, see the contributions to Biondo and Fiala, *Civility, Religious Pluralism, and Education.*

79 Shapri LoMaglio, "Christian Commitment to Pluralism Should Not Waiver," in *Pluralism in Peril*, 105, 107.

80 Ibid., 16–17.

81 Levine and Kawashima-Ginsberg, "The Republic Is (Still) at Risk," 18.

82 Ibid., 18.

An Australian Case Study on Law and Values

Debating a Bill of Rights

Frank Brennan

The International Plea: Human Rights Should Be Protected by the Rule of Law

The preamble to the 1948 Universal Declaration of Human Rights (UDHR)states: "Whereas it is essential, if man is not to be compelled to have recourse, as a last resort, to rebellion against tyranny and oppression, that human rights should be protected by the rule of law." Two years after the Declaration was proclaimed by the UN General Assembly, the Council of Europe was established, with member states signing on to the European Convention on Human Rights resolving "to take the first steps for the collective enforcement of certain of the rights stated in the Universal Declaration." Anthony Mason, when serving as chief justice of Australia, said, "It is unrealistic to interpret any instrument, whether it be a constitution, a statute, or a contract, by reference to words alone, without regard to fundamental values."[1] What, then, are the fundamental values which underpin these legal instruments which profess commitments to human rights protected by the rule of law and to collective enforcement of human rights set down in the UDHR? James Allsop, chief judge of the Federal Court in Australia, has told a Hong Kong audience: "The essential human values most particularly relevant to public law are: a rejection of unfairness and an insistence on essential equality; respect for the integrity and dignity of the individual; and mercy."[2]

Since 1950, it has been commonplace for nation-states to extend the rule of law domestically and internationally to the protection of human rights. Domestically, nation-states have struck differing balances between the domain of parlia-

---

1 Anthony Mason, "Future Directions in Australian Law," *Monash University Law Review* 13 (1987): 149, 158–59.

2 James Allsop, "Values in Law: How they Influence and Shape Rules and the Application of Law," Lecture at the Centre for Comparative and Public Law, University of Hong Kong, October 20, 2016, https://www.fedcourt.gov.au/digital-law-library/judges-speeches/chief-justice-allsop/allsop-cj-20161020.

ments and the domain of courts when restricting the government's capacity to limit the exercise of human rights. Internationally, nation-states have opted for a varying range of scrutiny by other nation-states and by international monitoring bodies. While respecting national sovereignty, the community of nations has increased the prospects for naming and shaming of those nation-states failing to respect human rights within their own borders. Many nation-states have opted for some form of bill of rights (constitutional or legislative) to enhance the protection of human rights under the umbrella of the rule of law. Australia is one nation which has not. Many nation-states have opted for maximum scrutiny of their human-rights records by signing on to optional protocol procedures which allow disaffected citizens to petition UN bodies to assess state action for human-rights compliance. Australia is one nation which has done so, though elected politicians sometimes then choose to disregard the findings of the international agencies.

The forty-seven member states of the Council of Europe subject themselves to scrutiny by the European Court of Human Rights at Strasbourg. In 1998, the United Kingdom enacted its own Human Rights Act "to give further effect to rights and freedoms guaranteed under the European Convention on Human Rights." The UK legislation attempts to strike the balance between parliamentary sovereignty and national independence, on one hand, and judicialized accountability and international scrutiny on the other. Even prior to 1998, many UK actions invasive of human rights (particularly in the troubled times in Northern Ireland) were subject to judicial scrutiny in Strasbourg. In fact, the United Kingdom had contributed significantly to the jurisprudence of the European Court of Human Rights even prior to 1998 because, unlike some of the more flagrant human rights violators in the Council of Europe, the British have taken seriously their duty to the court, and both government and the NGO sector in civil society have debated and scrutinized closely any decision of the Strasbourg court. The Strasbourg jurisprudence has helped shape not only British attitudes but also British values respectful of human rights. British values and attitudes in turn have helped develop the Strasbourg jurisprudence of human rights.

The British have usually ensured that a highly competent and respected judge has served on the Strasbourg court whenever British disputes are being adjudicated. For example, Lord Reed, the president of the UK Supreme Court, has served on the European Court of Human Rights as an ad hoc judge for twenty years. Three UK judges have served as president of the European Court for more than a decade of the court's existence. The British have contributed significantly to the Strasbourg jurisprudence of human rights, and the Strasbourg jurisprudence was impacting so much on the British debate about human rights that Westminster decided, in 1998, to enact legislation aimed at harmonizing judicial reasoning at home and abroad on human-rights issues. Even though the United Kingdom has opted for Brexit, and no matter the terms of exit from the European Union, the United Kingdom will still be a member of the Council of Europe and subject to the jurisdiction of the European Court of Human Rights. Even if the UK Parliament were to repeal the 1998 Human Rights Act, it would still enact legislation replicating in domestic law the key rights and freedoms set down in the European Charter, regardless of which party was in power.

Prior to 1998, countries such as New Zealand and Canada had developed their own national human-rights laws. Canada opted for a constitutional charter; New Zealand opted for legislation. Though Australian courts and parliaments were attentive to developments in these countries, which share something of a common legal heritage and present cultural disposition, the Australians remained content that their human-rights protections remained adequate, being not unlike those in the United Kingdom, but for the development of the Strasbourg jurisprudence. But once the United Kingdom had enacted the Human Rights Act, Australia was left isolated on the rock of parliamentary sovereignty and national independence. Ironically, by failing to legislate a human rights act, the Australian politicians have left the unelected judges to develop the law of human rights for themselves without the same assistance that they received in the past from judges in equivalent jurisdictions like the United Kingdom, Canada, and New Zealand. The reasoning of the judges in those jurisdictions is now guided by their bills of rights. The difficult judicial task for them is the balancing of the diverse rights set down in their human-rights legislation. The Australian judges are left judicially isolated, having to develop the law of human rights without the bright-line parameters of a human rights act and without the cross-fertilization of ideas from the ultimate courts of appeal in similar countries.

The Australian Experiment: A Nation Founded without Adequate Human-Rights Protections

The absence of a national bill of rights in Australia requires an ongoing national conversation as to how best to protect human rights under the rule of law, including an ongoing assessment of the utility of collective enforcement of these rights. In those nation-states with a bill of rights, the argument is often confined to whether the courts got it right in a particular dispute. Without a bill of rights, the argument is often more wide ranging, debating whether parliament should legislate to protect a particular right or to protect the common good or the public interest. Opponents of any bill of rights in Australia are not usually opposed to comprehensive protection of human rights. They tend to be people who question whether their own courts or the international tribunals get the balance correct when adjudicating human-rights claims, or whether these decision makers espouse the same values as they do when it comes to protecting rights such as freedom of religion, freedom of speech, freedom of association, and freedom to own and use property. Many bill opponents suspect that judicial decision makers, guided by the prevailing trends in the legal academy rather than by popular sentiment and attitudes, tend to espouse values at variance with theirs–for example, precluding religious groups from being able to maintain the ethos of their institutions, or restricting speech which might offend or insult particular groups regardless of the truth content of the speech.

The case study of Australia may be of broader interest because the public discussion of human rights is not restricted to the critique of judicial reasoning. Neither is the discussion cut short with the declaration that the stipulated, legislated "rights are trumps." Rather, the discussion culminates in a consideration of which community values are most prized, how those values are expressed in legal principle and policy priorities, and how conflicting values are held in tension by institutional arrangements and modes of public discourse. Judicialized accountability and international scrutiny have gone hand in hand in Australia, giving expression to community values with which even the most populist of politicians and media commentators have to contend. But without any form of national bill of rights, the contours for the debate remain more fluid, and the institutional arrangements for the resolution of conflict remain contested.

At the end of the nineteenth century, extensive debates occurred about the desirability of a federation being formed of the six British colonies established in Australia. Some of the interlocutors were very familiar with the U.S. Constitution, including the Bill of Rights, which was appended after the American Revolution. The Australian "founding fathers" (and they were all men) saw no need to define citizenship in the new nation. Everyone would continue to be British subjects. There was a suggestion that the proposed Australian constitution should include a provision ensuring that the British subjects in one state should enjoy the same rights and privileges as the British subjects in any other state. The values of equality and the innate human dignity of all British subjects were espoused. Drawing on the U.S. Constitution, Richard O'Connor (later one of the founding judges of the High Court of Australia) suggested that there be a provision providing: "A state shall not deprive any person of life, liberty, or property without due process of law, or deny to any person within its jurisdiction the equal protection of its laws."[3] Both suggestions failed to win majority support. One reason was the prevalent adverse attitude toward people of different races. For example, Sir John Forrest, a delegate from Western Australia, told the 1898 Convention:

---

3 *Official Record of the Debates of the Australasian Federal Convention*, Melbourne, Feb. 8, 1898, p. 673.

> It is of no use for us to shut our eyes to the fact that there is a great feeling all over Australia against the introduction of coloured persons. It goes without saying that we do not like to talk about it, but still it is so. I do not want this clause to pass in a shape which would undo what is about to be done in most of the colonies, and what has already been done in Western Australia, in regard to that class of persons.[4]

Isaac Isaacs, later a High Court judge and governor-general of Australia, impressed on the convention delegates that the U.S. provision of equal protection under the Fourteenth Amendment was the result of the Civil War and the freeing of slaves–a history very different from Australia's. While some delegates could see the need for some statement of principle about equality and nondiscrimination, other delegates thought that any such provision, no matter how worded, would interfere with the powers of the individual states.

O'Connor told the Convention:

> One word as to the first part of my amendment, which is to the effect that a state shall not deprive any person of life, liberty, or property without due process of law. In the ordinary course of things such a provision at this time of day would be unnecessary; but we all know that laws are passed by majorities and that communities are liable to sudden and very often to unjust impulses–as much so now as ever. The amendment is simply a declaration that no impulse of this kind which might lead to the passing of an unjust law shall deprive a citizen of his right to a fair trial.[5]

Isaacs retorted, "That is a very dangerous proposal–that the Supreme Court should control the Legislatures of the states within their own jurisdiction."[6] The pushback continued, with other delegates claiming that the constitutions of the individual states already protected the citizens. O'Connor asserted that the newly constituted nation needed to ensure that protection was maintained. He told the Convention:[7]

> We are now dealing with the prohibition against the alteration of these Constitutions. We are dealing with a provision which will prevent the alteration of these Constitutions in the direction of depriving any citizen of his life, liberty, or property without due process of law. Because if this provision in the Constitution is carried it will not be in the power of any state to pass a law to amend its Constitution to do that. It is a dec-

---

4 Ibid., 666.

5 Ibid., 683.

6 Ibid.

7 Ibid.

> laration of liberty and freedom in our dealing with citizens of the Commonwealth. Not only can there be no harm in placing it in the Constitution, but it is also necessary for the protection of the liberty of everybody who lives within the limits of any State.

O'Connor's amendment lost by a vote of seventeen for and twenty-four against. This was not simply a contest of differing attitudes. It was a contest of conflicting values. Isaacs and his supporters valued the freedom of individual states to determine their racial composition. O'Connor and his supporters valued the freedom of individuals to enjoy equal protection and respect under the law.

The newly constituted federation of Australia permitted racial discrimination against prospective migrants and denied recognition of the rights of the Aboriginal people to their lands. Under the Constitution, the Commonwealth Parliament had no power to make laws with respect to Aborigines. The Commonwealth Parliament did have power to make adverse discriminatory laws against people of other races for whom it was deemed necessary to make such laws. There was no due process or equal protection measure in the Constitution which limited the power of state legislatures.

Australian Developments: Protecting Human Rights without a Bill of Rights

After World War II, Australian officials participated fully in the international deliberations regarding the UDHR and played an active role in the formulation of all key international instruments setting out the range of human rights (including the International Covenant on Civil and Political Rights [ICCPR] and the International Covenant on Economic, Social and Cultural Rights [ICESCR]) and later the conventions banning various forms of adverse discrimination. Being a federation, Australia was always able to buy time for implementation, invoking the federalism clause to demonstrate that appropriate laws and policies for protecting human rights and outlawing adverse discrimination were matters for the states, and not for the national government or Parliament.

The civil unrest of the 1960 s often resulted in claims for better protection of civil liberties. The language of human rights and civil rights was foreign to Australian ears at that time. The International Convention on the Elimination of all Forms of Racial Discrimination (CERD) came into force for Australia in October 1975, whereupon the Australian Parliament legislated immediately the Racial Discrimination Act, which was the first piece of national human-rights legislation which limited the power of the state parliaments to deal adversely with Aborigines or with those of other races who had suffered ongoing adverse discrimination. For Australia, the ICESCR came into force in March 1976, and the ICCPR came into force in November 1980. The language of civil liberties started to be replaced with the language of human rights. Aboriginal protests drawing international attention were marked by the cry, "What do we want? Land Rights. When do we want it? Now." In 1973 and 1985, Labor governments did introduce human-rights bills, which would have worked a partial implementation of the key international instruments. A Constitutional Commission set up in 1985 recommended, in 1988, a suite of constitutional reforms, including a comprehensive list of human rights, but all these proposals were stillborn. Nonetheless, these attempts were an indicator of a sense that there was a shortfall in the architecture for the protection of human rights. While the Labor Party was moderately supportive of these comprehensive human-rights measures, the conservative Liberal/National Party Coalition was opposed. But the major political parties were agreed on the need for Australia to be a model international actor contributing to the drafting of and signing on to all the major international human-rights instruments.

The Convention on the Elimination of all Forms of Discrimination Against Women (CEDAW) came into force for Australia in August 1983; the Convention against Torture (CAT) came into force for Australia in September 1989; the Convention on the Rights of the Child (CRC) came into force for Australia in January 1991; and the Convention on the Rights of Persons with Disabilities (CPRD) came into force for Australia in August 2008. Australia was also at the forefront of those nations prepared to sign on to the optional protocols to various UN human-rights instruments permitting citizens to bring individual complaints to international tribunals once all domestic remedies had been exhausted. Undoubtedly, these moves helped to inform and educate the Australian public about human rights and the values underpinning the formulation of these instruments. A national human-rights commission was set up to educate the public about these human-rights measures and to process complaints from citizens alleging that government had failed to comply with the requirements of these measures.

In the absence of a national bill of rights, Australia's legislative protection of human rights became something of a patchwork quilt. For example, within a year of CEDAW coming into force for Australia, the Commonwealth Parliament enacted the Sex Discrimination Act in 1984 "to give effect to certain provisions of the Convention on the Elimination of All Forms of Discrimination Against Women and to provisions of other relevant international instruments." In the absence of any act prohibiting religious discrimination, the freedom of religious bodies to teach and implement their doctrine on marriage, gender, and sexuality was carved out by means of exceptions for various behaviors and exemptions for various entities in key provisions of the Sex Discrimination Act. The negotiation of these exceptions and exemptions over the last thirty-five years was the testing ground for community discussion, agitation, and clarification about the value and the limits of religious freedom. But over time, the public has lost sight of the positive right of religious freedom. As Australians have become less religious, and as the elite have become more secularist, key opinion makers and the media have been asking why religious folk should get special treatment by way of exceptions and exemptions in nondiscriminiation legislation. Whereas even a decade ago, many religious leaders saw benefit in opposing a national human-rights act, they now see benefit in agitating for a religious discrimination act or even a religious freedom act. They rightly argue that the value of religious freedom should not be seen simply in terms of an exemption or exception to discrimination legislation, any more than the value of equal respect and dignity should be treated only as an exception or exemption to religious-freedom legislation.

In the absence of a bill of rights, the Australian High Court performs three discrete functions. First, the Court interprets the Constitution, striking down any laws made by the Commonwealth or state parliaments inconsistent with provisions of the Constitution. The Court has even enunciated an implied freedom of political communication, as the Constitution specifies that the houses of Parliament are chosen by the people. How would the people exercise such a choice meaningfully unless there were a freedom of communication about political matters impacting on people's electoral choices? Thus, the implied freedom of communication about political matters which might help to inform the citizen's vote.

Second, the Court interprets valid legislation, and it interprets those laws as consistently as possible with the basic freedoms and protections one would expect to find in a democracy under the rule of law. As the High Court has said, "The courts should not impute to the legislature an intention to interfere with fundamental rights. Such an intention must be clearly manifested by unmistakable and unambiguous language.'[8] Chief Justice French described this as "a statement about the value attached by the courts to common law rights and freedoms. It was expressed out of respect for the Parliament as an assumption about the legislative approach to those rights and freedoms."[9] French's predecessor, Chief Justice Gleeson, said, "The presumption is not merely a common sense guide to what a Parliament in a liberal democracy is likely to have intended; it is a working hypothesis, the existence of which is known both to Parliament and the courts, upon which statutory language will be interpreted. The hypothesis is an aspect of the rule of law."[10]

Third, the Court develops the common law consistent with contemporary values of the Australian people while maintaining the consistency of the law.

---

8 *Coco v The Queen, Commonwealth Law Reports* 179 (1994): 427, 437, (Mason CJ, Brennan, Gaudron and McHugh JJ).

9 Robert French, "Law Making in a Representative Democracy: The Durability of Enduring Values," The Catherine Branson Lecture, Adelaide, Oct. 14, 2016, p. 12, http://www.hcourt.gov.au/assets/publications/speeches/current-justices/frenchcj/frenchcj14Oct2016.pdf.

10 *Electrolux Home Products Pty Ltd v Australian Workers' Union, Commonwealth Law Reports* 221 (2004): 309, 329.

How Contemporary Values Inform the Development of the Law Protecting Human Rights

A century ago, the Privy Council in London ruled on a land dispute in what was then Rhodesia. Lord Sumner wrote:[11]

> The estimation of the rights of aboriginal tribes is always inherently difficult. Some tribes are so low in the scale of social organization that their usages and conceptions of rights and duties are not to be reconciled with the institutions or the legal ideas of civilized society. Such a gulf cannot be bridged. It would be idle to impute to such people some shadow of the rights known to our law and then to transmute it into the substance of transferable rights of property as we know them.

Lord Sumner observed that there was "a wide tract of much ethnological interest" between these tribes and other indigenous peoples "whose legal conceptions, though differently developed, are hardly less precise than our own." He thought the natives in question "approximate rather to the lower than to the higher limit."[12] According to the Privy Council, the maintenance of native title rights "was fatally inconsistent with white settlement of the country," which "was the object of the whole forward movement, pioneered by the [South Africa] Company and controlled by the Crown with the result that the aboriginal system gave place to another prescribed by the Order in Council." The Privy Council concluded its consideration of the native title claim, "Whoever now owns the unalienated lands, the natives do not."[13] The natives were the people of one new polity without a voice, under one new law without rights. The values of the colonial power made no place for the recognition of the rights, dignity, and equality of the natives.

At the height of colonial expansion by European empires, those indigenous groups who bore some resemblance to their colonial masters were to enjoy some recognition and protection. Those differing from their new masters, who could barely comprehend their social reality, were to be denied any semblance of land rights and self-determination. Such Eurocentric notions put blinkers on the law's horizons of justice.

Seventy-four years after the Privy Council's decision about the fortunes of the British South Africa Company, the High Court of Australia had, for the first time, in the *Mabo* case, to consider the rights of the Australian "natives" to the "unalienated lands." In 1992, that court decided to discard the distinction between inhab-

---

11 *In re Southern Rhodesia, Appeal Cases* [1919]: 211, 233–34.

12 Ibid., 234.

13 Ibid., 235.

ited colonies that were deemed to be *terra nullius* and those which were not. Justice Brennan, in the lead judgment, wrote:[14]

> If it were permissible in past centuries to keep the common law in step with international law, it is imperative in today's world that the common law should neither be nor be seen to be frozen in an age of racial discrimination. The fiction by which the rights and interests of indigenous inhabitants in land were treated as non-existent was justified by a policy which has no place in the contemporary law of this country.

With the removal of the blinkers used by Lord Sumner and most Europeans of his time, Indigenous people are not guaranteed a better life, but they can be assured the legal and political preconditions for better participation in the life of the nation-state, while maintaining and adapting their traditional places and lifestyle. The contemporary Australian court went on to say:[15]

> Whatever the justification advanced in earlier days for refusing to recognize the rights and interests in land of the indigenous inhabitants of settled colonies, an unjust and discriminatory doctrine of that kind can no longer be accepted. The expectations of the international community accord in this respect with the contemporary values of the Australian people.

Does this reference to contemporary values imply that the judges thought the majority of Australians, if asked in an opinion poll, "Do you support Aboriginal land rights?," would have answered unequivocally, "Yes"? I do not think it can mean that. I am prepared to accept that the majority of Australians, if asked that question in 1992, would have answered no. We need to distinguish attitudes from values. Following the work of Milton Rokeach, John Braithwaite suggests, "While a value is a standard that transcends objects and situations, an attitude is not a standard. An attitude is simply an organised set of beliefs focused on the specific object or situation that gives the attitude its name."[16] The values that underpin the *Mabo* decision are respect for property, the desire for certainty in the conduct of relations relating to land, predictability in the application of the law by courts for the resolution of conflict, and nondiscrimination in the sense that governments should not treat persons differently unless there is a coherent rationale for such different treatment. In particular, governments should not treat people's property

14 Justice Brennan (Mason CJ and McHugh J concurring) in *Mabo* v *Queensland (No. 2), Commonwealth Law Reports* 175 (1992): 1, 41–42.

15 Ibid., 42.

16 John Braithwaite, "Community Values and Australian Jurisprudence," *Sydney Law Review* 17 (1995): 351, 354.

rights more adversely simply because they are members of a particular race. These are the enduring values of contemporary Australians.

The Australian High Court's legal reasoning, which developed the common law of native title for the benefit of Aborigines, would have delivered little to those who had been so long dispossessed, but for the effect of the 1975 Racial Discrimination Act (RDA), enacted by the Australian Parliament as a domestic implementation of CERD, the convention on the elimination of racial discrimination. The effect of the High Court decision was that all native title extinguished by the crown prior to 1975 was validly extinguished and without payment of compensation. But any native title which survived from the assertion of British sovereignty in 1788 until 1975 would then have enjoyed the double protection of the RDA. If title were extinguished after 1975, it could be done only on payment of compensation. Any surviving title could not be extinguished in future except in accordance with the ordinary laws governing the compulsory acquisition of private land by the government for public purposes. So the ultimate protection of Aboriginal land rights under the rule of law came about in Australia as the result of collective international enforcement in the formulation of CERD, parliamentary action to incorporate CERD into Australian domestic law, and court decision to reshape the common law in accordance with the contemporary values of the Australian people while maintaining the shape and consistency of the law.

There was great controversy in Australia when the High Court delivered this decision. Doyens of the mining and pastoral industry were very upset. They questioned the judges' reference to community values. Five months after the *Mabo* decision, Justice Brennan had cause in another case to observe:[17] "The contemporary values which justify judicial development of the law are not the transient notions which emerge in reaction to a particular event or which are inspired by a publicity campaign conducted by an interest group. They are the relatively permanent values of the Australian community." He went on to say:[18]

> Changes in the common law are not made whenever a judge thinks a change desirable. There must be constraints on the exercise of the power, else the Courts would cross "the Rubicon that divides the judicial and the legislative powers"... [T]he chief constraints are found in the traditional methods of judicial reasoning which ensure that judicial developments remain consonant not only with contemporary values but also with ... the skeleton of principle which gives the body of our law its shape and internal consistency. The law must be kept in logical order and form, for an aspect of justice is consistency in decisions affecting like cases and discrimination between unlike cases on bases that can be logically explained.

17 *Dietrich* v *The Queen, Commonwealth Law Reports* 177 (1992): 292, 319.

18 Ibid.

Replying to the criticism, the then Chief Justice Mason wrote about "values of an enduring kind," which help to inform the judicial task of legal development:[19]

> That values do play a part in the judicial process is well accepted. As Justice Stephen said in *Onus* v *Alcoa of Australia Pty Ltd?*, "Courts necessarily reflect community values and beliefs." The principal problem in discussing values and the law is that the term "values" is a rag-bag expression which is used to embrace a number of different ideas–moral and ethical values, standards, policy considerations (which vary greatly) and attitudes. Another major problem arises from the uses to which these ideas may be put in circumstances which may differ quite radically.

Conclusion

Australia's elected politicians and civil servants have maintained an active presence at the table of international deliberation formulating and ratifying international human-rights instruments. Australia's major political parties are committed to domestic legal implementation of international human-rights instruments to which the country has voluntarily subscribed. The Australian judiciary interprets the Constitution, reads down statutes, and develops the common law consistent with these international instruments. The combined effect of these actions of the executive, Parliament, and the judiciary is the expansion of the patchwork quilt of human-rights protection under the rule of law and the enhancement of the commitment to collective enforcement. This has been achieved in ways consistent with the substantive and instrumental values espoused by elected politicians and unelected judges. The elected politicians need to look to their consciences, contemporary values, the policy of their party caucus, and the attitudes of their constituency. The unelected judges need to look to their consciences, contemporary values, and the rule of law. Together they give voice to contemporary values and apply those values to shape laws and policies acceptable to the people who prize their national independence and the sovereignty of their parliaments, and who affirm the equality and dignity of all, including those whose interests are most overlooked in a popularly elected parliament.

Without the complex U.S. jurisprudence of due process and equal protection, and without the oversight of Strasbourg, we Australians seem to have landed in much the same place on most contested moral and political issues in the public square agitating and applying shared values in international fora, in the parliaments, and in the courts. Since the same-sex marriage debate in Australia, there has been some rethinking by religious conservatives on the need for legislation,

19 Anthony Mason, "The Judge as Lawmaker," *James Cook University Law Review* 3 (1996): 1, 12.

including a human rights act, to protect religious freedom, ensuring that equality does not trump religious freedom and conceding that religious freedom ought not trump equality. But that is simply a reflection of the political calculation that the elected politicians are now no more likely than the unelected judges to privilege religion over equality. There has also been a hardening of views by some human-rights activists who are now opposing any expansion of the patchwork quilt of antidiscrimination laws to include discrimination on the basis of religion. Michael Kirby, a long-time advocate for human-rights legislation, has warned:

> Never forget that apartheid in South Africa was ultimately justified by reference to the supposed religious condemnation of miscegeny and that racial intolerance was based on the alleged inferiority of black people traced to contestable Biblical texts ... There is a need for considerable caution in elevating every religious opinion to an enshrined legal right to hurt and harm others.[20]

There is still hard work to be done to convince both politicians and judges that religious folk are entitled to equal protection of the laws, especially when their religious views are at variance with those of the general public and the intellectual elite of an increasingly secular society and secularist state. That may be because there is not only a change of attitude toward religion in an increasingly secular Australia, but also a change of values. Fewer Australians now value the entitlement of religious folk to maintain the religious ethos of their institutions, which are in receipt of taxpayer funds to provide services to the general community regardless of their religious affiliations. More draw the line at religious employers or religious service providers that discriminate against individuals on the basis of unchangeable personal attributes in the name of religious freedom. More Australians now value equality and respect for all persons who want to access services or seek employment regardless of their gender or sexual orientation. If the values are changing, so too will the laws and policies. That would be the case whether or not Australia had a constitutional or legislative bill of rights. Then again, recourse to community values should not be a foil for majoritarian sentiment wanting to deny the just entitlements of an unpopular misunderstood minority. In the month before he recognized the rights of Aboriginal Australians to their traditional lands in accord with community values, Justice Brennan dissented in a case where his fellow judges authorized a nontherapeutic sterilization of a child with mental disability. He said:[21]

---

20 Michael Kirby, Letter to the editor, *Australian Law Journal*, Nov. 11, 2019, http://sites.thomsonreuters.com.au/journals/2019/11/11/a-letter-from-the-hon-michael-kirby-ac-cmg/.

21 *Department of Health & Community Services* v *JWB & SMB ('Marion's Case'), Commonwealth Law Reports* 175 (1992): 218, 277.

> [T]he rule must give priority to the right to physical integrity and the human dignity it protects, even though such a rule imposes burdens on parents, guardians and those having the care of the intellectually disabled child who are entitled to the active support of the State which must bear the ultimate burden.

Such a rule, it may be said, is too idealistic and is out of touch with contemporary community standards. There is much force in that criticism but this is an area of the law in which it is necessary to guard against the tyranny which majority opinion may impose on a weak and voiceless minority.

We must all be eternally vigilant against the tyranny of the majority, especially when their populist sentiment has the backing of the elites in society. And we must continue to keep an eye out for those who are weak and voiceless, whether because of their race, religion, or any other attribute which ought to be irrelevant when determining how to respect their dignity and equality in a pluralist democracy under the rule of law. That vigilance is required whether or not there is a bill of rights.

The gravest danger to human rights is the constraint placed on discourse and debate about the conditions under which people can participate in shaping the kind of society in which they live. That discourse and debate must continue, whether or not a country has a bill of rights, and most especially in relation to issues which are deemed politically correct. In the absence of a bill of rights, there is a need to enhance public conversation, law, and policy making without one. Through respectful dialogue in the public square, in our parliaments, and in our courts, we might succeed in rejecting unfairness, insisting on the essential equality of all, and respecting the integrity and dignity of those most different from us, while extending mercy to those who most need it, even if they may not be the most deserving.

The German Constitution as Value System

Ute Mager

The question of the impact of law on character formation comprises two aspects: first, what formative values the legal system itself contains; second how the law enables or hinders the transmission of values, including those not considered valuable in a particular legal system.

Values in the German Constitution

In Germany, not only legal scholars but a great number of people regard the Constitution as a new value system that consciously turned away from the unjust and criminal Nazi regime. This set of values constitutes the state organization as a free democracy based on the rule of law (Article 20[1–3] of the Basic Law), with the obligation to respect and protect human dignity (Article 1[1]) as well as classical human rights, in particular equal treatment (Article 3), personal freedoms (Article 2), freedom of belief (Article 4), freedom of speech (Article 5[1]), freedom of assembly (Article 8), freedom of association (Article 9), and a guarantee of private property (Article 14). The value system also includes the welfare state (Article 20[1]) and environmental protection (Article 20a).

Constitutional Obligations for the Legislature

Two provisions highlight the character of the Constitution as a set of values. The first is Article 79(3) of the Basic Law: "Amendments to this Basic Law affecting the division of the Federation into *Länder*, their participation on principle in the legislative process, or the principles laid down in Articles 1 and 20 shall be inadmissible." Accordingly, the legislature amending the Constitution is subject to control by the Federal Constitutional Court. In particular, the state obligation to respect and to protect human dignity (in Article 1) thus becomes an unchangeable value.

Furthermore, amendments to the Constitution must be explicit and need a two-thirds majority vote of the members of the Bundestag and of the Bundesrat.

However, the saying that "where there is no plaintiff, there is no judge" also applies to proceedings before the Federal Constitutional Court. Thus, it can happen that the legislature changes a constitutional value decision by simple legislation. This happened in 2017, when the German federal parliament made an amendment to the Civil Code with regard to the extension of marriage to same-sex partners. (Registered same sex partnerships for life have been possible since 2001.) Article 6(1) of the Basic Law reads, "Marriage and the family are under the special protection of the state order." According to historical, but also systematic, interpretation of this article, which had been approved many times by the Federal Constitutional Court,[1] the constitutional concept of marriage refers to the union of a man and a woman. The introduction of so-called "marriage for all" by simple legislation presents the problem: the constitutional concept of marriage has become arbitrary. Therefore, an explicit constitutional amendment would have been preferable.

Besides Article 79, Article 1(3) of the Basic Law also is relevant. It says, "The following basic rights shall bind the legislature, the executive and the judiciary as directly applicable law." Accordingly, fundamental rights are binding law for the legislature. The Weimar Constitution of 1919 did not contain such a provision. The restriction of fundamental rights was thus entirely in the hands of the legislature. With the fundamental rights as the legal standard for legislation, the Federal Constitutional Court attains the competence to declare void such legislation that infringes these rights in a disproportionate way. A consequence of this competence is that the legislator is obligated to explain the goals and the necessity for his legislation. However, the legislator may be granted a certain benefit of the doubt, depending on the severity of the intervention that has its basis in his direct democratic legitimation.

Influence of International Human Rights Systems

The interpretation and application of the fundamental rights of the Basic Law are not detached from the understanding of international human-rights systems. This applies above all to the 1950 European Convention on Human Rights (ECHR). This Convention established a minimum standard of human-rights obligations that are binding on the Federal Republic of Germany, and all other member-states of the Council of Europe. In view of the high human-rights standards in Germany,

---

[1] BVerfGE (Bundesverfassungsgerichtsentscheidungen = Federal Constitutional Court of Justice, Collection of Decisions) 10, 59 (66); 53, 224 (245); 62, 323 (330); 87, 234 (264); 105, 313 (348).

there are rarely divergences in the interpretation of the fundamental rights of the Basic Law and the interpretation of human rights under the ECHR. The Federal Constitutional Court endeavors to interpret fundamental rights in such a way that they are consistent with the interpretation of corresponding rights of the ECHR by the European Court of Human Rights.[2] Occasionally, the Court's interpretation of the fundamental rights of the Basic Law also takes into account the 1966 International Covenant on Civil and Political Rights and the 1966 International Covenant on Social, Economic, and Cultural Rights.[3]

Constitutional Values as a Foundation of the German Legal Order

Due to the binding force of the fundamental rights and constitutional obligations for the legislature, the constitutional system of values shapes the entire legal system. This applies to public law, private law, and criminal law alike.

Public Law

Public law reflects in all its regulations the primacy of individual freedom and self-determination, so that every state intervention must be justified with public-welfare purposes and has to be the result of an appropriate balancing between individual interests and the public policies. The guarantee of private property, for example, forms the benchmark for public-building law and construction-planning law. Equally, the many regulations governing the different professions may restrict the freedom to choose and practice one's profession only in a proportionate manner. Not least, all police action must be proportionate to the various fundamental rights that may be affected.

However, the state has the duty not only to respect the freedom of its citizens but also to pursue positive goals and thus strengthen values. In particular, the extensive regulations for protection of the environment has its constitutional basis in Article 20a of the Basic Law: "Mindful of its responsibility toward future generations, the state shall protect the natural foundations of life." This article has done much to promote increased awareness of the value of the environment.

---

2 BVerfGE 111, 307 ff.–Görgülü; 128, 326 ff.–preventive detention; 148, 296 ff.–strike ban for civil servants.

3 BVerfGE 122, 210 ff.–concerning student fees; 132, 134 ff.–concerning social assistance for asylum seeker; BVerfG, Neue Juristische Wochenschrift (NJW) 2018, 2542–limitation of employment; BVerfG, NJW 2001, 1848–genocide; BVerfG, Neue Zeitschrift für Verwaltungsrecht (NVwZ) 2008, 71–extradition; BVerfG, NJW 2019, 1201–right to vote.

Another important part of public law concerns the welfare state. While the welfare state promotes the values of distributive justice and care for the needy, it is quite ambivalent concerning the value of solidarity that arises in an exchange of give and take. The famous sociologist Niklas Luhmann emphasizes that one of the peculiarities of organized help is that it does not create solidarity.[4] Citizens who need to claim state aid are often encumbered by heavy bureaucratic procedures, which do not generate solidarity or gratitude. Moreover, such claims may weaken solidarity within the family and broader kinship networks. Nevertheless, social welfare legislation is of paramount importance for social peace, and a critical safety net for the temporarily or permanently disadvantaged.

Civil Law

The constitutional protection of fundamental rights not only binds state authorities in their interactions with members of society, but it also has an indirect effect on the legal relations between private individuals. In this respect, the legislature has the duty to delimit the spheres of freedom in accordance with the principle of autonomy, which is fundamental in civil law, and the principle of equality. The mutual respect of the spheres of freedom, both presupposed and realized in law, demands tolerance from human beings in their behavior toward one another. By enacting civil law regulations, the legislature often fulfills its duty to protect fundamental rights. Examples are tort laws that allow victims of harm to be compensated for injuries to their persons, properties, or reputations; labor and employment laws that protect workers' rights and guard against abuses or arbitrary dismissal by employers; copyright and other intellectual property projects that allow parties to enjoy the fruits of their labor, inventions, or creativity; as well as disclosure obligations for public limited companies.

Special prohibitions against discrimination—in particular with regard to gender, race, and faith—not only bind the state but also apply to the relationships between private individuals. It is again the duty of the legislature to regulate these problems. An example is the General Equal Treatment Act, which has its basis in a directive of the European Union[5] that applies to the areas of employment, social security, education, and access to services offered to the public. In fact, discrimination is not to be tolerated in the public sphere. But it is sometimes harder to apply this nondiscrimination value in the private sphere. Take a last will and testament that provides for disinheritance if the son of African American parents marries a white woman or a white man. According to German inheritance law,

---

4 Niklas Luhmann, *Soziologie des Risikos* (Berlin: De Gruyter, 1991), 113.

5 Directive 2000/78/EC establishing a general framework for equal treatment in employment and occupation.

such a will would be effective, since the disinherited child has at least a claim to his compulsory portion, which amounts to half of the statutory portion of the inheritance. This example shows how private arbitrariness can be respected and limited concurrently.

Criminal Law

Criminal law follows the principle of guilt, based on the value of a human subject who is capable of moral agency and assuming responsibility. This is constitutionally based in Article 1(1) of the Basic Law that guarantees human dignity. It follows that punishment has to be proportionate to personal guilt. From the recognition of the individual as a responsible subject follows the principle of "no punishment without a statute" that makes clear for everyone which acts are forbidden.

On the other hand, many criminal offenses are an expression of the state's duty to protect fundamental rights and their values. The punishment of homicide serves to protect the value of life; the punishment of theft to protect property; the punishment of insult, slander, or defamation to protect personal integrity and honor. Criminal law both respects the defendant as an individual person with moral agency and responsibility based on dignity and establishes a minimum standard of social behavior based on constitutional values that the state has a duty to protect.

Conclusion

As shown in the examples above, constitutional values shape the entire German legal system, whose daily application in private and public life, including judicial enforcement, influences people's sense of justice. Conversely, serious deficiencies in law enforcement can lead to the erosion of people's orientation toward the values enshrined in the Constitution and in law.

Value Transmission in School

School is the place where the older generation has the possibility to convey to the following generation the knowledge, skills, attitudes, values, and convictions the elders believe to be necessary for the continuation of state and society. Accordingly, the goals of formation and education reflect the functional structure of a society, and its constitutional system and the promotion of common values with the aim of societal cohesion are essential components of school education.

According to Article 7(1) of the Basic Law, the entire school system is under the supervision of the state. The constitutions of the federal states (*Bundesländer*) contain values as educational objectives, which in part reflect the constitutional order of values, such as respect for human dignity, respect for religious conviction, education for freedom and democracy, social justice, and responsibility for nature and the environment. But there are also objectives that go beyond the constitutional values–for example, respect for God, self-control, sense of responsibility and helpfulness, love of one's homeland, willingness to work for the common good, interest in the culture of one's own people and foreign peoples, truthfulness, charity, tolerance, and a spirit of peace.[6]

In the concrete implementation of these educational goals–at least in individual cases–they can come into conflict with parental educational goals, which in turn enjoy protection by way of the parents' right and duty to care for and educate their children, as Article 6(2) says. Courts have to solve those conflicts by taking into account the constitutional value system, in particular the freedom of religion.

For example, the courts had to decide whether Muslim parents could prevent their daughters from participating in coeducational swimming lessons or in school trips. Members of other faiths as well have asked for exemptions from school lessons in individual cases or for home schooling. In Germany, school attendance is compulsory according to Article 7(1) of the Basic Law; therefore, home schooling is forbidden.[7] The state has an educational mandate that, with

---

6 For example:

Art. 131 Constitution of the Free State of Bavaria:

(1) Schools shall not only impart knowledge and skills, but also form heart and character.

(2) The highest educational goals are reverence for God, respect for religious conviction and human dignity, self-control, a sense of responsibility and a willingness to take responsibility, helpfulness, openness for all that is true, good, and beautiful, and a sense of responsibility for nature and the environment.

(3) The pupils are to be educated in the spirit of democracy, in love for the Bavarian homeland and the German people, and in the spirit of reconciliation between peoples.

(4) The girls and boys shall also receive special instruction in infant care, child rearing, and housekeeping.

Art.22 Constitution of the Free State of Thüringen:

(1) Education and training must promote independent thought and action, respect for human dignity and tolerance toward the convictions of others, recognition of democracy and freedom, the will to social justice, peacefulness in the coexistence of cultures and peoples, and responsibility for the natural foundations of human life and the environment.

(2) The teaching of history must reflect an unadulterated portrayal of the past.

(3) Teachers must take into account the religious and ideological feelings of all pupils.

7 BVerwG (Bundesverwaltungsgericht = Federal Administrative Court), NVwZ (Neue Zeitschrift für Verwaltungsrecht = New Administrative Law Journal) 2010, 525 (526).

the exception of religious instruction, is in principle of equal rank with parents' rights. The aim of the obligation to attend school with others is to promote social integration and prevent the emergence of parallel societies. However, schools have to take the educational goals of the parents into consideration, especially with regard to religious convictions. Therefore, after balancing parental and state educational objectives, the courts have decided that Muslim girls must take part in swimming lessons, although they may do so in clothing (burkini) that does justice to their religious convictions.[8] On the other hand, they do not have a right not to see other girls and boys in swimwear. It is worth mentioning that in earlier cases, the courts decided more "liberally," or perhaps more carelessly, in stating that schools had to grant exemptions from swimming lessons for Muslim girls.[9] It seems to be the consequence of growing diversity, pluralism, and, not least, fundamentalism in society that courts now try harder to harmonize educational goals of schools with those of parents.

In another very revealing case, courts had to decide whether parents could refuse to allow their child to watch a film showing dark magic. The judges denied the claim for exemption. At first glance, this seems unconvincing, as the issue looks inconsequential. However, the judges of the Federal Administrative Court argued,[10] on one hand, that the state must maintain neutrality and tolerance in the organization of teaching, above all in religious and ideological terms, and must refrain from any influence in the service of a certain religious-ideological direction. In fact, schools have an obligation to take religious rules of conduct into account. But, on the other hand, this obligation has limits: a categorical duty to observe all religious rules of conduct that parents submit would amount to a principled primacy of each individual position of faith over the state's power and right to determine the necessary education of its citizens. A school would then have to content itself with teaching arrangements that appear acceptable from all positions of faith; the curriculum would ultimately be dependent on the consensus of all individual participants. This is neither practically possible in a pluralistic society nor constitutionally intended with regard to the integration function of the school. The integrative effectiveness of schools not only proves itself in the inclusion of minorities and in respecting their peculiarities, but also presupposes that minorities do not close themselves off from confronting educational content with which they have religious, ideological, or cultural reservations. The attempt to make taboo certain literary or cinematic representations or other educational content is not foreign to many faiths. If the school were to grant exemption from teaching in all cases, the core of the state's educational mandate would

---

8 BVerwGE (Bundesverwaltungsgerichtsentscheidungen = Federal Administrative Court, Collection of decisions) 147, 362 (374 f.).

9 BVerwGE 94, 82 (83).

10 BVerwG, NVwZ 2014, 804 (806).

be affected. Accordingly, an exemption from school instruction can be considered only in exceptional cases and only if it concerns central religious commandments. A mere displeasure, as in the case of the film, is insufficient. Moreover, neither the film nor the school had associated the use of black magic with any positive evaluation.

How to Deal with the Opponents of a Liberal Society?

As became obvious in the previous section, freedom of religion and freedom of communication–in particular freedom of speech, assembly, and association–facilitate the transmission of values that are in conflict with a liberal society. In this respect, the problem arises as to how much freedom the state must or can grant to opponents of a liberal society without endangering the liberal constitution or becoming unfree.

The answer to this question arises in part from the scope of protection (*Schutzbereich*) of fundamental rights. As the freedom of speech does not cover wrong facts, the denial of the Holocaust (so-called Auschwitz lies) does not fall within the scope of this right.[11]

The freedom of assembly guarantees that "All Germans shall have the right to assemble peacefully and unarmed without prior notification or permission." Therefore, violent demonstrations are not within the scope of the right.

However, the range of protection is generally determined by balancing divergent interests and values. Each restriction of fundamental rights has to pursue a legitimate purpose and has to be necessary and appropriate in consideration of the impairment of the fundamental right in question (principle of proportionality) as already mentioned above. This holds true also for opponents of liberal society.

Articles 9(2), 18, and 21(2) of the Basic Law mark the limits of tolerance. Article 9(2) states: "Associations whose aims or activities contravene the criminal laws, or that are directed against the constitutional order or the concept of international understanding, shall be prohibited."[12] Article 18 determines: "Whoever abuses the freedom of expression, in particular the freedom of the press (Article 5[1]), the freedom of teaching (Article 5[3]), the freedom of assembly (Article 8), the freedom of association (Article 9), the privacy of correspondence, posts and telecommunications (Article 10), the rights of property (Article 14), or the right of asylum (Article 16a) in order to combat the free democratic basic order shall forfeit these basic rights. This forfeiture and its extent shall be declared by the Federal Constitutional Court." Article 21(2) declares:

11 BVerfGE 90, 241 (249).

12 See for the interpretation of this article BVerfGE 80, 244 (253); 149, 160 ff.

> "Parties that, by their aims or the behavior of their adherents, seek to undermine or abolish the free democratic basic order or to endanger the existence of the Federal Republic of Germany shall be unconstitutional. The Federal Constitutional Court shall rule on the question of unconstitutionality."[13]

It is worth emphasizing that only the Federal Constitutional Court has the competence to apply Article 18 and Article 21(2) of the Basic Law. To date, Article 18 of the Basic Law has never been used. It is the federal home secretary or the home secretary of a *Bundesland* who has the competence to prohibit associations. They may have recourse to the courts based on the freedom of association.

Final Remark

As a whole, liberal democracy must keep open space for value orientations of the most diverse kind, which, however, must have a common denominator to assure compatibility. These common denominators are, on one hand, the fundamental respect of law, which reflects and concretizes the constitutional values, and, on the other hand, respect for the conviction of the other–not necessarily as equivalent but as requiring the renunciation of persecution or violent conversion.

---

13 For the interpretation of this article, see BVerfGE 9, 162 (165); 12, 296 (305); 13, 46 (52); 47, 130 (139); 144, 20 margin 527.

Parables about Promises

Religious Ethics and Contract Enforceability

E. Allan Farnsworth[1]

Introduction

Lee Taylor assaulted his wife, who then took refuge in Lena Harrington's house. Taylor gained entry into the house and began another assault on his wife. The wife knocked Taylor down with an axe and was about to cut his head open when Harrington deflected the axe, saving Taylor's life but badly mutilating her hand. Taylor then orally promised to pay Harrington damages, but paid only a small sum. When she sued him on his promise, the trial court sustained his demurrer, and the Supreme Court of North Carolina affirmed, being "of the opinion that, however much the defendant should be impelled by common gratitude to alleviate the plaintiff's misfortune, a humanitarian act of this kind, voluntarily performed, is not such consideration as would entitle her to recover at law."[2]

Students encountering this case in the casebook by Calamari, Perillo, and Bender are likely to be critical of this result.[3] Those who track the case down in the one-volume Calamari and Perillo treatise may be further distressed to find it cited as one of "the majority of cases" that reject "the moral obligation concept" and refuse to enforce such promises.[4]

On encountering the doctrine of consideration, and in particular its application to cases of moral obligation, students often experience dissatisfaction with the treatment of promise-keeping in common law. Is one not morally obligated to keep one's promises? Should the law not reflect that moral obligation? Some

---

1 We are grateful to the editors of the *Fordham Law Review* for permission to republish this article, which appeared initially under the same title in *Fordham Law Review* 71 (2002): 695–707.

2 *Harrington v. Taylor*, 36 S.E.2d 227, 227 (N.C. 1945).

3 John D. Calamari, Joseph M. Perillo, and Helen Hadjiyannakis Bender, *Cases and Problems on Contracts*, 3rd ed. (St. Paul, MN: West, 2000), 259.

4 John D. Calamari and Joseph M. Perillo, *The Law of Contracts*, 4th ed. (St. Paul, MN: West, 1998), § 5.4, at 228.

students may come with answers to these questions derived from philosophers from Aristotle through Kant.[5] Others may come with answers based on what they perceive to be conventional religious teachings. This chapter is designed for the latter. I propose to consider the extent to which traditional religious sources are relevant in answering these two questions. I confine my discussion to promises made between private parties, the kinds of promises that are governed by the law of contracts.

Views differ on the extent to which religion has influenced the law on promise-keeping. Near the beginning of the Calamari and Perillo treatise, mention is made of the view of "canon lawyers and rabbinical scholars in the late Middle Ages and the Renaissance [that] promises were binding in natural law as well as in morality because failure to perform a promise made by a free act of the will was an offense against the Deity."[6] That there was a shift in emphasis during the Enlightenment "from a theological to a humanistic basis" does "not imply that the religious basis was abandoned."[7] James Gordley, however, concludes that medieval jurists did not arrive at the conclusion that promises were binding "by borrowing the teaching of the Canon law that it is sinful to break a promise," and common lawyers "did not borrow the ideas that consent was binding because of a virtue of promise-keeping."[8] Indeed, nineteenth-century jurists "did not ground their legal doctrines on any definite philosophical or political commitments."[9]

I begin my own reflections with this parable:

> There was once a wayfaring seaman who fell ill among strangers in Samaria, where a good man at some expense gave him shelter and comfort. Hearing of this, the seaman's father wrote to the Samaritan promising out of gratitude to pay his expenses. When the father, later regretting his decision, refused to pay, the Samaritan took the father to court. But the court refused to enforce the father's promise, saying that the Samaritan had not given anything in exchange for it. As a wise judge explained, the

---

5 Much has been written on promise-keeping by scholars using philosophical and other sources, and I will not here examine their work. Two representative works are P. S. Atiyah, *Promises, Morals, and Law* (Oxford: Clarendon Press, 1981) and Charles Fried, *Contract as Promise: A Theory of Contractual Obligation* (New York: Oxford University Press, 1981).

6 Calamari and Perillo, *The Law of Contracts,* 8.

7 Ibid. See also Joseph M. Perillo, "The Statute of Frauds in the Light of the Functions and Dysfunctions of Form," *Fordham Law Review* 43 (1974): 39, 66n155 (describing the influence of canon law).

8 James Gordley, *The Philosophical Origins of Modern Contract Doctrine* (Oxford: Clarendon Press, 1991), 41, 135, 227.

9 Ibid.

> father might be under a moral obligation to pay, but "the law of society has left most of such obligations to the interior forum, as the tribunal of the consciences has been aptly called."

This parable, of course, is not from scripture but from the venerable case of *Mills v. Wyman*, decided by the Supreme Judicial Court of Massachusetts in 1825 and speaking through its Chief Justice, Isaac Parker.[10] The lesson of the parable is that, at least where promises are concerned, there is a barrier that separates moral obligations from legal ones.

We do not know whether Chief Justice Parker, a devout New England Unitarian, saw a religious basis for the father's moral obligation–he made no mention of any religious source for what the "tribunal of the conscience" might require. Nor do we know whether he approved of the barrier between the legal and the moral–he did no more than yield to it.[11] I argue, at the risk of offending some readers, that sources in the Judeo-Christian tradition–particularly those with which students are likely to be familiar–have surprisingly little to say about my moral obligation to perform my promises; that they have even less to say about when the law should enforce my promises; and that, at least as to the second of these points, it is just as well for our society that they do not have much to say.

In my days at Sunday school, I surely supposed that someone in biblical times had said that I should honor my promises. But who was it? God? Moses? Jesus? Had I looked in scripture, I would have been hard pressed to support my supposition.

Another Realm

Here is a parable from another realm:

> There was once a strange and distant realm in which Holy Writ told the people that God said: "O ye who have attained to faith! Be true to your covenants." And when the people heard this, they hung these words upon the walls of their courts so that their judges and all who attend court might know that promises were to be honored.

This parable fairly accurately describes the situation in many Islamic lands, where the quoted Qur'anic injunction, which "emphatically upholds the moral ob-

---

10 *Mills v. Wyman*, 20 Mass. (3 Pick.) 207, 210 (1825).

11 As to Parker's religious affiliation, see Curtis W. Nyquist, "Contract Theory, Single Case Research and the Massachusetts Archives," *Massachusetts Legal History* 3 (1997): 53, 83–85. See also Geoffrey R. Watson, "On the Tribunal of Conscience: Mills v. Wyman Reconsidered," *Tulane Law Review* 71 (1997): 1749, 1781.

ligation to fulfill one's contracts,"[12] is indeed said to be found on the walls of courts.[13] One lesson of the parable is that a great religion need not ignore the obligation to honor promises. I do not contend that a system of contract law can be deduced from such general phrases alone,[14] but Islamic law as later elaborated to deal with the enforceability of contracts has a distinctly religious basis.

Biblical Sources

One can find in the Bible a tradition of honoring promises. God said to Noah: "Then will I remember the covenant which I have made between myself and you and living things of every kind."[15] God said to Abraham: "I will give you and your descendants after you ... all the land of Canaan, and I will be God to your descendants."'[16] And this time God wanted something in return: "For your part, you must keep my covenant, you and your descendants after you, generation by

---

12 Frank E. Vogel and Samuel L. Hayes III, *Islamic Law and Finance* 66 (Leiden: Brill, 1998); *see* Qur'an, Al-Ma'idah (The Repast), 5:1, translated in Muhammad Asad, *The Message of the Qur'an: The Full Account of the Revealed Arabic Text Accompanied by Parallel Transliteration* (Bristol: Book Foundation,1980). The covenants referred to include those "between the individual and his fellow-men." Ibid., n1. It is said that the quoted phrase "has been justly admired for its terseness and comprehensiveness," the Arabic including obligations not only to God but also those among persons. "We make a promise, we enter into a commercial social contract ..., we must faithfully fulfil all obligations in all these relationships." Abdullah Yusuf Ali, *The Holy Qur'an: Text, Translation and Commentary,* 3rd ed., 2 vols. (Lahore: Muhammad Ashraf, 1938), 1:238n682. For similar Qur'anic injunctions, see 9:4 ("[O]bserve, then, your covenant with them [idolaters with whom you have made a covenant and who have not failed you] until the end of the term agreed with them."); 17:34 ("[B]e true to every promise," for on Judgment Day "you will be called to account for every promise which you have made!").

13 On the practice of putting the phrase quoted in the text on the walls of courts in the Middle East, see Saba Habachy, "Property, Right, and Contract in Muslim Law," *Columbia Law Review* 62 (1962): 450.

14 The system of contract law elaborated by jurists is based on the general Qur'anic injunctions and the Sunnah (Traditions) of Muhammad. For conflicting interpretations of the Quranic injunctions, see Muhammad Yasuf Masa, "The Liberty of the Individual in Contracts and Conditions According to Islamic Law," *Islamic Law Quarterly* 2 (1955): 79.

15 Genesis 9:15; Genesis 9:11 ("I will make my covenant with you: never again shall all living creatures be destroyed by the waters of the flood, never again shall there be a flood to lay waste to the earth.") Biblical quotations are taken from the New English Bible (1970) unless otherwise indicated.

16 Genesis 17:8

generation."[17] And the same was true when God spoke to Moses on Sinai: "Here and now I make a covenant .... Observe all I command you this day."[18] The focus in the Hebrew Bible is not on promise-keeping between private parties, not on what we think of as contracts. It is rather on promises by God and to God. As Moses cautioned the people of Israel, "When a man makes a vow with the Lord or swears an oath and puts himself under a binding obligation, he must not break his word."[19] But there is no eleventh commandment like the injunction in the Qur'an to honor our contracts with others.

The focus of the New Testament is the same. John speaks of "the promise that he himself gave us, the promise of eternal life."[20] And Paul tells us that "it was not through law that Abraham, or his posterity, was given the promise that the world should be his inheritance, but through the righteousness that came from faith .... The promise was made on the ground of faith, in order that it might be a matter of sheer grace."[21]

It is not easy to find biblical authority for the specific proposition that I should perform the promises that I make to other persons. Perhaps this is not surprising in an account of events primarily of religious significance in relatively primitive societies. But as a lawyer, I have no difficulty in inferring such a proposition. The Bible is, after all, replete with references to the righteousness of a God who performs his promises. Thus, Solomon said, "Blessed be the Lord who has given his people Israel rest, as he promised: not one of the promises he made through his servant Moses has failed."[22]

And since Jesus, in the Sermon on the Mount, urged his followers to be "perfect, even as your Father which is in heaven is perfect,"[23] I infer that he was urging them as a general matter to honor their promises as God honors his. I have, however, found no Christian theologian who advances this argument, and so I turn to other sources.

The Hebrew Bible does recount a few agreements to which God was not a party.[24] Two of these involve Abraham, described by Hannah Arendt as

---

17 Genesis 17:9.

18 Exodus 34:10–11.

19 Numbers 30:2–3.

20 1 John 2:25.

21 Romans 4:13–16.

22 1 Kings 8:56.

23 Matthew 5:48 (King James).

24 Sometimes promises were mixed–in part to God and in part to others. When the Gadites and the Reubenites promised to be drafted as a force to go into battle with the Israelites, Moses replied: "If you stand by your promise ... then you may come back and be quit of your obligation *to the Lord and to Israel;* and this land shall be your possession in the sight of the Lord. But I warn you, if you fail to do all this, you will have sinned *against the Lord,*

> the man from Ur, whose whole story ... shows such a passionate drive toward making covenants that it is as though he departed from his country for no other reason than to try out the power of mutual promise in the wilderness of the world, until eventually God himself agreed to make a Covenant with him.[25]

One is the pact that Abraham made with Abimilech for the use of the well at Beersheba (which seems to have been the only biblical place named after a contract).[26] The other is the agreement that Abraham made with Ephron the Hittite for the cave at Machpelah to bury his dead. Abraham, declining a gift, said to the Hittites: "I give you the price of the land .... [And he] came to an agreement with him and weighed out the amount that Ephron had named."[27]

Another agreement to which God was not a party was that between Rahab the prostitute and Joshua's spies. Two spies sent by Joshua to reconnoiter the country around Jericho spent the night at the home of a Rahab, who said to them:

> Swear to me now by the Lord that you will keep faith with my family, as I have kept faith with you. Give me a token of good faith; promise that you will spare the lives of my father and mother, my brothers and sisters and all who belong to them, and save us from death. To this the spies replied, "Our lives for yours, so long as you do not betray our business," warning her "that they would be released from the oath she had made them take unless she did what they told her." And because she did as they said, her family was spared when Jericho fell.[28]

The New Testament has less to say about the obligation to perform one's promises than it does about the obligation to release others from their promises. (Only the

---

and your sin will find you out. So ... carry out your promise" (Numbers 32:20–24, emphasis added). See also the treatment of Joshua's oath that the Gibeonites acquired through deception in Joshua 9:19–23: "The chiefs replied, 'But we swore an oath to them *by the Lord the God of Israel*; we cannot touch them now. What we will do is this: we will spare their lives ... [but] they shall be set to chop wood and draw water for the house of my God'" (emphasis added).

25 Hannah Arendt, *The Human Condition* (Chicago: University of Chicago Press, 1958): 243–44.

26 Genesis 21:28–32: To settle Abraham's complaint against Abimelech about a well, "the two of them made a pact .... Therefore that place was called Beersheba [meaning Well of an Oath], because there the two of them swore an oath."

27 Genesis 23:13–16.

28 Joshua 2:12–18. See also, on the pact arranged by Moses with the Gadites and Reubenites, Numbers 32:20–24: "Moses answered, 'If you stand by your promise ... this land shall be your possession in the sight of the Lord. But I warn you, if you fail to do all this, you will have sinned against the Lord.'"

contract with Judas comes to mind.)[29] According to Luke, Jesus told his followers to "lend without expecting any return,"[30] and according to Matthew, Jesus taught us to ask that we be forgiven "our debts, as we forgive our debtors."[31] Consider, then, this parable:

> There was once a landowner who went out early one morning to hire laborers for his vineyard, agreeing to pay each the usual day's wage of one denarius. An hour before sunset, he went out and found another group of laborers and told them to join the others. When evening came, he called the laborers to give them their pay. Those who started work an hour before sunset came forward and were paid one denarius each. When the men who came first were also paid one denarius, they grumbled because they expected something extra, saying: "These latecomers have done only one hour's work, yet you have put them on a level with us, who have sweated the whole day long in the blazing sun." The owner turned to one of them and replied, "My friend, I am not being unfair to you. You agreed on one denarius, did you not?"

This is a condensed version of the parable told by Jesus to his disciples according to Matthew. The lesson, said Jesus, is, "The kingdom of Heaven is like this .... Thus will the last be first, and the first last."[32] But any lawyer can tell you that there is here also an earthly lesson–that one who has made a contract with another cannot simply disregard the contract and claim restitution for performance rendered under the contract. But to apply that lesson to this parable is to say that the landowner was right to hold to their promises the laborers who had come in the morning, because they had "agreed on one denarius." Might it not seem un-Christian to disregard the benefit that they had conferred by sweating in the blazing sun the whole day long? Would not a truly Christian landowner have released them from their promise? I return to this parable below, but I want first to turn to another parable.

---

29 A rare New Testament contract is that made with Judas. See Luke 22:5–6: "They ... undertook to pay him a sum of money. He agreed." See also, on Paul's apology for failing to keep his commitment to the Corinthians, 2 Corinthians1:17–18: "That was my intention; did I lightly change my mind?"

30 Luke 6:35.

31 Matthew 6:11 (King James).

32 Matthew 20.

Fidei Laesio

The next parable is this:

> There was once a virtuous merchant who sold sheep, lambs, and hogs to another merchant, who paid only part of what he had promised. When the virtuous merchant demanded the balance, the other promised "by my faith" to pay it by a certain day, but when the day came, he had not done so. When the virtuous merchant took the other to court, the judge ordered the other "to observe this promise and faith before an appointed day under pain of major excommunication."

This parable is loosely based on a case brought in an English ecclesiastical court in 1511.[33] The lesson of this parable is plain. Though no court would sanction the breach of a *promise*–even one to a virtuous merchant–the church would sanction as a sin the breach of an *oath* made in the face of God,[34] if not by excommunication, then perhaps by public whippings or the wearing of penitential garb in a parish procession.[35] Because the king's central common-law courts afforded no satisfactory basis for enforcing promises, litigants went by default to other courts, including merchant and ecclesiastical courts. For centuries after the colonization, if not conquest, of the New World, church courts maintained a foothold in the domain of contract by enforcing such "promissory oaths," by which a Christian could pledge his hope of salvation to secure the fulfillment of a promise. Although Jesus had said to his disciples, "You are not to swear at all,"[36] canon law had become, in the words of one scholar, "an 'oath-dominated' sort of justice."[37] During the fifteenth and sixteenth centuries, hundreds of these *fidei laesio* (breach-of-faith) cases, typically arising out of informal oral "promissory oaths" involving small sums, were brought each year to the ecclesiastical courts, where they came to dominate litigation. Although in 1164, long before the case on which my para-

---

33 The case is set out in R. H. Helmholz, "*Assumpsit and* Fidei Laesio," *Law Quarterly Review* 91 (1975): 406, 413. For the judge's order, taken from one in a 1497 case, see ibid. at 424. The "by my faith" was sufficient as an oath. See R. H. Helmholz, *The Spirit of Classical Canon Law* (Athens: University of Georgia Press, 1996), 161.

34 See Deuteronomy 23:21–22: "When you make a vow to the Lord your God, do not put off its fulfillment; otherwise the Lord your God will require satisfaction of you, and you will be guilty of sin. If you choose not to make a vow, you will not be guilty of sin." See also Numbers 30:2: "When a man makes a vow to the Lord or swears an oath and so puts himself under a binding obligation, he must not break his word. Every word he has spoken he must make good."

35 For mention of cases imposing such sanction, see Helmholz, "*Fidei Laesio*," 424.

36 Matthew 5:34; see also James 5:12 ("Above all things, my brothers, do not use oaths.").

37 Helmholz, *Classical Canon Law*, 145–46 (discussing the lawfulness of the oath).

ble is based, the Constitutions of Clarendon had forbidden the church to hear such cases, church courts heard them largely unmolested. Half a century after 1511, all the judges in Exchequer Chamber united to formally reaffirm that *fidei laesio* could not be the means of giving the church courts general jurisdiction over contracts.[38] Not until the common-law courts provided a satisfactory alternative in the form of assumpsit, which took them nearly one hundred more years after 1511, did the church courts lose their foothold in the domain of contract.[39]

The church courts had not been alone in infusing religious notions into the common law. In 1489 it was argued in Chancery that where one of two executors had released a debtor of the deceased testator, the common law allowed no remedy, this being one of those matters that "lie in conscience between a man and his confessor." To this, Chancellor John Morton, then archbishop of Canterbury, replied,

> Sir, I know well that each Law is, or ought to be, in accord with the Law of God; and the Law of God is that an executor, who is of evil disposition, must not waste all the goods, etc. And I know well that if he does so waste and makes no amends or satisfaction ... or will not make restitution ... he shall be damned in Hell. And to make remedy for such an act ... is well done according to conscience.[40]

The matter was not to be left to "the tribunal of the conscience," as Chief Justice Parker left the obligation of the father of the wayfaring seaman four centuries later.

But even in theocentric England, more and more lawyers and judges were laymen, learned in the common law at the expense of the canon law. As Holdsworth said, "Thus the ecclesiastical and the common law go their separate ways. We can no longer expect to find royal judges who can show an accurate knowledge of papal legislation; nor will ideas drawn from canonical jurisprudence be used to develop our law."[41]

Legal historians have sometimes argued that the common law of contracts showed significant influences of the canon law,[42] and there is disagreement as

---

38 W. S. Holdsworth, *A History of English Law,* 16 vols. (London: Methuen, 1909), 2:252.

39 See Slade's Case, 76 Eng. Rep. 1074,1077 (K.B. 1602).

40 Y. B. Hil. 4 Hen. 7, f.4, p.8 (1489), reprinted in C. H. S. Fifoot, *History and Sources of the Common Law: Tort and Contract* (London: Stevens & Sons, 1949), 326.

41 Holdsworth, *A History of English Law,* 2:254.

42 Helmholz, "*Fidei Laesio,*" 408, arguing that "there is a connection between the *causa fidei laesionis* and the early history of assumpsit in the royal courts." See also Charles Donahue Jr., "*Ius Commune,* Canon Law, and Common Law in England," *Tulane Law Review* 66 (1992): 1745, 1766: "The idea of the independent promise seems pretty clearly to have been derived from the church court actions for breach of faith." But see Holdsworth, *A*

to the extent to which religious notions of morality influenced common-law courts after the sixteenth century.[43] It is noteworthy, however, that when Lord Mansfield, in 1765, made his memorable, if short-lived, attempt to expunge the doctrine of consideration from promises made among merchants, he invoked neither the "Law of God" nor damnation "in Hell," nor did he refer to any other religious or moral ideas.

After the demise of *fidei laesio,* what religious leader urged his followers to perform their promises to other persons? Martin Luther? John Calvin? John Wesley? During the seventeenth and eighteenth centuries, Christians made generous use of the notion of "covenant" for the organization of religious groups.[44] But I have found only one religious leader who generally urged his followers to honor their promises to each other. It was Brigham Young, who said, "Fulfil your contracts and sacredly keep your word .... I have no fellowship for a man that will make a promise and not fulfil it."[45]

Contemporary Scholarship

Why, as a matter of religious ethics, should my promising–my mere declaration that I undertake an obligation–have the effect of imposing an obligation on me to

---

History of the English Law, 3:319: "Nor was English law influenced by the theories of the canon law; for in spite of their continual efforts, the ecclesiastical courts were not allowed to interfere with ordinary agreements."

43 On developments in the seventeenth and eighteenth centuries, see Harold J. Berman, "The Religious Sources of General Contract Law: An Historical Perspective," *Journal of Law and Religion* 4 (1986): 103, 112–22. For discussion of the nineteenth-century notion that Christianity is part of the common law, see Stuart Banner, "When Christianity Was Part of the Common Law," *Law and History Review* 16 (1998): 27, from which it appears that this notion played no role in the enforcement of contracts. For one view of this history, see Duncan Kennedy, "Form and Substance in Private Law Adjudication," *Harvard Law Review* 89 (1976): 1685, 1725: "Positive law [in the eighteenth century] was of a piece with God's moral law as understood through reason and revelation .... The sense of a conflict between systems of thought emerged only at the beginning of the nineteenth century." For a different view, see Atiyah, *Promises, Morals, and Law,* 4, arguing that by 1800 "the common lawyers had largely come round to the modem viewpoint, that promises *per se* are morally binding, and that insofar as the doctrine of consideration fails to give effect to this moral ideal, it is an anomaly."

44 For the Jewish tradition, see Daniel J. Elazar, "Covenant as the Basis of the Jewish Political Tradition," *The Jewish Journal of Sociology* 20 (1978): 5.

45 John A. Widtsoe, ed., *Discourses of Brigham Young* (Salt Lake City, UT: Deseret Book Company, 1925), 358; see also ibid. at 467: "Pay your debts ... but do not run into debt anymore."

perform my promise, even if I have later changed my mind and regret having made the promise? Contemporary writers on Christian ethics have had some interesting things to say on this question, but I have several difficulties with what they say.

First, a number of distinguished scholars use what I would call a technique of avoidance, sometimes with disdain. This is common among covenant theologians. According to Robin Lovin,

> [T]he self-interested, rational individual who calculates the value of proposed social arrangements in terms of his or her own purposes and makes commitments accordingly could not be the covenant-partner [the theologians] had in mind .... Covenant theology and contract theory thus offer us two alternative accounts of how persons move voluntarily and in history from an unacceptable state of nature to life in political community.[46]

Joseph Allen agrees that

> [T]o work from [the] covenant model is also to reject *some contractual* ideas as adequate conceptions for the whole of the moral life–those, for example, in which the social contract is seen as a relationship only of bargaining ... in which the rights and obligations of each person are limited to what has been agreed to, or would be agreed to, in the bargain.[47]

Another covenant scholar emphasizes "the difference between a compact and a contract"; the latter has only two sides, being of limited scope and duration, and being "legalistic in nature," binding "only with the letter of the agreement, not the spirit," while a "compact is contrary to every characteristic just noted for a contract."[48] Such discussions do not easily produce insights into what religious ethics has to say about my contracts.

Second, those scholars that confront the ethical questions raised by contracts sometimes resort to circularity. Margaret Farley argues that "if we ask why I 'ought' to keep my commitments, the first and most obvious answer is that this is what commitment *means;* what commitment *does* is produce an 'ought.'" It does not help me when I find this supported with the statement that "When I make a

46 Robin W. Lovin, "Equality and Covenant Theology," *Journal of Law and Religion* 2 (1984): 241, 245, 248.

47 Joseph L. Allen, *Love and Conflict: A Covenantal Model of Christian Ethics* (Nashville, TN: Abingdon Press, 1984), 17.

48 Donald Lutz, "The Evolution of Covenant Form and Content as the Basis for Early American Political Culture," in *Covenant in the Nineteenth Century: The Decline of an American Political Tradition*, ed. Daniel J. Elazar (Lanham, MD: Rowman & Littlefield, 1994), 45 n.4.

commitment to another person, I dwell in the other by means of my word."[49] In similar fashion, Donald Evans reasons that "In saying, 'I promise to do X,' I create a moral obligation to do X."[50]

Third, when writers on Christian ethics marshal noncircular arguments, the arguments are often the same as those commonly made in purely secular analyses. Margaret Farley points out that if I do not honor my promises, "I stand to lose my reputation, or the trust of others, or my own self-respect,"[51] but I have difficulty grasping the religious aspect of this. Donald Evans describes promising as "a linguistic act which takes place according to various conventions," saying it has "performative force" and citing J. L. Austin's work,[52] and Joseph Allen endorses this analysis.[53] But this analysis, too, is a familiar one in secular argument. Allen avoids the circularity of Evans's argument by arguing that in covenanting, "we entrust ourselves ... to someone else," risking that "we might be betrayed"[54] This strikes me as a slight recasting of the widely accepted argument of contract scholars that at least one basis for the enforceability of a promise ("covenant") is that it induces reliance ("entrusting") in the promise.

What Is Needed

It seems to me that one of two elements is needed for religious ethics to make a contribution to the first of my two questions: When do I have a moral obligation to perform my promises?

As to the first element, I begin with agapism: "Love your neighbor as yourself."[55] I have no difficulty in deriving from this the principle that one should be truthful and not tell lies. One should therefore not make promises that one does not intend to perform. But this is not to say that, having intended to perform my promise when I made it, I am bound to perform it if I later change my mind. Nonperformance where there has been such a change of mind is distinguishable from nonperformance where there was never any intention to perform. Although Aristotle appears to have ignored this distinction, it is well known to lawyers who

---

49 Margaret A. Farley, *Personal Commitments: Beginning, Keeping, Changing* (San Francisco, CA: Harper & Row, 1986), 17, 71.

50 Donald Evans, "Love, Situation and Rules," in *Norm and Context in Christian Ethics*, ed. Gene H. Outka and Paul Ramsey (London: SCM Press, 1968), 367, 383.

51 Farley, *Personal Commitments*, 18.

52 Evans, "Love, Situation and Rules," 383.

53 Allen, *Love and Conflict*, 34.

54 Ibid., 33.

55 Matthew 22:39.

call the misrepresentation implicit in the latter "promissory fraud."[56] There may be cases of what we may call a "loving promise"—a promise made in recognition of an obligation imposed by love that defines the scope of that obligation. The parable of the wayfaring seaman may be an example, and on that basis the father can be viewed as under a moral obligation. But most contracts are made, as writers such as Robin Lovin and Joseph Allen have stressed, not out of love for others but out of self-interest. What can agapism have to say to me about why I should perform such promises?

That brings me to the second element. If agapism is not a sufficient principle, is there some other principle that is relevant? And, if so, what is the source of that principle in theology? The principle, I assume, must be that of justice, the basis of most of the nonreligious discussions of the question. It is difficult for me to see how this is a peculiarly religious principle, or even one to which theology has much of its own to contribute. Frederick Carney has described a

> Supposed duality [under which] love is a teleological principle, or a general norm that looks to consequences and causes us ... to seek the welfare of what we value, [while] justice is a deontological principle, or a general norm that calls attention to an immediately perceived duty ... without itself considering consequences.[57]

My difficulty is in finding a religious mandate for justice in the contract context.

Conclusion: A Good Thing

Up to this point, I have been concerned with my *moral obligation* to perform my promises. What of my second question: when should the law *enforce* my promises? Recent years have seen much concern with the relationship between con-

---

56 In describing promise-keeping, Aristotle argued that "a person who breaks his word is not truthful," but while Thomas Aquinas "explained that promises are binding as a matter of ... honesty," and that promise-breaking "is like lying," he seems to have recognized the distinction between what lawyers know as promissory fraud and a mere change of mind. See Gordley, *Philosophical Origins,* 11–12; see also E. Allan Farnsworth, *Changing Your Mind: The Law of Regretted Decisions* (New Haven, CT: Yale University Press, 1998), 30. For an argument, unconvincing in my view, that the nature of a promissory obligation "seems simply to be the requirement of *veracity,*" so that the "reason why I should *do* what I have said I *will* do is thus ... essentially the same as the reason why I should *say* I have done what I actually *have* done," see G. J. Warnock, *The Object of Morality* (London: Methuen, 1971), 109, 111.

57 Frederick S. Carney, "Deciding in the Situation: What is Required?" in Outka and Ramsey, *Norm and Context in Christian Ethics,* 3, 8.

tract law and economics. Little attention has been paid to the relation of contract law and morality–in particular contract law and religious ethics. According to Stanley Fish, "morality is something to which the law wishes to be related, but not too closely" for "a legal system whose judgments perfectly meshed with our moral intuitions would be thereby rendered superfluous."[58] Would we want a society in which the dictates of religion were as specific as in the parable from another realm or in that of the virtuous sixteenth-century English merchant? I note that the influence of Christianity on contract law did not vanish entirely with *fidei laesio.* It lived on in laws prohibiting gambling and usury and the making of contracts on Sunday. Whether such laws suggest that a religious influence is appropriate for a diverse and secular society is at least questionable.

Finally, one must ask: Whose religious ethics? Principal goals of contract law are predictability and certainty. Advocates of "situation ethics," such as Joseph Fletcher, resist the notion that rules to meet these goals can or should be crafted.[59] Edward Leroy Long Jr. states that "no Christian theologian wants to call himself a legalist," noting Luther's view that "law is the antithesis of gospel" and Calvin's rejection of "law righteousness."[60] This is not a view likely to earn favor with those responsible for the workings of our legal system.

Indeed, what lawyer would not react to such views with relief that, as Jesus said to Pilate, "My kingdom does not belong to this world."[61] Nonetheless, we who live in an increasingly diverse America can be grateful that most of the time, most of us regard honoring our promises as a serious matter, whatever we see as the religious or moral basis of our doing so.[62]

---

58 Stanley Fish, *There's No Such Thing as Free Speech and It's a Good Thing, Too* (New York: Oxford University Press, 1994), 141–42.

59 Joseph Fletcher, *Situation Ethics: The New Morality* (London: SCM Press, 1966).

60 Edward Leroy Long Jr., "Soteriological Implications of Norm and Context," in Outka and Ramsey, *Norm and Context in Christian Ethics,* 265, 272, 275, 278.

61 John 18:36.

62 See Richard A. Posner, *Law and Legal Theory in England and America* (Oxford: Clarendon Press, 1996), 95 (reporting that a private rating of the risk of the nonenforceability of contracts placed the United States second best, after Switzerland and tied with the United Kingdom).

The Law of Contracts and Ethics

Interrelation in Spite of Separation

Thomas Pfeiffer

In the world of legal scholarship, discussing the relation between law and ethics is usually a matter for philosophers of law and scholars in the area of jurisprudence, which I am not. Instead, the following is a result of insights or views won by research in the area of contract law. It should also be noted that defining the relation between law and ethics is closely intertwined with one's general view of the law. A legal positivist's position–that is, the position of a person believing that law is exclusively based on rules, which are set by a competent person or body–will in this respect be very different from, for example, a follower of a theory of law as integrity.[1] The following is not meant to comment on these discussions on an abstract level but rather refers to examples of contract law to elaborate why law and morality, in spite of an interrelation, cannot and should not be identical.

The Need for a Distinction Between Law and Ethics

One of the most basic principles in modern legal development is the distinction between law and ethics. This distinction is accepted also by authors who argue in favor of a close interrelation between law and morality.[2] There are several reasons why law, on one hand, and ethics, on the other, cannot be identical in modern societies.

The most significant reason relates to societal pluralism and individual freedom. In a free and pluralistic society, there may be more than one legitimate answer to ethical questions. In contract law (and in private law in general), legal choices may be influenced, for example, by considerations of communicative jus-

1 See, for example, Ronald Dworkin, *Law's Empire* (Cambridge, MA: Harvard University Press, 1986), 176–275.

2 See Ronald Dworkin, *Taking Rights Seriously* (Cambridge, MA: Harvard University Press, 1977), 93; Dworkin distinguishes "abstract" moral rights from specific institutional rights, which also include legal rights.

tice (*iustitia communitativa*) or, instead, distributive justice (*iustitia distributiva*).[3] Translating ethical rules into legal rules would amount to imposing all rules of a certain ethical system on every citizen. Moreover, if all ethical rules automatically resulted in identical legal rules, legislative decisions would be determined by a certain ethical system and not by a majority of voters or representatives. That would be contrary not only to democratic principles but, even more importantly, to everybody's fundamental freedom to pursue happiness according to their own choices. Distinguishing and separating law and ethics is therefore a necessary characteristic of free and pluralistic societies. This is why societies which automatically translate ethical views, in particular those of a certain religious system, into legal rules usually are authoritarian in nature.

Jurisprudence provides for additional (potential) reasons for distinguishing between law and ethics, in particular: (a) that morals are something "interior" within a person's mind or consciousness, whereas law regulates the "exterior," that is, the consequences of a person's actions; (b) that moral obligations are valid per se, whereas legal obligations are often owed to a specific person or institution only; (c) that the grounds for being obligated are different in ethics and law because morality requires (or may require) a certain ethos of a person, whereas for law, the legality of one's conduct is sufficient; and, finally, (d) that morality has its sources in one's autonomous ethos, whereas legal rules provide for heteronomous standards.[4]

The separation between law and ethics also has a very practical dimension. This can be demonstrated by a look at certain ethical rules which are broadly accepted in Christian culture. The first example is the idea that "to give is more blessed than to receive" (Acts 20:35). From the perspective of contract law, that rule seems acceptable insofar as the legal rules for donations, in most legal systems, aim at protecting the donor against liability claims of the receiver. However, that protection has its limits. In case of a legal controversy between donor and receiver, the law must not base its determinations on the moral comparison between donor and receiver but has to treat both parties equally and look at how the applicable legal rules balance the legitimate interest of either side.

A second example is the "golden rule"—that one must treat others the way one would like to be treated. Following this rule in contract law would result in obvious difficulties. If I sell a certain object for a hundred euros, I simultaneously express that I prefer having a hundred euros over having the object. At the same time, I expect the other contract party to agree to the opposite—that is, to prefer

3 Aristotle, *Nikomachische Ethik*, German translation, edited by Günter Bien (Hamburg: Verlag Felix Meiner, 1972).

4 See Gustav Radbruch, *Rechtsphilosophie*, 3rd ed. (Leipzig: Quelle & Meyer, 1932), cited from Radbruch, *Rechtsphilosophie. Studienausgabe*, ed. Ralf Dreier and Stanley L. Paulson, 2nd ed. (Heidelberg: CF Müller Verlag, 2003), 41–49.

having the object over having a hundred euros. In other words, the whole idea of contractual exchange is built on the principle that our preferences are different, so that I do not have to treat others as I wish to be treated with regard to the specifics of my transactions. Only on a rather abstract level can freedom of contract and following my own preferences be reconciled with the golden rule, and that is if I understand that I am morally obliged to sell at a fair price since I expect to be charged fair prices myself. But that principle would indeed be too abstract to work as a rule of contract law.[5]

Contract Law and Other Areas of Law

It is not by accident that this chapter refers to contract law as an example for distinguishing law and ethics. Probably the most influential book on the relation between law and morality, Immanuel Kant's *Die Metaphysik der Sitten* (*The Metaphysics of Morals*),[6] lays out the doctrine of laws first and only then continues with the doctrine of virtue. In the first part of the work, Kant begins with private law as opposed to public law. The first category he addresses in the first part is *Begehrungsvermögen*–"the capability to desire" or, in other words, the capability to have personal or individual preferences. The relevance of this category for legal purposes stems from the effects of legal rights, which enable a person to enforce his or her desires regardless of the views of others or of a majority.

Contract law is an area where individual preferences, on one hand, and the law, on the other, are intertwined very closely. Therefore, it is an ideal example for demonstrating that law and ethics need to be distinguished and are, to a certain extent, different. Using contract law as an example for discussing the separation and interrelation of law and ethics, however, raises a particular problem. In contract law, the rights and obligations of the parties have to be determined pursuant to the contractual agreement and, as far as relevant, by applicable statutory provisions ("fall-back rules"). The question of the relation between this contractual regime and ethics, therefore, is twofold. First, it concerns the relation between the parties' agreement (and their underlying motives, intentions, and interests) and ethical principles; second, one has to look at the statutory rules of contract law.

Whereas an autonomous determination of rights and obligations occurs in other areas of private law–for example, in succession law–there are certain areas where autonomous determination is less significant, such as tort law. It is obviously easier to identify interrelations between law and ethics in these areas. However, there are still differences between law and ethics in these areas: whereas all

5 See Dworkin, *Taking Rights Seriously*, 93.

6 Immanuel Kant, *Die Metaphysik der Sitten* (1798), ed. Wilhelm Weischedel, 18th ed. (Frankfurt am Main: Suhrkamp, 2017).

legal systems provide for certain rules in order to compensate tort victims, there are significant differences regarding, for example, the standard of liability (in particular: fault or no-fault), or causation (including the proof of causation), or the measurement of monetary and nonmonetary damages. The general principle that wrongdoers should compensate their victims is probably known to law as well as to ethics, yet very significant legal questions may be influenced by other matters, such as the practicality of certain rules or their impact on general economic development.

Conversely, contract law is an area in which individual preferences play a more important role. Although giving weight to individual preferences may in itself be a moral obligation, the differences between legal and moral obligations can be demonstrated more easily in an area where these preferences play a more important role.

Legal Rights as Originating from Moral Principles

Whereas law and ethics are not identical and, in this sense, are different and separate, there still is a connection. In spite of the necessary distinction between law and ethics, a very good argument can be made that legal rights are a particular derivative of moral or political rights. A society may consider certain moral decisions to be so significant that it opts to accept them as legally enforceable also. In contract law, a good example is the old Roman law principle that contracts are binding (*pacta sunt servanda*), which could also be seen as a consequence of the principle that one has to honor one's promises. Only if that rule is both a moral and a legal rule can binding and enforceable contracts exist. To that extent, there is certainly an interrelation between morals and the legal obligation to keep one's contractual promises. From this viewpoint, moral rights can be described as abstract background rights, to which certain specific legal rights are related.[7]

Again, however, there are also limits to this view. If one took literally the principle that promises must be kept, the debtor would always have to actually perform a contract, unless there is a case of impossibility or the like. In particular, one may consider unacceptable a legal system that would allow a so-called efficient breach of contract, which may result if a legal system does not provide for a claim for specific performance but limits the creditor to a claim for damages. Yet from a legal perspective, this line of reasoning is circular, because the question is what signing a contract means. A legal rule that obligates a debtor to compensate the creditor only for losses in case of nonperformance may also have an impact on the legal content of the promise given. According to such a rule, the contractual promise is only to provide for compensation and does not include a promise for

7 Dworkin, *Taking Rights Seriously*, 93.

specific performance. In fact, for good reasons most legal systems do not follow a black-and-white pattern regarding specific performance but distinguish between situations in which specific performance is necessary and others in which compensation is sufficient. The exact delineation between specific performance and mere compensation differs, however, among legal systems.

In more general terms, given these differences, the legal content of a promise cannot be separated from its legal background. The content of what is legally expected from a promisor will also depend on the relevant legal rules. If a legal system provides for compensation only, a promise to do something amounts only to a promise to compensate the other party in case of nonperformance. The same is true with various other aspects of contractual promises. The promise to deliver a certain good may imply a warranty that the good is of a minimum quality. Yet whether, and under which circumstances, a promise includes an implied warranty may depend on the applicable legal rules. From a broader perspective, contract-law rules, even if their core has some moral foundation, may be influenced by a variety of factors, such as the political goal of protecting consumers or providing an encouraging environment for the supply side of the market. Certain fundamental contract-law rules certainly originate from or are influenced by ethical rules, even though most legal rules are not simply a derivative of ethical rules.

What is a Fair Price?

The most significant question for the parties to a contract usually relates to the quid pro quo or, in more common language, the price. This brings us to a further problem: what is a fair price? Consider a baker who intends to sell a loaf of bread. The costs for producing the loaf of bread may be–including raw materials, wages for employees, depreciation of equipment, rooms, energy, taxes, etc.–1 euro per loaf. Economically, the baker might be able to survive on a very low level if he charges 1.50 euros per loaf. To make a reasonable average profit, however, it might be necessary to charge a minimum of 2 euros per loaf. The average price for a loaf of bread in the vicinity of, say, ten kilometers may be 2.20 euros for a loaf of bread. In the village where our bakery is located, customers may be willing to pay between 2.50 and 3 euros per loaf, depending on the customer, in order to avoid driving to the next town for bread at a lower price. The baker may make the most profit by offering the bread for 2.69 euros because this is the price that most customers would be willing to pay. The only other baker in the same village may charge 2.76 euros. The highest price offered in the vicinity of twenty kilometers may be 3.15 euros, and the lowest 1.89 euros per loaf.

One could endlessly discuss which of the figures I mentioned, if any, is the fairest or most appropriate or just price. The impossibility of determining *the* fair price becomes even more obvious if we include in our considerations that there are significant differences between the quality of our baker and that of other bakers or the next supermarket. To complicate things a little more, we have to consider that not only does the quality of bread differ from baker to baker but so do our personal preferences for the taste or texture of bread. As a consequence, we have to accept that, for legal purposes, there is no such thing as *the* fair price. We usually are best off if we let every baker decide for himself the price he wishes to charge and leave it to the market to determine what happens. We consider that fair in legal systems because contracts are not imposed on the parties, who usually are free to decide whether or not to accept a contract. Of course, there are sectors where pricing is regulated by legal rules. But these are exceptions based on the particularities of certain sectors that cannot be generalized. In general, the justification for the binding effect and the legal recognition of contracts lies in the consent of both parties. Or, as the Romans said: *Stat pro ratione voluntas* ("The will stands in place of reason"). We do not need check the appropriateness of contracts, because they are justified by the parties' consent.

In other words, at the outset, it is not the law that has to educate parties as to the appropriateness of a certain contract. In a free society, it is rather the other way around. By concluding a contract, the parties inform the market and society about which contract terms they consider appropriate.

Limits to the Sufficiency of Consent

There are, however, cases where we wonder whether the parties' consent is indeed sufficient to justify the binding effects of a contract. In this respect, one could distinguish between contracts that might be contrary to certain public goods (or have harmful effects on third parties) and contracts that are grossly unfair to one of the parties. As in other areas of the law, such as torts, the law states the outer limits of what we deem to be acceptable between individuals. For this reason, modern contract law has stated certain limits to the freedom of contract, in particular in the fields of labor law, consumer law, and landlord/tenant law.[8] Apart from these areas, moral values may indeed justify considering a contract unacceptable, even though both parties freely consent to it.

From an international perspective, a controversial and therefore very helpful example of this phenomenon is–if you will forgive my use of both the example and the terminology–so-called dwarf tossing, or (more specifically) contracts for the organization or performance of dwarf-tossing.[9] At first glance, one might not

---

8 For this development, see, for example, Uwe Wesel, *Geschichte des Rechts in Europa: von den Griechen bis zum Vertrag von Lissabon* (Munich: C. H. Beck, 2010), 670.

9 For Germany, see, for example, Verwaltungsgericht Neustadt (Weinstraße), Order of May 21, 1992, Case 7 L 1271/92.NW, *Neue Zeitschrift für Verwaltungsrecht* (1993):

see a problem. The audience and the customers are happy because they enjoy the entertainment. The producer of the event is happy because he makes a profit. The dwarfs are happy because they are paid for being tossed and have consented to that. Still, there is considerable hesitation in various legal systems over whether dwarf tossing is legally acceptable and whether the underlying contracts are or should be valid. Little people may have good reason to feel offended by such an event or the underlying offer, even if they are not involved personally. One may very well argue that dwarf tossing not only humiliates those little people who have agreed to be tossed but makes a mockery of all little people–and perhaps of handicapped persons in general–and implies that they are mere objects and can be used or disposed of very easily. There may also be cases where a little person agrees to a contract only to provide for urgent needs of his or her family. On the other hand, one might argue that there is still consent by all participants and that, after all, we are dealing only with a joke, a very bad one certainly, but still a joke, so that in most cases no one really implies an offending statement that would be meant seriously. Be that as it may, even if dwarf tossing was unacceptable only on an ethical level, there are certainly contracts that the law cannot and does not accept. In this respect, several mechanisms operate.

The Need for a Free Contractual Choice

First, most legal systems provide for rules to ensure that a party's consent to a contract is in fact based on that party's real and free contractual choices. Contracts to which a party consents only on the basis of threat or the use of force are not acceptable. Furthermore, most contract-law systems have rules providing for the ineffectiveness or avoidability of contracts where the consent of one of the parties is based on a significant error.

However, one of the most basic problems for contract law is that most of our choices are influenced by external factors to a certain degree. If I go out without an umbrella, and a heavy rain starts, my practical choices may be paying a taxi fare that I consider an outrage, or buying an umbrella in a color that I do not like, or returning home drenched. In spite of these limitations, contract law would usually find a party's consent to a taxi or the umbrella contract sufficient and valid. One of the most important tasks of contract law is distinguishing between influencing factors that are acceptable and others that are not.

98–100; for France, see Conseil d'État, Decision of October 27, 1995, no. 136727–Commune de Morsang-sur-Orge; for a view from the United States, see Robert W. McGee, "If Dwarf Tossing Is Outlawed, Only Outlaws Will Toss Dwarfs: Is Dwarf Tossing a Victimless Crime?," *American Journal of Jurisprudence* 38 (1993): 335.

Market and Competition

Another important mechanism is provided by competition and the market. When I, as a mere law professor, negotiate with a big company, there is an obvious imbalance between the company's economic power and my own, but still I have options. When you buy a car, you cannot compete with the manufacturer's or dealer's economic power. But what you can do is exit the negotiations and go from Porsche to Mercedes. Competition and market therefore are most essential for our practical freedom of contract. Of course, that mechanism requires a functioning market so that the law–antitrust or anticartel law–may or must step in if, as in cases of a monopoly, market control does not work.

In these cases, however, the function of the law is not so much to direct the play but rather to set an appropriate stage on which the different players cannot avoid the control mechanisms of the market. Interestingly, one of the most significant aspects for determining an abuse of a monopoly position in anticartel law is the comparison of contracts, concluded by a monopolist, with a parallel contract on a real or hypothetical market. Again, it is the market that informs the law about appropriate contract practices. However, these contract practices are observed, analyzed, and transformed under a certain legal rule or legal practice by the competent authorities (legislatures, state agencies, courts). Acceptable legal practice will then certainly be respected or, at least, considered by actors on the market. This effect will, in many instances, operate by way of regulation rather than education.

Unacceptable Content

These two mechanisms–that is, a contract law that aims at determining real consent of the parties, and the indirect control of contractual choices by competition and a functioning market–do not always result in contracts that we find acceptable. As the example of dwarf tossing indicates, there are situations where we find it necessary to make certain contracts illegal because they do serious harm to society or to individuals. Examples are contracts on the sale of drugs or contracts involving human trafficking.

Whereas in contract law it is, in most instances, sufficient that the law refuses the enforcement of contracts that harm individuals or society, there are other areas of law in which the role of binding legal provisions goes beyond the mere prevention of harm or damages. For example, under family law, parents must provide for their children; in public law, the state must make minimum provision for education, welfare, care for the needy, health care, etc. Yet even in the field of contracts, the law may pursue certain goals for political reasons. In European law, certain contract provisions are mandatory in the sense that the parties may not derogate from them, even though they may have good reasons for doing so because these provisions aim at establishing an internal market.[10]

However, since legislation is not able to provide for all possible situations of unacceptable contracts, all legal systems have general rules that contracts may be declared invalid or voided because of unacceptable content. Anglo-American contract law, for example, includes the doctrine of unconscionability. Romanic contract laws refer to the doctrine that a contract needs to have a valid "cause," which means that contracts are invalid if they are based on an illicit or illegal cause. German law and related legal systems provide for statutory rules on the invalidity of contracts that are contrary to good morals. Moreover, civil-law systems–including Germanic and Romanic legal systems–typically also apply the doctrine of good faith to contracts.

Unacceptable Content and Educational Effects?

The question, however, is whether and how far these doctrines are meant to have a pedagogical effect on individuals or society. From a legal perspective, the traditional approach would be that law has a twofold role in society. First, it protects legitimate expectations of individuals or groups. Contract law, for instance, protects the legitimate expectation that individuals are bound by their contractual promises so that each party can rely on the other's performance of a promise and its enforceability, if necessary. These functions are closely related to concepts such as legal clarity and legal security. Liberty and freedom require that we know or could know the framework under which our present or future actions and conduct will or must take place, and that reasonable expectations will not be disappointed.

Second, the law aims at influencing the conduct of persons. We provide for the enforceability of contracts, if necessary by force, not only because parties may legitimately expect each other to keep their contractual promises, but also because, for the good of society, we want parties to perform contracts or meet their contractual liabilities. And we also want them to do so voluntarily, without the exercise of state powers. The question is which mechanism stands behind that voluntary performance of legal obligations. Is it the threat that the other party may resort to courts and state enforcement, if necessary, in case the debtor fails or refuses to perform? Or is it that putting an enforcement mechanism in place also has a pedagogical effect, so that most people agree that performing their obligations is appropriate and, as a consequence, actually comply with their contractual obligations? Or more shortly: is the aim deterrence or education?

---

10 For an example, see European Court of Justice, Judgement of Sept. 5, 2019, Case C-28/18 –Verein für Konsumenteninformation v. Deutsche Bahn AG.

The traditional legal view would probably be that it is rather the threat than the pedagogical effect behind it that operates in these cases. One reason for this is that we take it for granted anyway that people have to comply with their obligations. The rule that contracts are enforced by state powers is considered a reflection of an already existing culture that contracts are binding, and not the source of that expectation. Eventually, however, we probably have a communicating system of influence where every case of state enforcement also makes manifest that state power exists and therefore exercises a pedagogical influence on society.

The law itself is silent on these matters. In its practical application, these questions do not really matter. Eventually, the relation between these several lines of influence cannot be answered by lawyers alone without support by other academics, in particular social scientists and psychologists.

Usages versus "Good" Morals

Another aspect of the pedagogical questions revolving around the use of these general clauses concerns their specific content. Concepts like good morals or good faith have an empirical aspect. The morals of different societies may differ. What is moral may also be defined by the usages of a certain society. This can be seen from the fact that the legal understanding of good morals may change through the course of time.

A typical example is the legal treatment of unmarried couples. In Germany, an unmarried couple's renting a hotel room was considered contrary to good morals until the late sixties or even the early seventies, so that the underlying contract was considered to be invalid; today, that attitude as well as the legal assessment following from it has changed completely.

Interestingly, however, most legal systems have an understanding of concepts such as good morals or good faith that includes certain reservations in this respect. German courts have ruled that a particular casual habit or usage, even if it is common in society or parts of society or in a specific commercial sector, cannot count as good morals. Only a few years ago, for example, a German court ruled that agreements to the effect that the family of the bridegroom has to pay money for the bride's willingness to marry are contrary to good morals, although such agreements are very common among migrant families from certain countries.[11]

11 For example, Oberlandesgericht Hamm, OLG Hamm, Jan. 13, 2011, case 18 U 88/10, I-18 U 88/10, NJW-Rechtsprechungsreport 2011, pp. 1197–202.

Objective Good Morals

The perennial question, however, of what constitutes "good" or "bad" cannot be answered solely on a philosophical or ethical basis, if these terms are used as legal categories. Of course, every society needs a certain minimum ethical and cultural standard on which to build life in that society, and this standard is reflected by the society's legal rules. To this extent, an ethical judgment may indeed bring about a legal rule. Legal experience demonstrates that we can live best if the legal understanding of "acceptable" or "good" is, too a very large extent, understood as a normative, rule-based concept. That means that "good" morals are those which are generally in line with the general approach and philosophical underpinnings of the legal system as a whole.

Conclusion

Law and ethics are separate and different but interrelated. In contract law, the distinction between both is necessary, first of all, to allow us the pursuit of our different interests and desires. Second, in a free and pluralistic society, the law cannot simply impose a certain ethical system on every citizen.

However, it is also the role of the law to define the unacceptable, which will always reflect certain ethical values or standards. In this respect, particularly in contract law, influence is exercised in both directions: on one hand, contract practice informs us about which agreements, rules, and mechanisms are desirable and practical; this information and practice in turn will influence the shaping of contract-law rules. On the other hand, contract-law rules will influence contract-law practice by enforcement as well as by information and education.

"The True Freedom of the Christian Spirit"

Martin Luther's Vision of Redistributive Taxation

Allen Calhoun

Introduction

This chapter begins with a story–one that arose from Martin Luther's concern to provide for the poor through social assistance as well as charity. That concern first surfaced in Luther's sermons on usury in 1519 and 1520.[1] Luther then elaborated on his vision for social reform in his "Open Letter to the Christian Nobility of the German Nation Concerning the Reform of the Christian Estate" (1520).[2]

The Wittenberg town council, not surprisingly, was the first to respond to Luther's "Open Letter." It did so by drafting an ordinance that would "ensure the regulation of public assistance to the city's house poor."[3] The Wittenberg ordinance was published in 1522, and other towns soon approached Luther hoping for his assistance in drafting legislation. One of these was Leisnig, a town south of Wittenberg with a parish that also included eleven surrounding villages.[4] In response, Luther spent a week in Leisnig preparing a church order that included a "common chest,"[5] and in 1523 he wrote a "Preface to the Ordinance of a Common Chest" and had the Leisnig ordinance printed and published with his preface.[6]

---

1 See Carter Lindberg, *Beyond Charity: Reformation Initiatives for the Poor* (Minneapolis: Fortress Press, 1993), 119.

2 Martin Luther, "Open Letter to the Christian Nobility," *LW* 44:211. Unless otherwise noted, citations from the works of Martin Luther are from *Luther's Works* (*LW*) (American Edition), ed. Jaroslav Pelikan and Helmut T. Lehman, 55 vols. (Philadelphia: Muhlenberg Press and Fortress Press, and St. Louis: Concordia Publishing House, 1955–86).

3 Lindberg, *Beyond Charity*, 119.

4 Ibid., 123–24.

5 Ibid., 124.

6 Walther I. Brandt, introduction to "Ordinance of a Common Chest, Preface," *LW* 45:165.

The Leisnig ordinance explicitly provided for ongoing taxation:[7]

> We the nobility, council, craft supervisors, gentry, and commoners dwelling in the city and villages of our whole parish, have unitedly resolved and consented that every noble, townsman, and peasant living in the parish shall, according to his ability and means, remit in taxes ... a certain sum of money to the chest each year, in order that the total amount can be arrived at and procured which the deliberations and decisions of the general parish assembly, on the basis of investigation in and experience with the annual statements, have determined to be necessary and sufficient .... By the grace of God these practices have now been restored to the true freedom of the Christian spirit.[8]

The provision, to be sure, contains patent ambiguities: whether the tax is an emergency measure designed to maintain chest resources at a certain level or a regular contribution from the inception of the program; whether the amount of the tax is set or means-tested; and whether the assembly has the authority to adjust the amount. Nevertheless, two themes emerge. First, ability and needs are both in view; the tax is to be paid according to each taxpayer's "ability and means" but also explicitly for the maintenance of the "needy poor." Second, the levy is to be measured and consistent. Third, the ordinance's annual tax provision assumes that the revenue collected will be redistributed; the resources of the common chest must be maintained at a level sufficient to meet the needs of the poor, as determined by the investigation and experience of the parish assembly. Luther himself, in his preface, acknowledged that funds in the common chest could be used in a number of ways but concluded that need-based redistribution was preferable to all others:

> The third way is the best, however, to devote all the remaining property to the common fund of a common chest, out of which gifts and loans could be made in Christian love to all the needy in the land, be they nobles or commoners .... Now there is no greater service of God than Christian love which helps and serves the needy, as Christ himself will judge and testify at the last day, Matthew 25. This is why the possessions of the church were formerly called *bona ecclesiae*, that is, common property, a common chest, as it were, for all who were needy among the Christians.[9]

Implementation of the ordinance proved more difficult than its drafting. An impasse arose between the congregation and the Leisnig town council. Appeals to the elector were futile. Another visit by Luther was unsuccessful. In November

---

7 Lindberg, *Beyond Charity*, 123–25.

8 Martin Luther, "Fraternal Agreement on the Common Chest," *LW* 45:192.

9 Martin Luther, "Ordinance of a Common Chest, Preface," *LW* 45:172–73.

1524, Luther wrote to the elector's adviser, Georg Spalatin, that he "deeply regretted that the Leisnig attempt, the first of its kind, which should have been such an example of success, had turned out to be such a miserable example of failure."[10] It was not until 1529 that the existence and operation of the common chest were confirmed.[11]

Taxes and Redistribution

The link between this piece of history and taxation today turns on the present meaning of equity. The institution of taxation occupies a unique position among areas of law in modern pluralistic societies. To begin with, taxes are inherently redistributive. Apart from a lump-sum tax, every tax system imaginable inevitably changes taxpayers' economic positions. We can call this feature of taxation "inherent redistribution." At the same time, taxes–in conjunction with spending policies–offer societies the opportunity to redistribute resources deliberately–for example, by taking from the rich and giving to the poor. This use of taxation can be termed "deliberate redistribution."

Both types of redistribution suggest that such a thing as *equity* exists in tax systems. The term "equity" is used in various senses, but there are two of note. First, a tax system is taken to be equitable when it allocates the burden of taxation according to some measure of *fairness*. One such measure is the *benefit principle*, according to which those who benefit the most from the government's use of its tax revenue should pay the most taxes. Another measure–dominant in defenses of progressive income tax systems over the past century and a half–is the *ability-to-pay* principle, which holds that the greatest tax burden should be allocated to those who will sacrifice the least by paying taxes. Equity-as-fairness reflects the reality that taxes are inherently redistributive. A tax system may also be called equitable, however, when it is used deliberately as a mechanism for reallocating resources from those who have much to those who have little–in other words, when it is deliberately redistributive.

Equity of both types aside, modern pluralistic societies also require tax systems to raise a desired amount of revenue with as little negative impact as possible on the incentive of society's members to produce and thus grow the economy. This tension dictates that tax systems be as *efficient* as possible, that is, that they be minimally distortionary. The best tax, according to the efficiency principle, is one that allows taxpayers to make virtually the same decisions about how much to spend, earn, and save that they would have made were there no tax at all.

---

10 Brandt, introduction to "Ordinance of a Common Chest," 167.

11 Ibid.

Efficiency in tax systems works at cross-purposes with the deliberately redistributive kind of equity but not, to the same degree, with the inherently redistributive kind. The great attraction of the ability-to-pay principle lies in the fortuitous coincidence of efficiency and inherently distributive equity that it offers. Those with the most pretax wealth are the least likely to be burdened by paying taxes *and* the least likely to see their financial decisions distorted by taxes. Nevertheless, a tension remains. In a progressive income-tax system, which is the hallmark of ability-to-pay taxation in modern pluralistic democracies, any tax has some distortionary effect. The perennial question is: how high should tax rates be, particularly in the higher income brackets, before the negative effect on economic growth outweighs the benefit of the tax revenue?

These tensions, and tensions within tensions, can be conceptualized in terms of a triangular interplay of interests: (1) the interest of the state in raising revenue; (2) the interest of taxpayers in minimizing the amount of taxes that they are required to pay; and (3) the interest of the socially and economically needy in seeing tax revenue used to improve their circumstances. Each of these three interests has its place in policymaking. The policymaker is generally committed to providing some level (usually a disputed level) of infrastructure and security necessary for all citizens to live in peace and relative ease; the policymaker typically believes that the taxpayer should be burdened as little as possible so that she can contribute to economic prosperity for the benefit of all; and policymakers are likely to acknowledge that the poor should be provided for at least to preserve a measure of contentment throughout society and thus stave off political instability, which would undermine the conditions necessary for economic growth.

In part because of the ability-to-pay principle, one edge of the triangle–the line running from the state to the taxpayer–has collapsed in many modern societies. Policymakers no longer need to refer to separate equity considerations in balancing government revenue needs against taxpayer ability. The term "efficiency" covers both considerations. The government and the taxpayer are allies for two reasons: (1) the more money the taxpayer makes, the more revenue the government can collect; and (2) the taxpayer realizes that some degree of government investment in society is necessary for her individual economic success. Deliberate redistribution occasionally enters the policy discussion,[12] but when it does, it does so primarily in an instrumental way. Its purpose is to reduce economic inequality to further political stability and overall prosperity. At least in the American context, the poor are in view only in an indirect way; they will benefit because "a rising tide lifts all boats."

A triangular "tax relationship" not unlike the one described above arose in sixteenth-century Germany. Winfried Schulze argues that the growth of monetary

12 See, for instance, the proposals of some 2020 U.S. presidential candidates for a federal wealth tax.

exchange and favorable agrarian market conditions rendered the feudal lords of that time and place "eager to make the best possible use of obligatory dues and services."[13] At the same time, the peasants wanted to secure individual and collective claims to land, inheritance rights, and rights to use and sell their products under favorable market conditions. The central monarchy and territorial rulers, meanwhile, "had a major interest in an economically healthy population which was able to pay taxes."[14]

It was in this emerging social, economic, and political landscape that Luther preached and wrote. Some of the seismic shift was apparent to Luther. He saw around him a world that was "profoundly worried about the scarcity of resources," to use Paul Warde's phrase.[15] Population was growing more rapidly than the food supply, and prices were rising. Local regulation by the communes was no longer adequate for poor relief; "from 1562 onwards dearth and its consequences became a regular concern of the central government."[16] Evident in Luther's writings and sermons is a deep suspicion of two trends–one toward the increasing interest of the princes and emperor in an abundant and steady stream of revenue from taxes, the other toward the burgeoning profit economy. Concerned about the direction in which the rulers were moving, Luther called for the subordination of the state's other revenue needs to the necessities of the poor. "If we have to spend such large sums every year on guns, roads, bridges, dams, and countless similar items to insure the temporal peace and prosperity of a city," he asked, "why should not much more be devoted to our poor neglected youth?"[17]

At the same time, Luther saw a reorientation underway in the economy of his day away from the needs of the poor. Carter Lindberg writes: "Luther was convinced that the new profit economy divorced money from use for human needs, necessitated an economy of acquisition, fed the mortal sin of avarice, and eroded the common good."[18] Abandonment of the guiding principle of *need* could only mean capitulation to the idea that economic principles and laws are autonomous–a perspective that Luther considered "idolatrous."[19] It would be anachronistic to suppose that Luther saw the advent of an alliance between the state and its

13 Winfried Schulze, "Peasant Resistance in Sixteenth- and Seventeenth-Century Germany in a European Context," in *Religion, Politics, and Social Protest: Three Studies on Early Modern Germany*, ed. Kaspar von Greyerz (London: George Allen & Unwin, 1984), 70.

14 Ibid., 71.

15 Paul Warde, *Ecology, Economy and State Formation in Early Modern Germany* (Cambridge: Cambridge University Press, 2006), 38.

16 Ibid., 97.

17 Martin Luther, "To the Councilmen in All Germany That They Should Establish and Maintain Christian Schools," *LW* 45:350.

18 Carter Lindberg, "Luther on a Market Economy," *Lutheran Quarterly* 30 (2016): 380.

19 Ibid., 382; Lindberg, *Beyond Charity*, 113.

citizens with means, an alliance that we term “efficiency.” He did, however, see greed as the motive behind both obtaining profit from trade and increasing tax revenues. These twin developments were born of the same evil impulse, in Luther’s view, and they threatened to push the poor from social policy considerations altogether.

Luther’s denunciation of Germany’s incipient profit economy was unequivocal, but his stance toward regular, universal taxation was nuanced. In fact, as reflected in the Leisnig ordinance and his preface to it, Luther advocated regular, universal taxation. His complaint against the rulers was not that they used taxation to meet their administrative objectives; it was the nature of those objectives.

The connection between Luther’s theological statements–anyone’s theological statements, for that matter–and the momentous changes in the political economy of sixteenth-century Europe remain contested. Hans-Christoph Rublack considers German legislation of the period driven by “the everyday experience of social action.”[20] Theological reasoning, in Rublack’s view, did little more than legitimate the norms that society prudentially developed.[21] Peter Brickle, on the other hand, contends that Luther, no less than Zwingli or even Müntzer, took the Bible “to be the standard, and the deductive exegetical process the method employed, in solving this-worldly problems.”[22]

The rapid move to centrally administered welfare in German towns that embraced the evangelical cause in the 1520 s must be seen as primarily a theological shift. Redistribution of resources for the benefit of the poor was a spiritually motivated act for Luther. After the initial failure of the Leisnig ordinance, Luther preached a sermon in which he offered ideas on how a city could establish a system of poor relief. He added ruefully, “But we do not have the personnel for this, therefore I do not think we can put it into effect until God makes Christians.”[23] It seems unlikely that someone so captivated by his spiritual discoveries would have had the time and luxury to devote himself to understanding and resolving the socioeconomic shifts in his world and cloaking his solutions in theological language. What, then, called forth such a persistent desire for the governing authorities to use their ongoing tax revenue systematically for the poor under their jurisdiction?

---

20 Hans-Christoph Rublack, “Political and Social Norms in Urban Communities in the Holy Roman Empire,” in von Greyerz, *Religion, Politics, and Social Protest*, 24.

21 Ibid., 41–42.

22 Peter Brickle, “Social Protest and Reformation Theology,” in von Greyerz, *Religion, Politics, and Social Protest*, 15.

23 Brandt, introduction to “Ordinance of a Common Chest, Preface,” *LW* 45:167, quoting Luther, “Sermon for St. Stephen’s Day, Dec. 26, 1522,” *Weimarer Ausgabe* (WA) 12:693.

Redistributive Currents in Luther's Theology

Part of the answer to that question lies with Luther's abhorrence of abuses in the medieval system of almsgiving. Almsgiving rather than redistribution through tax-and-transfer systems had been the important instrument of poor relief in the Middle Ages. Taxation had a different purpose, that of funding the state. The triangular tax relationship was not yet fully in view. As Jacques Le Goff notes, in the feudal period kings were expected to live off their own resources, but in the thirteenth and fourteenth centuries an increase in the number of servants prompted interest in taxation.[24] The first justification of exceptional taxes was war, particularly the crusades. By the end of the thirteenth century, however, it was typical of rulers to extend these taxes to maintain order.[25] By the fifteenth century, in much of Europe "the income drawn directly from the landed estates of the prince was overtaken by taxation as the main source of finance for the activities of central governments."[26] It was left to sixteenth-century Europeans to begin using taxation for poor relief.

Even in the "Ninety-Five Theses," Luther was already reacting against the idea that the poor are the treasure of the church, supplying the rich with the opportunity to do good works through almsgiving.[27] Whereas late medieval reform efforts tried merely to control begging, Luther sought the abolition of begging.[28] This shift, Carter Lindberg notes, was prompted not so much by sensitivity to the "deleterious effects of widespread begging" as by an awareness of the implications of Luther's "theology of justification by grace alone, which precludes any salvific benefits to poverty and to alms."[29] Thus, the Lutheran towns established common chests as an expression of the "brotherly love" that is the "fruit" of realizing that "all temporal and eternal blessings won by our Lord and Savior Christ out of pure grace and mercy are granted unto us by the eternal God."[30]

The word "granted" hints at a theme of redistribution, not just of spiritual goods but of material goods as well, that runs throughout Luther's theology. This section examines that theme in general; the following section focuses on what was for Luther the paradigm of redistributive theology: the Lord's Supper.

---

24 Jacques Le Goff, *Money and the Middle Ages: An Essay in Historical Anthropology*, trans. Jean Birrell (Cambridge: Polity Press, 2012), 90–91.

25 Ibid., 91.

26 Ibid., 96.

27 See, for example, Martin Luther, "The Ninety-Five Theses," 59, in *Documents of the Christian Church*, ed. Henry Bettenson, 2nd ed. (London: Oxford University Press, 1963). See also Lindberg, *Beyond Charity*, 99.

28 Lindberg, *Beyond Charity*, 106.

29 Ibid.

30 "Fraternal Agreement on the Common Chest," *LW* 45:178.

Through faith, Luther wrote, the soul is united with Christ "as a bride is united with her bridegroom," and, thus, "everything they have they hold in common, the good as well as the evil."[31] This "happy exchange" (*fröhliche Wechsel*) between Christ and the believer is based on the originally Christological doctrine of the *communicatio idiomatum* (communication of attributes).[32] The doctrine is not original with Luther, but he places it in the center, not just of his Christology, but of his whole theology.[33] Embracing the full implications of the *communicatio*, Luther insisted that whatever we say about Christ "as a human being" must also be said about Christ as God, and whatever we say of Christ as God we must also say about Christ the human being.[34]

The exchange between bridegroom and bride (Christ and the believer) models the exchange between the two natures of Christ.[35] Thus, according to Luther, Christ distributes to Christians the "prerogatives" of "priesthood" and "kingship" that he obtained.[36] The prerogative of kingship is a spiritual kingship that means that the believer is, in the space of faith and liberty, subject to none.[37] Christ "obtained" this prerogative, and the believer receives it because Christ "imparts" and "shares" it through the legal consequences of the act of "marrying" the believer.[38] Christ's distribution to the believer of the prerogative of priesthood carries the redistributive dynamic beyond the relationship between Christ and believer: priesthood itself implies a redistribution of what is received. By virtue of the priesthood of all believers, bestowed on Christians by Christ, Christians in turn distribute to others what they have received.[39]

The believer's focus on the neighbor's need is the outcome of the distributive logic in Luther's *communicatio idiomatum*; the "merry exchange" through trust in Christ's word bestows on the believer "Christ's benefits and attributes" and gives

---

31 Martin Luther, "The Freedom of a Christian," *LW* 31:351.

32 See Bernd Wannenwetsch, "Luther's Moral Theology," in *The Cambridge Companion to Martin Luther*, ed. Donald K. McKim (Cambridge: Cambridge University Press, 2003), 120; Martin Wendte, "Mystical Foundations of Politics? Luther on God's Presence and the Place of Human Beings," *Studies in Christian Ethics*, Aug. 7, 2018, journals.sagepub.com/doi/10.1177/0953946818792628.

33 Oswald Bayer, *Martin Luther's Theology: A Contemporary Interpretation*, trans. Thomas H. Trapp (Grand Rapids, MI: William B. Eerdmans Publishing Co., 2008), 236.

34 Martin Luther, "On the Councils and the Church," in *The Christian Theology Reader*, ed. Alister E. McGrath, 2nd ed. (Malden, MA: Blackwell Publishing, 2001), 281.

35 Wendte, "Mystical Foundations of Politics," 7.

36 Luther, "The Freedom of a Christian," *LW* 31:354.

37 Ibid.

38 Ibid.

39 Ibid., 355.

the believer the ability to "make the *need* of the other person his own."[40] The "good things" flowing from Christ to the believer "flow on to those who have need of them,"[41] by which Luther means that the believer's faith and righteousness should cover the sins of the believer's neighbor. This nonreciprocal, unidirectional attention to the neighbor's needs is love. The Christian "lives in Christ through faith, in his neighbor through love."[42]

Because the believer is *distributee* as well as *distributor*, she lives in a place of abundance, free from all the anxieties that her own distributing of good things would cause if she were in a place of scarcity. The neighbor's necessity, consequently, can now become the sole, consuming focus of the believer. For Luther, the goods of the church are (or should be) common property, not explicitly because of a preexisting state of communal ownership,[43] but because "there is no greater service of God than Christian love which helps and serves the needy."[44] The common chest, therefore, is "for all who were needy among the Christians."[45]

Thus far, the exact nature of the overflow of good things is ambiguous. On one hand, the "good things" redistributed seem at times to be spiritual things. Introduction of the common chest, on the other hand, means that an overflow of material goods follows the same redistributive pattern. The following section explores the redistribution of specifically material goods in Luther's highly material and tangible conception of the Lord's Supper.

Eucharist and Redistribution

Luther wrote:

> In this sacrament [of the Lord's Supper], therefore, man is given through the priest a sure sign from God himself that he is thus united with Christ and his saints and has all things in common, that Christ's sufferings and life are his own, together with the lives and sufferings of all the saints .... But in times past this sacrament was so properly

---

40 Bernd Wannenwetsch, *Political Worship*, trans. Margaret Kohl (Oxford: Oxford University Press, 2004), 331.

41 Luther, "The Freedom of a Christian," *LW* 31:371.

42 Ibid.

43 Compare Thomas Aquinas's view of property in the *Summa theologica* (Latin-English Edition), trans. Fathers of the English-Dominican Province (NovAntiqua, 2013), II–II, questions 58 and 66.

44 Luther, "Ordinance of a Common Chest, Preface," *LW* 45:172.

45 Ibid., 173.

> used, and the people were taught to understand this fellowship so well, that they even gathered food and material goods in the church, and there–as St. Paul writes in 1 Corinthians 11–distributed among those who were in need.[46]

As early as 1519, in "The Blessed Sacrament of the Holy and True Body of Christ, and the Brotherhoods," Luther drew a tight parallel between communion in the sacrament of the Lord's Supper on one hand and the common citizenship of those in political community on the other.[47]

Approaching redistribution from a position of abundance revolutionizes distributive justice. Rather than serving "as the management of the distribution struggle," politics can allow members of society to regard each other as "partner[s] or accomplice[s]," and not as "threat[s]," when "abundance" instead of "deficiency" is the "fundamental point of departure."[48] When scarcity is in the fore, the neighbor's needs are a threat, self-interest drives society, and justice becomes the resolution of conflict between each person's self-interest. When abundance underlies the political dynamic, on the other hand, the neighbor's need is not a threat, and justice merges into other-seeking love. Luther called his extended metaphor in "The Blessed Sacrament" a "homely figure," in which the fellowship with Christ and the saints in the Lord's Supper "is like a city where every citizen shares with all the others the city's name, honor, freedom, trade, customs, usages, help, support, protection, and the like, while at the same time he shares all the dangers of fire and blood, enemies and death, losses, taxes, and the like."[49]

The connection of the Lord's Supper's to life in political community is more than analogical for Luther. In the next paragraph, Luther moved beyond the Lord's Supper as merely a "figure" of solidarity and commonality. Now it is a "sign" that the believer does, in fact, hold all things in common with Christ and the saints.[50] The "things in common" possessed by the believer are not only spiritual things. Distribution of material goods is a proper "use" of the Lord's Supper. Luther bemoaned the loss of the proper use of the sacrament in "times past," when

46 Martin Luther, "The Blessed Sacrament of the Holy and True Body of Christ, and the Brotherhoods," *LW* 35:52, 57.

47 Ibid., 50–51.

48 Wannenwetsch, *Political Worship*, 332–33.

49 Luther, "Blessed Sacrament," *LW* 35:51–52.

50 Ibid., 52. Wannenwetsch describes the "inner logic of this citizenship" as an instance of the *communicatio idiomatum*, observing that "Luther makes clear that celebrating the Eucharist is nothing less than a political act in which the communicants actualize and suffer the citizenship that has been bestowed on them by baptism." Wannenwetsch, "Luther's Moral Theology," 134. Wendte considers the sacrament of communion the "paradigmatic point of intensification" of the "merry exchange." Wendte, "Mystical Foundations of Politics?," 8.

the people "even gathered food and material goods in the church, and ... distributed among those who were in need."[51] Striking in Luther's account is the complete absence of differentiation between spiritual and physical benefits and burdens. Those who approach the sacrament selfishly, Luther wrote, "will not help the poor, put up with sinners, care for the sorrowing, suffer with the suffering, intercede for others, defend the truth, and at the risk of life, property, and honor seek the betterment of the church and of all Christians."[52] The Lord's Supper is paradigmatic of the continuity between "the sacred and profane spheres."[53] The sacrament erases that distinction, according to Martin Wendte, because it is the most salient example of the way in which "God and God's Word are always working for humankind in a materially mediated way."[54]

Luther did distinguish, not between spiritual and physical distribution but between the Lord's Supper as "testament and sacrament" and "the sacrifice and good works" that may be done "in connection with it."[55] The distinction here is between *sacrament* and *sign*. The Lord's Supper, according to Luther, is both—something "external" yet containing "something spiritual."[56] Many things that are not also sacraments can be signs.

Signs, in this sense, resemble sacraments, except that they are not means of salvation.[57] The estates are appointed, and they accompany the Word. God gives many signs "for the greater assurance and strengthening of our faith."[58] Scripture, Luther wrote, is full of these signs "given along with the promises"—the sign of the rainbow given to Noah, the sign of circumcision given to Abraham, the rain on Gideon's fleece, to name just three.[59] These signs, in Michael Laffin's words, intermingle "the Word with the elemental world."[60] Luther's recognition of quasi-sacramental signs reflects his "discovery of the positive meaning of worldly re-

---

51 Luther, "Blessed Sacrament," *LW* 35:57.

52 Ibid.

53 Wendte, "Mystical Foundations of Politics?," 9.

54 Ibid.

55 Martin Luther, "A Treatise on the New Testament, That Is, the Holy Mass," *LW* 35:102.

56 Ibid., 86.

57 In his discussion of Luther's three "estates" (or "institutions," sometimes "orders"), Michael Laffin argues that the estates' "quasi-sacramental character" comes from their "connection with the Word." Michael Laffin, *The Promise of Martin Luther's Political Theology: Freeing Luther from the Modern Political Narrative* (London: Bloomsbury T&T Clark, 2016), 170. They are not sacraments, because they are not means of salvation, but they are "means of God's self-giving, that is, ... means of grace." Ibid.

58 Luther, "Treatise on the New Testament," *LW* 35:86.

59 Ibid.

60 Laffin, *Promise of Martin Luther's Political Theology*, 170.

ality and its spiritual importance."[61] For Luther, the physical and material world mediates the Word in a sense, so that there is something accompanying the Word "to which we may cling and around which we may gather."[62]

Distributive logic undergirds Luther's theology of the Lord's Supper, understood as both sign and sacrament. Only the distribution of the spiritual benefits Christ has won is a means of salvation in the sacrament, but the distribution of material goods to the needy is also a means of grace. The formal logic is the same; what changes in the shift from sacrament to sign is the soteriological content. Thus, Luther could affirm on one hand that distributing "alms to the poor" and "food and other necessities ... to the needy" is "quite another thing from the testament and sacrament, which no one can offer or give either to God or to men,"[63] while bemoaning with equal force the fact that "the custom of gathering food and money at the mass has fallen into disuse" and that, in the mass, possessions are no longer "given, with thanksgiving to God and with his blessing, to the needy who ought to be receiving them."[64]

Thus, the tangible distribution of material goods to the needy not only reflects the distribution of good things won by Christ and distributed to believers with the words "This is my body, this is my blood," but also accompanies those words themselves. The recipients of Christ's body and blood further the distributive dynamic in the "overflow" to others of the "superfluity" those recipients have in "God's gifts."[65]

Conclusion: What Hath Leisnig to Do with Berlin, London, or Washington?

The social and economic policies of a community, regardless of its size, communicate something about that community's ideological commitments. In our time, the way in which revenue, efficiency, and equity considerations are articulated in tax policy reflects our societies' priorities. When some version of efficiency is foregrounded, the society announces that it places a premium on economic prosperity.[66] A society that highlights taxation as a vehicle for relieving the material suffering of the needy in its midst proclaims a different hierarchy of concerns.

---

61 Ibid.

62 Luther, "Treatise on the New Testament," *LW* 35:86.

63 Ibid., 93–94.

64 Ibid., 96.

65 Wannenwetsch, *Political Worship*, 335.

66 This is not necessarily a selfish valuation; conventional wisdom may well assert that a prosperous nation benefits all its members.

"Tax expressivity" of this sort also reinforces the commitments that it articulates. When a society elevates efficiency in its tax laws above other considerations, it reminds itself of its guiding principles and recommits itself to honoring them. Elizabeth Anderson writes: "To have an evaluative attitude toward something is in part to govern one's deliberations and actions by social norms that communicate distinctive meanings to others."[67] Anderson calls this perspective on social norms "an expressive theory of rational action."[68] The institution of taxation is especially communicative in this sense, because it can move nimbly between expressing a commitment to efficiency on one hand and prioritizing equity on the other.

Luther saw that Christians communicate something through the payment of taxes. Throughout his political theology in general, "Christians should be subject to the governing authorities and be ready to do every good work," because "they shall by so doing serve others and the authorities themselves and obey their will freely and out of love."[69] He illustrates this point by reference to the Temple tax episode in Matthew 17. "This incident," Luther writes, "fits our subject beautifully for Christ here calls himself and those who are his children sons of the king, who need nothing; and yet he freely submits and pays the tribute."[70] Taxation is an *instrument* from the believing subject's perspective. The Christian "uses" taxation to express and implement love for others in a way that other people, living in fear of the sword, cannot.

The expressive quality of quasi-sacramental redistributive taxation in Luther's political theology must not, however, be emphasized to the exclusion of its social and economic effects. The redistributive pattern manifested in Leisnig's ordinance was capable of shaping the ethos of a whole society precisely because it depended so heavily on the theology of the Lord's Supper, which always had a formative quality in Luther's teaching. It is beyond the scope of this chapter to consider the direct impact that Luther's redistributive vision may have had on German politics.[71] However, by illustrating, for all earthly authorities to see, how

---

67 Elizabeth Anderson, *Value in Ethics and Economics* (Cambridge, MA: Harvard University Press, 1993), 18.

68 Ibid., 17.

69 Luther, "The Freedom of a Christian," *LW* 31:369.

70 Ibid.

71 Carter Lindberg asserts that Luther "initiated social welfare programs that provided the seeds for the later welfare state." Lindberg, "Luther on a Market Economy," 379. Social and theological historian Samuel Torvend concurs, writing that Luther "brought considerable energy to this project [of economic reform] that would be imitated throughout Germany and the Nordic countries and, in time, become what North Americans and Western Europeans know as stated-funded social assistance." Samuel Torvend, "'Greed Is An Unbelieving Scoundrel,'" in *The Forgotten Luther: Reclaiming the Social-Economic Dimension*

taxation could be used to relieve the needy, Luther reminds us even in our time that taxation theologically conceived should be a triangular relationship.

That triangular relationship has a pragmatic purpose. Taxation, the theologians tell us, must always be a balance. If the needs of the poor are not part of the policy equation, the other two points of the triangle become dominant. In fact, the triangle is in danger of becoming a line; and, once it has become a line, it may then become a single point. To state the matter less geometrically, tax policy that has sidelined poor relief tends to fall captive to either the revenue demands of the state or the efficiency requirements of the economy. In the former case, the power to tax becomes "simply the power to 'take,'" the government reveals itself "as a revenue-maximizing Leviathan," and "the power to tax is the most familiar manifestation of the government's power to coerce."[72] In the latter case, tax policy becomes virtually meaningless; efficiency "is an incoherent standard for a tax system" because "[e]very tax system actually in use impedes growth in some way, so a growth norm favors repeal of every existing tax."[73] Even those most utilitarian of tax doctrines–ability-to-pay and its successor, the optimal tax models[74]–require a counterbalance to efficiency in the form of equity (albeit a weak, inherently redistributive form of equity).

In addition to supplying the much-needed counterbalance to revenue-maximization and efficiency, however, Luther's redistributive theology teaches us to reimagine a political and economic institution–the institution of taxation–in a way that focuses our attention on the need of our neighbors and trains us to express our concern through that institution and use it accordingly. The voice of equity in the tax policies of modern pluralistic societies is recessive. That it remains a voice at all, however, is a testimony to the theologians' speaking truth to power. Their persistent interjection of the needs of the poor is exemplified by Luther's call to restore the Lord's Supper to its original material function and his advocacy of common chests for poor relief. For both pragmatic and theological reasons, that call still echoes. It refuses to permit the death of equity in modern

of the Reformation, ed. Carter Lindberg and Paul A. Wee (Edina, MN: Lutheran University Press, 2016), 38.

72 Geoffrey Brennan and James M. Buchanan, *The Power to Tax: Analytical Foundations of a Fiscal Constitution* (Indianapolis: Liberty Fund, 1980), xxii, 11.

73 Linda Sugin, "Tax Expenditures, Reform, and Distributive Justice," *Columbia Journal of Tax Law* 3 (2011): 36.

74 The optimal tax models provide a formula that purports to generate the optimum rate structure once desired values for equity and efficiency are plugged in. The models, according to Linda Sugin, are "the one real-world tool that is regularly employed toward achieving [distributive justice]." Linda Sugin, "Theories of Distributive Justice and Limitations on Taxation: What Rawls Demands from Tax Systems," *Fordham Law Review* 72, no. 5 (1994): 2013–14.

social consciousness and political debates, even if equity is diluted to the point of vanishing. Although equity is a shadow of its former self, our collective memory of the sixteenth century seems unwilling to let our kings take all the money and go to war.

Teaching Sexual Morality in Church and State Historically and Today

John Witte Jr.

Sex has long excited an intimate union between theology and law in the Western legal tradition. For two millennia, both churches and states issued detailed private laws and guidelines to define and facilitate licit sex within an enduring and exclusive marital bed. They also issued elaborate penal laws and procedures to prohibit and punish illicit sex. Church and state officials periodically fought over whose laws governed sexuality. And they periodically shifted the line between sexual *sins*, which remained under church law alone, and sexual *crimes*, which were punished by the state (as well). Nonetheless, until the twentieth century, churches and states alike played formidable roles in defining and regulating licit and illicit sex.

A typical early modern list of sex crimes–in civil-law and common-law lands alike–included abduction, abortion, adultery, bestiality, buggery, child abuse, concubinage, contraception, feticide, fornication, homosexual acts, illegitimacy, incest, infanticide, malicious desertion, masturbation, obscenity, polygamy, pornography, prostitution, rape, seduction, and sodomy. Sometimes more exotic offenses were added, such as castration, transvestism, mixed bathing, public nudity, sexual contact by or with clerics or monastics, and others. Sometimes defendants were charged with catch-all sex crimes like perversion, indecency, lewdness, "abomination," or "unnatural sex." Many of these sex crimes had shifting and sometimes eliding definitions over time and across legal systems and were variously classified as offenses against God, religion, morality, nature, public order, or persons.[1] Until a century ago, sex offenders faced severe criminal punishment–execution in egregious cases.

---

[1] See, for example, J. Kohler and Willy Scheel, *Die peinliche gerichtsordnung kaiser Karls V. Constitutio criminalis Carolina* (Halle: Verlag der Buchhandlung des Waisenhauses, 1900), 62–64; Paul Johann Anselm von Feuerbach, *Lehrbuch des gemeinen in Deutschland geltenden peinlichen Rechts* (Giessen: G. F. Heyer, 1801), 484–508, §§ 413–36; G. Mueller, ed., *The French Penal Code* [1801] (New York: Fred B. Rothman & Co., 1976), Arts. 283–90, 316–17, 330–40; William Blackstone, *Commentaries on the Laws of Eng-*

Today, most of these traditional sex crimes have been eclipsed by the dramatic rise of new constitutional laws and cultural norms of sexual liberty. Traditional crimes of contraception, abortion, fornication, and sodomy have been struck down as antiquated and unconstitutional. Prohibitions on adultery, concubinage, and nonmarital sex and cohabitation have become dead letters, and modern law no longer visits "the sins of the fathers" or mothers upon nonmarital children. Free-speech laws protect all manner of sexual expression, short of obscenity, although the wildest unregulated frontiers of prurience are now only a mouse-click away. Privacy laws protect most forms of sexual conduct among consenting adults, including adult prostitution in some democracies. The classic sex crimes of incest and polygamy still remain on the books, but they are now the subjects of growing constitutional and cultural battles. Only one traditional sex crime has strengthened in recent decades: the crime of rape, now joined by strong new prohibitions against sexual assault, battery, stalking, and harassment, as well as the sexual abuse and statutory rape of children. The sex crimes that remain, however, are now usually labelled as crimes against persons, dignity, or sexual autonomy rather than crimes against God, morality, or nature.

This radical reduction of traditional sex crimes over the past century reflects not only the rise of modern constitutional liberty but also the shift of modern criminal law away from a fault-based to a harm-based system of liability. Traditional fault-based logic swept in many consensual and victimless sex acts that were considered to be just wrong (*malum in se*)–adultery, fornication, sodomy, bestiality, buggery, group sex, same-sex relations, and other perceived sexual taboos. Modern harm-based logic ignores most such acts and instead focuses on crimes that inflict involuntary harm, particularly to vulnerable victims like young children or rape victims. To be sure, some traditional crimes remain hard to classify today: scholars debate whether pornography, prostitution, and polygamy are *harm* crimes that should remain on the books or *fault* crimes that need to be removed. But many other traditional sex crimes based on moral fault have fallen aside.

Finally, the reduction of modern sex crimes reflects the transformation of modern family law. Historically, Western family law promoted the integration of marriage, sex, and procreation within an enduring and exclusive marital household. Criminal law, in turn, prohibited sexual conduct that threatened or undermined this integrated domestic ideal. Today, family law countenances a far wider range of sexual activities and domestic relationships. And it accommodates sev-

---

land, 4 vols. (Boston: Beacon Press, 1962; first published 1765–69), vol. 4, chap. 4.11, 15; James Fitzjames Stephen, *A History of the Criminal Law of England*, 3 vols. (Cambridge: Cambridge University Press, 2014; first published 1883), 3:10, 117–18.

eral "striking new separations in the sexual field"[2]—separations between (1) marriage and sex; (2) marriage and childbirth; (3) marriage and childrearing; (4) childbirth and parenting; (5) sex and physical contact, given the advent of cybersex; and (6) childbirth, sexual intercourse, and biological filiation, given the rise of artificial reproductive technology, sperm banks, and surrogacy. This new family-law regime has far less room and need for many traditional sex crimes.

Modern Christians living in Western liberal societies have variously celebrated or lamented all of these changes. Some Christians have been at the forefront of the sexual revolution and advocated and embraced at least some of these new sexual norms, while offering innovative theological arguments in support of them. Some churches have largely gone with the cultural flow on issues of sexuality and sexual liberty, with or without much change to their official teachings. Some churches have retained or reemphasized strict standards of traditional sexual morality, with internal church laws holding their congregants to these standards as a condition for leadership, if not membership. Many churches have also been deeply challenged, and sometimes divided, over pressing new legal and moral issues about abortion, contraception, artificial reproductive technology, women's rights, children's rights, same-sex marriage, no-fault divorce, remarriage, and more. Finally, several churches have been roiled by massive scandals and criminal prosecution for clerical pedophilia and cover-ups by church leaders, as well as sexual and psychological abuses by pastors, counselors, teachers, coaches, and charity workers in religious organizations.

I touch lightly on these latter difficult topics at the end, knowing that they deserve much fuller treatment. I first review the main historical teachings on sex crimes in the Bible and the Western legal tradition. I then explore how teaching traditional sexual morality may still be viable for modern liberal states and Christian churches.

Sex Crimes in the Bible

Many traditional Western sex crimes were rooted in the Bible. The Old Testament grounded its sexual prohibitions in religious narratives of personal purity and communal fidelity to God's covenant. The Mosaic law treated bestiality, buggery, and most forms of incest as capital crimes. Adultery was a capital crime, too, although the sexual double-standard of the day restricted this offense to extramarital intercourse by the wife, not her husband. Similarly, it was a capital offense for a betrothed woman, but not her fiancé, to have consensual sex with another before

---

2 Don S. Browning, "Family Law and Christian Jurisprudence," in *Christianity and Law: An Introduction*, ed. John Witte Jr. and Frank S. Alexander (Cambridge: Cambridge University Press, 2008), 165.

the wedding. The Mosaic law prohibited castration, sex during menstruation, harm to a fetus, and child sacrifice, and joined pre-Mosaic customs in condemning men for "spilling [their] seed on the ground" (Genesis 38:9) after sexual contact. It further prohibited harlotry, interreligious marriage, and sex between divorced persons. It called for variant punishments of rape and seduction of a woman. If the victim was married, her innocent husband or the authorities could mete out (capital) punishment. If the victim was single, the rapist had to pay a dowry to her father; marry the victim if she and her father would have him; and waive his right to divorce. In most other cases, a husband could divorce his wife for her "indecency," leaving both parties free to remarry another. A husband could also take multiple wives, and was obliged to do so in some cases of seduction, enslavement, famine, childless marriage, or premature death of his married brother.[3]

The Mosaic law repeatedly called God's chosen covenant people of Israel to a higher plane of sexual morality than the Gentiles around them. "Do not defile yourselves by any of these things," reads Leviticus 18:24–29 after a lengthy recitation of "sins of the flesh." "For whoever shall do any of these abominations, the persons that do them shall be cut off from among their people. So keep my charge never to practice any of these abominable customs which were practiced before you, and never to defile yourselves by them," lest the holy land "vomit you out."

The New Testament echoed some of these Mosaic sexual prohibitions, but also called for greater equitable and egalitarian application of them. For example, the Gospel of Matthew reports that Joseph could have had Mary, his fiancée, stoned for her presumptive premarital adultery, but he endeavored to break the engagement quietly without dishonoring her. Jesus rescued an adulterous woman sentenced to death. "[H]e who is without sin, cast the first stone," Jesus challenged her accusers, before ordering her to sin no more (John 8:7). Jesus called his followers to live by the letter and spirit of the laws on sexual purity. "You have heard that it was said, 'You shall not commit adultery.' But I say to you that everyone who looks at a woman lustfully has already committed adultery with her in his heart" (Matthew 5:27–28). He also ordered men to rein in divorce: "Everyone who divorces his wife, except on the ground of unchastity, makes her an adulteress; and whoever marries a divorced woman commits adultery" (Matthew 19:3–9).

Saint Paul offered similar teachings. While encouraging celibacy for the single and widowed, and repeating conventional norms about male headship, Paul also insisted that "the husband should give to the wife her conjugal rights" (1 Cor-

---

3 Exod. 20:14; 21:7–12, 22; 22:16–19; Lev. 18:6–23, 19:20–22, 29; 20:1–6, 10–22; Deut. 5:18; 7:3–4; 17:17, 21:15–16; 22:20–29; 23:17–18; 24:1–23; 27:21; Prov. 6:32–35, with discussion in Louis M. Epstein, *Sex Laws and Customs in Judaism* (New York: KTAV Publishing House, 1967); Ralph W. Scott, *A New Look at Biblical Crime* (Chicago: Nelson-Hall, 1979); Carolyn Pressler, "Sexual Legislation," in *The Oxford Encyclopedia of the Bible and Law*, ed. Brent A. Strawn, 2 vols. (Oxford: Oxford University Press, 2015), 2:290–302.

inthians 7:3) and told husbands "to love your wives, as Christ loved the church, and gave himself up for her" (Ephesians 5:25). He also glossed Jesus's prohibitions on adultery and lust with denunciations of incest, sodomy, prostitution, polygamy, seduction, immoderate dress and grooming, and other forms of sexual immorality and perversion.[4] "Flee fornication!" (1 Corinthians 6:18) was Paul's most famous admonition, which he directed to men and women alike. "Do you not know that he who joins himself to a prostitute becomes one body with her?" Paul challenged his male readers. "For, as it is written, 'The two shall become one flesh.' Every other sin which a man commits is outside the body; but the immoral man sins against his own body. Do you not know that your body is a temple of the Holy Spirit within you? ... Therefore, honor God with your bodies" (1 Corinthians 6:16–20).

While repeating this general call for bodily purity and spiritual chastity, the early Church Fathers and Talmud Rabbis offered further biblical rationales for specific sex crimes.[5] Bestiality, they argued, defied the differences between species that God had separated at creation; after all, Adam could find no beast in Paradise like him, which had led God to create Eve, whom Adam recognized as "bone of my bones, flesh of my flesh" (Genesis 2:23). Homosexual acts confused the genders that God had separated–"male and female he created them" (Genesis 1:27). Sex during menstruation, *coitus interruptus*, and masturbation were lustful acts that defied the primal divine command to "be fruitful and multiply" (Genesis 1:28). Contraception, abortion, feticide, and infanticide also defied the primal command of procreation and raising up the next generation of God's people. Rape, fornication, and adultery brought harm and shame to the innocent victim and her family, and could produce "bastards" who suffered significant legal disabilities, since "no bastard shall enter the assembly of the Lord" (Genesis 23:2). Incestuous marriages corrupted the blood, commingled the property, weakened the family tree, and compromised the legacy and inheritance of the marital family and the strength of its alliances with other families and communities. These early interpretations of biblical sex crimes were incorporated into early Christian canon laws and penitential books, and into later Christianized Roman law as well.

---

4 Rom. 1:24–27; 1 Cor. 5:1; 6:9, 15–20, 7:1–6; Eph. 5:3–4, 25; Col. 3:5–6; 1 Tim. 2:9–10; 3:2; 1 Thess. 4:3–8; Hebr. 13:4.

5 Sample texts in David G. Hunter, *Marriage in the Early Church* (Minneapolis: Fortress Press, 1992); Epstein, *Sex Laws and Customs.* The seventeenth-century English jurist John Selden offered a brilliant synthesis of these early teachings in his *On Jewish Marriage Law: The Uxor Hebraica*, trans. Jonathan R. Ziskind (Leiden: Brill, 1991).

Sex Crimes in the Western Legal Tradition

Thomas Aquinas

At the height of the Middle Ages, the Dominican friar Thomas Aquinas (1225–74) integrated these biblical teachings into a natural-law theory of sex crimes that became axiomatic in the Western legal tradition. Thomas knew the Roman law of sex crimes and the medieval civilian jurisprudence it had inspired. Emperor Justinian's sixth-century collection of laws, for example, outlawed as "contrary to nature itself" all forms of bestiality, sodomy, adultery, incest, rape, prostitution, and seduction of virgins; sex with nuns, slaves, and minors; and sex in groups or in public places, like baths. These crimes Justinian variously branded as "abominable," "wicked," "execrable," and "insane" forms of "debauchery" that were "hateful to God" and God's laws. Any children born of such unions, he declared, were "bastards" who were "irredeemable" and "nonheritable."[6]

Thomas also knew the church's canon laws on sex offenses. By his day, the scholastics had arranged these offenses in a hierarchy. Most began with the baseline of simple fornication and then added crimes of escalating gravity: prostitution, concubinage, seduction, bigamy, adultery, rape, and incest. Graver still were "unnatural" sexual acts (gay and lesbian relations, bestiality, oral sex, anal sex, and sex with children). Gravest of all were non- or antiprocreative sex acts (masturbation, contraception, sterilization, abortion, and infanticide). Each of these offenses was worse still when committed by ordained clergy, avowed monastics, or recidivists, whether clerical or lay; or when aggravated by the commission of other crimes like battery, theft, kidnapping, or homicide.[7]

To sort out this legal inheritance and to devise his theory of sex crimes, Thomas began with several facts about the nature of human sexuality and reproduction. First, he observed, most humans crave sex all the time, especially when they are young and most fertile. Unlike other animals, humans do not have a short rutting or mating season followed by a prolonged period of sexual inactivity. Second, human babies are born weak, fragile, and utterly dependent for many years. Unlike most other animals, they cannot run, swim, or fly away on their own at birth

---

6 Bruce W. Frier et al., ed. and trans., *The Codex of Justinian: A New Annotated Translation, with Parallel Latin and Greek Text* (Cambridge: Cambridge University Press, 2016), 6.57.5.1, 5.27; Fred H. Blume, trans., *Justinian's Novels* (1952, unpublished), http://www.uwyo.edu/lawlib/blume-justinian/ajc-edition-1/novels/index.html (accessed January 23, 2019), 74, 77.1, 89.5, 141.

7 James A. Brundage, *Law, Sex, and Christian Society in Medieval Europe* (Chicago: University of Chicago Press, 1987) 207, 212–14, 225–26, 241–51; Vern L. Bullough and James A. Brundage, *Sexual Practices and the Medieval Church* (Buffalo, NY: Prometheus Books, 1982), 89–101, 129–60, 176–87.

or shortly thereafter. They need protection, food, shelter, clothing, and education in order to survive, let alone thrive. Third, most human mothers have difficulty caring fully for their children on their own, especially if they already have other children. They need help, especially from fathers and their kin networks. Fourth, however, most human fathers will bond and help care for children only if they are certain of their paternity. Put a baby cradle in a public place and most women will stop out of natural empathy. Most men will walk by, unless they are unusually charitable or deputized to provide care. Once assured of their paternity, however, most men will bond deeply with their children, help with their care and support, and defend them at great sacrifice. For they will see their children as a continuation and extension of themselves–of their being, name, property, and heritage.[8]

Given these facts, Thomas concluded, rational humans have learned to develop enduring and exclusive marital unions as a good and advantageous form of sexual bonding and reproductive success. Such unions serve the ongoing sexual needs and desires of husband and wife. They ensure that both a father and a mother are certain that a baby born to them is theirs. They ensure that both parents will care for, nurture, and educate their children until they mature. And these unions deter both spouses from dangerous sex outside the marital bed.[9]

But nature creates only a wobbly normative framework, given our perennial human sex drives and temptations, Thomas argued. Both church and state thus need to enact firm and clear positive laws to guide and govern their members. The church must offer comprehensive spiritual direction about sexual vices and virtues, drawing not only on natural law but also on sacramental, moral, and biblical teachings. Accordingly, the church's confessional books and canon laws contain far more detailed and expansive instructions about sex than what appears in the state's criminal law. The state has a more limited jurisdiction over sex based on natural law and natural justice alone, making its roll of sex crimes shorter and more focused. Thomas worked through these sex crimes, one by one, often leavening his arguments from nature with prudential and practical considerations.

"Simple fornication" between a single man and a single woman, he said, was criminal because it jeopardizes the health and future of the woman and "tends to injure the life of the offspring to be born of this union." If a fornicating woman becomes pregnant, she may well be left alone to care for her child, which is risky for her and the child. Yes, a wedding could be hastily arranged before birth. This, however, risks a nonconsensual marriage, and the woman may be suspected of fornication with others, too, making it harder to determine the father of her child

8 Thomas Aquinas, *Summa Theologica*, trans. Fathers of the English Dominican Province (London: Thomas Moore, 1948) (hereafter *ST*), I, q. 99, a. 1; V Supp., q. 41, a. 1–2; q. 49, a. 1–6; Thomas Aquinas, *Summa Contra Gentiles*, trans. Vernon J. Bourke (Notre Dame, IN: University of Notre Dame Press, 1975) (hereafter *SCG*), III.II.122–23.

9 *SCG* III.123; *ST* II–II, q. 26, a. 7–9; V, q. 49, a. 1–2.

who will provide vital care when the infant child needs it most. Yes, an unmarried father or a stepfather might still provide child support and education to his illegitimate child, but doing so was not typical of most males. So, Thomas concluded, "human nature rebels against an indeterminate union of the sexes" in fornication, and the state must prohibit it clearly, though punish it quite lightly through fines or forms of public shaming or community service.[10]

Thomas was surprisingly tolerant of prostitution. He considered it a necessity of social order, given the realities that some men will always be unattached and will inevitably seek sex somewhere. Prostitution was rather like a sewer in a castle, Thomas said; without it, the castle would be filled with filth. Similarly, a society without prostitution would be filled with fornication, adultery, sodomy, and other sex crimes, and sometimes with violence, too, born of rape or seduction of innocent women. It was better, on balance, to allow prostitution to continue discreetly and allow prostitutes to keep their fees instead of banning the practice and imposing higher risks and costs on all others.[11]

For Thomas, it was a graver offense when an unmarried man seduced a virgin or manipulated or tricked her into bed. Not only did this sexual encounter carry the same risk of harm to any child born of the union, but an additional "two-fold injustice attaches to it," Thomas wrote. The victim was now hindered from contracting a lawful marriage and likely put on the road to "a wanton life," since a nonvirgin in that day had a much harder time finding a husband. The seduction was also unjust to the father, guardian, or fiancé of the victim, whose investment in and relationship with her was damaged. The crime was even worse, other scholastics argued, when committed against a younger girl who could be more easily manipulated, or a "kept" woman like a maid, ward, patient, tenant, or passenger who had no real choice but to yield to a man's sexual predations. Seduction was a serious offense in Thomas's day, punishable by heavy fines and seizure of the criminal's property, and sometimes banishment from the community.[12]

Rape was worse than fornication and seduction, Thomas argued, because it involved violence against the woman or against her family and was often accompanied by other violent crimes like abduction or aggravated battery. Such violence exacerbated the harm and constituted an additional crime against the body of the victim and against the property and other interests of her family. Forcible rape was a major capital crime in the medieval world, on the same order of gravity as assassination and treason, and brazen or repeat offenders could face execution.[13]

---

10 *ST* II–II, q. 154, a. 2.

11 *ST* II–II, q. 10, a. 2; II–II, q. 60, a. 2, 5; II–II, q. 87, a. 2; II–II, q. 108, a. 8.

12 *ST* II–II, q. 154, a. 6.

13 *ST* II–II, q. 154, a. 7; *SCG* III.122

"Adultery is more serious than seduction," Thomas continued, and even worse when "aggravated by the use of violence." When either the husband or the wife gained "access to another's marriage-bed," it breached marital fidelity and trust and caused harm to the entire family. It brought in sexual diseases that affected the innocent spouse and future offspring. It risked bastard children, who were either cast out of the home with slender chances of success or left in the home to become rivals to legitimate children and their mother. Adultery often led to separation of the married couple, yielding further dissipation of parental resources and care for children, and still greater temptation for both spouses to test the neighbor's bed. Even worse, it could lead to private revenge by the betrayed spouse, or murder of the betrayed spouse by the adulterous lovers. Adultery was thus a capital crime, Thomas argued.[14]

Polygamy constituted serial adultery, Thomas believed, and was a capital crime, too. Polyandry (one woman with multiple men), though rare, was unjust to children. A woman having sex with several husbands would undermine paternal certainty and investment in the children's care. The children would suffer from neglect, and the wife would be overburdened trying to care for them and to tend to her multiple husbands and their sexual needs. Polygyny (one man with multiple women) was unjust to wives as well as children. Polygyny did not necessarily erode paternal certainty, Aquinas allowed. So long as his multiple wives were faithful to him alone, a man could feel assured of being the father of any child born in his household. But this would require a man to pen up his wives like cattle, isolating them from other roving males, even when his own energies to tend to them were dissipated over the several women and children in his household. While locked up at home, the wives would be reduced to servants and set in perpetual competition with each other and with rival children for resources and access to their shared husband. This is not marriage but "a sort of slavery," said Aquinas.

So, if it is not lawful for the wife to have several husbands, since this is contrary to the certainty as to offspring, it would not be lawful, on the other hand, for a man to have several wives, for the friendship of husband and wife would not be free, but somewhat servile. And this argument is corroborated by experience, for among husbands having plural wives the wives have a status like that of servants.

"Natural justice" thus calls for monogamy alone, and criminal law must punish polygamists.[15]

Incest was an unnatural sex crime, too, Thomas argued. "There is something essentially unbecoming and contrary to natural reason in sexual intercourse between persons related by blood." If allowed, it would obstruct the proper relationships of authority and obedience between parents and children, elders and youth.

---

14 *ST* II–II, q. 154, a. 8, 12; II–II, q. 160; V q. 60, a. 1–2; V, q. 64, a. 1–4; V, q. 68.

15 *SCG* III.123–4; *ST* V, q. 44, a. 1; V, q. 49, a. 2; V, q. 65, a. 1–2.

It would heighten the temptations to lust and produce an "excessive ardor of love" among relatives who lived together or near each other. It would also "hinder a man from having many friends" beyond his relatives, and in a peaceful society "it is most necessary that there be friendship among many peoples." Even animals, with only natural instincts to guide them, are "horrified" by sexual contact with their close blood relatives, Aquinas added. Rational human beings have built on this natural instinct to develop more refined impediments of consanguinity and affinity to avoid sex and marriage among even distant relatives.[16]

The gravest offenses of all were what Thomas called "unnatural" acts of masturbation, sodomy, bestiality, and "effeminacy." Thomas treated them only briefly as scandalous violations of the natural use of the sexual body and the natural procreative ends of sexual interaction. Even worse, these were offenses against God himself and the natural order of creation. Thomas quoted favorably Saint Augustine's harsh instructions: "Those foul offenses that are against nature should be everywhere at all times detested and punished," with the state emulating God's fiery wrath against "the people of Sodom."[17]

Enduring Western Teachings on Sexual Morality

Thomas's wide-ranging arguments to encourage and enforce exclusive and enduring marriages while prohibiting and punishing extramarital sex remained a staple for the Western legal tradition until the twentieth century. Let me illustrate with a few statements by leading architects of the Anglo-American common law and political liberalism.

Many of these later writers started with the same facts about human nature, sexuality, and pair-bonding. Leading Scottish philosopher David Hume (1711–76) put it concisely: "The long and helpless infancy requires the combination of parents for the subsistence of their young; and that combination requires the virtue of chastity or fidelity to the marriage bed."[18] "The God of nature has enforced conjugal society, not only by making it agreeable, but by the principle of *chastity* inherent in our nature" as rational humans, Scottish judge Henry Home (1696–1782) expounded. "*Chastity and mutual fidelity* [are] essential to ... the continuation of the human race. As the carnal appetite is always alive, the sexes would wallow in pleasure *and* be soon rendered unfit for procreation were it not for the

16 *ST* II–II, q. 154, a. 10; *SCG*, III.125.6; *ST* V, q. 54–55.

17 *ST* II–II, q. 154, a. 12, reply obj. 1; *SCG* III.122, 126.

18 David Hume, *Enquiries Concerning the Human Understanding and Concerning the Principles of Morals*, ed. L. A. Selby-Bigge, 2nd ed. (Oxford: Clarendon Press, 1902; first published 1748), 206–07.

restraint of *chastity*" born of the natural law.[19] Both family law and criminal law underscore this natural reality, echoed by the leading common-law jurist William Blackstone (1723–80): "The main end and design of marriage [is] to ascertain and fix upon some certain person, to whom the care, the protection, the maintenance, and the education of the children should belong." "The duty of parents to provide for the maintenance of their children is a principle of natural law." Family law facilitates that duty; criminal law enforces it.[20]

Indeed, criminal law must prohibit and punish all sex crimes that harm this natural configuration of sex, marriage, and family life, others argued. English political philosopher John Locke (1632–1704) urged the state to punish all sex crimes that threaten the rights and interests of wives and children or erode a man's "natural obligation to continue in conjugal society with the same woman." Locke called for firm punishment of the "dishonesty and debauchery" of prostitution, concubinage, "simple fornication," incest, rape, and "domestic abuse" in order to protect "the welfare and safety" of the victims and to spare a community the "greater inconveniences" of care for violated women and their children. Locke also castigated rape, adultery, and polygamy as violations of the "natural rights" of women and children. Religious groups, he said pointedly, are not "exempt from the magistrate's power of punishing" such sex crimes just because they regard these activities as "articles of faith, or ways of worship." "[A] toleration of men in all that which they pretend out of conscience they cannot submit to, will wholly take away all the civil laws and all the magistrate's power."[21]

Other writers further developed the logic of individual sex crimes. English philosopher William Paley (1743–1805) defended the criminalization of simple fornication in order to encourage marriage. "The male part of the species will not undertake the encumbrance, expense and restraint of married life, if they can gratify their [sexual] passions at a cheaper price; and they will undertake anything rather than not gratify them." Paley recognized that he was appealing to general utility, but he thought that decriminalization of fornication would lead to forms of sexual libertinism that exploited and harmed women and children. "The libertine may not be conscious that these irregularities hinder his own marriage, ... much less does he perceive how *his* indulgences can hinder other men from marrying, but what will he say would be the consequence, if the same licentious-

19 Henry Home, *Sketches of the History of Man*, ed. James A. Harris (Indianapolis: Liberty Fund, 2007), 264–70.

20 Blackstone, *Commentaries*, vol. 1, chap. 15.1, ch. 16.1, 3.

21 John Locke, *A Letter Concerning Toleration and Other Writings*, ed. Mark Goldie (Indianapolis: Liberty Fund, 2010), 69, 84, 110–11; John Locke, *An Essay Concerning Human Understanding*, in *The Works of John Locke*, 10 vols. (London: Thomas Tegg, 1823), 2:96; John Locke, *Two Treatises of Government*, ed. Thomas Hollis (London, 1764), 264.

ness were universal? or what should hinder it becoming universal, if it be innocent or allowable in him?"[22]

Fornication can furthermore lead one or both parties to prostitution, Paley went on, with its accompanying degradation of women, erosion of morals, transmission of disease, and production of unwanted and uncared-for children. Fornication is no better if it devolves into concubinage—the "kept mistress," who can be dismissed at the man's pleasure or retained "in a state of humiliation and dependence inconsistent with the rights which marriage would confer upon her" and her children. It is best to cut off all this sexual pathos at the root, Paley concluded, by prohibiting sex outside the marital bed and encouraging fit and capable couples to marry instead.[23]

Adultery is even worse than fornication, said Paley, because it causes harm to an existing family. To the betrayed spouse, adultery is "a wound in his [or her] sensibility and affections, the most painful and incurable that human nature knows." To the children of an adulterous parent it brings shame and unhappiness, as the vice is inevitably detected and discussed. To the adulterous party it is a form of "perjury" that violates the marital vow and covenant. To all parties in the household, adultery will often provoke retaliation and imitation—another step in the erosion of marriage and endangerment of children and society. Adultery is thus a serious crime.[24]

This same concern for mutual fidelity and family stability informed the ongoing criminal prohibition on polygamy. Scottish philosopher Frances Hutcheson (1694–1746) argued that polygamy

> destroys all friendship in marriage; must be the cause of perpetual contentions; must tempt women so injuriously treated into adulteries; must corrupt the minds of men with wandering lust, destroying their natural affection to their children; and must occasion to some an offspring too numerous, which therefore will be neglected, and be void of all sense of duty to such dissolute parents.

Moreover, given the roughly equal numbers of men and women, polygamy would tend to exclude many men from the institution of marriage, "which chiefly civilize[s] and unite[s] men in society." Society will suffer gravely if too many men cannot marry because eligible women have been hoarded into the harems of men

22 William Paley, *The Principles of Moral and Political Philosophy*, ed. D. L. Le Mahieu (Indianapolis: Liberty Fund, 2002), 169–72.

23 Ibid., 172–74.

24 Ibid., 176–80.

who may or may not be virtuous or capable of maintaining them and their children.[25]

The crime of incest has a more straightforward argument, wrote the leading utilitarian Jeremy Bentham (1748–1832). "Every people pretend to follow in this respect, what they call the law of nature, and they look with a sort of horror upon everything not conformed to the matrimonial laws of their own country" or with the laws of the Bible or the church. But state prohibitions on incest are better rooted in four interrelated principles of utility, Bentham argued: (1) to reduce real or suspected rivalry among family members at the cost of household harmony; (2) to avoid seduction of young girls within the home which will prevent them from forming "permanent and advantageous" marriages when they grow up; (3) to avoid confusions in domestic relations "between those who ought to command and those who ought to obey"; and (4) to avoid physical injury from "premature indulgences" in sex. Utility was the best judge of incest laws, Bentham insisted. Worries about sexual taboos, "natural repugnance," "vulgar morality," weakened blood, or fewer alliances are all just "pious frauds." It is worth noting, however, that almost all of Bentham's utilitarian arguments against incest echoed Thomas Aquinas's natural-law arguments from five centuries earlier.[26]

While Western jurists and philosophers differed in their rationales for criminalizing fornication, prostitution, concubinage, adultery, incest, rape, and abuse of wives and children, few writers before the twentieth century argued for the relaxation or removal of these crimes from the books. Iconoclastic experimenters in "sexual communism" and "free love radicalism" did exist, but they were the exception, not the rule before the twentieth century.[27] This is less true about the traditional crimes of bestiality, sodomy, masturbation, contraception, polygamy, obscenity, and other prohibited forms of unnatural perversion, indecency, lewdness, and abomination. These crimes remained on the books in common-law and civil-law lands into the twentieth century. But a growing number of early modern detractors began to press for their removal, anticipating modern developments that struck many of these crimes for good.

---

25 Frances Hutcheson, *A Short Introduction to Moral Philosophy, in Three Books; Containing the Elements of Ethicks and the Law of Nature* (Glasgow: R. Foulis 1747), 248–60.

26 Jeremy Bentham, *Theory of Legislation*, trans. R. Hildreth (Boston: Weeks, Jordan, & Co., 1840), 248–61.

27 See, for example, Faramerz Dabhoiwala, *The Origins of Sex: A History of the First Sexual Revolution* (Oxford: Oxford University Press, 2012).

Church, State, and Sexual Morality Today

> In 1955 the American Law Institute declared that its new *Model Penal Code* does not attempt to use the power of the state to enforce purely moral or religious standards. We deem it inappropriate for the government to attempt to control behavior that has no substantial significance except as to the morality of the private actor. Such matters are best left to religious, educational, and other social influences.[28]

This striking statement about the limits of modern criminal law is now a commonplace in modern pluralistic liberal societies. This statement seems especially apt for the sexual field, where a half-century of sexual liberty jurisprudence has strengthened the perceived separation of sin and crime, morality and liberty, tradition and modernity. Many modern liberal countries have also firmly committed to *laïcité* or the disestablishment of religion, yielding a further separation of the roles of church and state in dealing with sex.[29] Sexual morality is now commonly thought to be for private actors to work out for themselves, drawing as they wish "on religious, educational, and other social influences." Even if one wanted to pursue a neo-Puritan sexual path today–I, for one, do not!–a new state criminalization of a number of traditional sex offenses could not pass constitutional or cultural muster in modern liberal societies.

But this does not mean that all the sex crimes listed in the Bible and articulated by the Christian tradition are now just relics of a bygone age. It is too simple to say that traditional moral standards have no place in modern criminal law. Some of the most serious crimes that liberal states actively prosecute today–murder, theft, rape, kidnapping, treason, conspiracy, perjury, and others–are, in fact, deeply rooted in the moral teachings of the Bible and other religious texts, even if they now have other rationales. Moreover, many traditional sex crimes were not only inspired by divine imperatives of sexual morality, bodily purity, and godly chastity but also infused with prudential and practical concerns that remain important for criminal law still today. These included, as we have seen, concerns for the person, property, and reputation of victims and other third parties; for the rights, liberties, and interests of defendants, victims, and their families; for the health, safety, and welfare of the community; and more. Traditional sexual morality is part of modern criminal law on sex, whether we like it or not.

A more helpful distinction is between "the morality of duty" and "the morality of aspiration," as Lon Fuller once put it. The *morality of duty* guides and even coerces humans to avoid their worst inclinations. It "lays down the basic rules with-

---

28 American Law Institute, *Model Penal Code. Tentative Draft No. 4* (Philadelphia: ALI, 1955), 207.

29 See, for example, Norman Doe, *Law and Religion in Europe: A Comparative Introduction* (Oxford: Oxford University Press, 2012).

out which an ordered society is impossible, or without which an ordered society directed toward certain goals" of protecting life, liberty, and property or pursuing justice, peace, and rule of law "must fail of its mark." By contrast, the *morality of aspiration* encourages humans to ascend to "the Good Life, of excellence, of the fullest realization of human powers."[30] It is directed to the Jekyll who sits alongside the Hyde within each of us–the saint who remains at perennial war with the sinner "within our members" (Romans 7:23). It not only coerces persons against acts of violence and violation but also cultivates in them virtues of charity and love. It not only punishes harmful acts of murder and theft but also discourages evil thoughts of hatred and covetousness. The morality of duty is like the rules of grammar: without them, there can be no coherent speech and literature. The morality of aspiration is like the quests for eloquence: with them, we get Shakespeare and Goethe.

The Role of the State

This simple framework gives us a different way to think through the distinctions between crime and sin, tradition and modernity, and the respective roles of state and church in the sexual field. At the most elementary level, the state does and should use criminal law to enforce a baseline sexual morality of duty–laying down "the basic rules without which an ordered society is impossible" and without which basic goods of life, liberty, and property, justice, peace, and rule of law are imperiled. Included in most liberal penal codes today are prohibitions against the traditional sex crimes of abduction (now usually called kidnapping), castration (now punished along with involuntary sterilization as aggravated battery), incest, infanticide (now usually a form of homicide), malicious desertion (now including failure to pay child support), obscenity, polygamy, prostitution (still a crime in many nations), rape, and sexual assault and battery. Each of these offenses, if not prohibited and punished, would indeed harm the basic individual and collective goods of life, liberty, and property, justice, peace, and rule of law. While some of these traditional offenses are now contested as violations of sexual liberty and autonomy, there are strong reasons–not least the concern for the rights and liberties of vulnerable victims–for these crimes to remain on the books.[31]

The modern liberal state can, and in my view should, use other tools besides criminal law to "nudge" and channel its citizens toward a higher sexual morality of aspiration. Nudging is now a common legal strategy of promoting desirable

---

30 Lon L. Fuller, *The Morality of Law*, 2nd ed. (New Haven: Yale University Press,1964), 3–32.

31 See John Witte Jr., *The Western Case for Monogamy over Polygamy* (Cambridge: Cambridge University Press, 2015).

public and private goods in many areas of life.[32] The liberal state facilitates, licenses, encourages, and sometimes even pays for or rewards all kinds of desirable behavior: think of voting in a state election, getting a free vaccine, or going to college on a state scholarship. The state imposes taxes or fines or withholds state benefits or opportunities for those who indulge in undesirable behavior: think of smoking, not wearing seat belts, or dropping out of high school. The theory of nudging or "legal channelling" stipulates that, over time, the desirable behavior encouraged by the state will become more customary, even natural or reflexive among citizens, and the undesirable behavior will be viewed as aberrant and perhaps even stigmatized.

Without encroaching on sexual liberty, the modern liberal state can nudge citizens to integrate their sex, marriage, and family lives as a public and private good to which they aspire.[33] The state can provide much stronger tax and social benefits for married couples. It can tighten its marital formation and dissolution rules to discourage an easy-in/easy-out marital culture. It can provide better comprehensive sex and family-planning education as a matter of public and private health and safety. It can offer free contraceptives to vulnerable populations, especially among the youth gathered, say, in high school proms or mixed-gender college dormitories. It can provide more expansive pregnancy and maternal care and financial services, and more efficient and humane adoption options for women contemplating abortion. It can create a much more sophisticated system of biotechnology and information technology to find and hold fathers accountable for the children they produce. It can do much more to put all "children's interests first"[34] and to help protect and vindicate the fundamental rights of children. It can do much more to encourage better elder and intergenerational care. And state officials can and should model and promote responsible sex, marriage, and family norms and habits in their own lives as a vital form of political and legal pedagogy.

But in the end, the state and its laws can do only so much in the sexual field. Human families also need broader communities and narratives to stabilize, deepen, and exemplify the natural inclinations and rational norms we have about responsible sex and procreation. Human families need models and exemplars of love and fidelity, trust and sacrifice, commitment and community to give these

---

32 Richard H. Thaler and Cass R. Sunstein, *Nudge: Improving Decisions about Health, Wealth, and Happiness* (New York: Penguin Books, 2008); Eric A. Posner, ed., *Social Norms, Nonlegal Sanctions, and the Law* (Cheltenham: Edward Elgar, 2007) and a sampling of recent literature in Eyal Zamir and Doron Teichman, eds., *Oxford Handbook of Behavioral Economics and the Law* (Oxford: Oxford University Press, 2014).

33 Carl E. Schneider, "The Channeling Function in Family Law," *Hofstra Law Review* 20 (1992): 495–532.

34 Helen Alvare, *Putting Children's Interests First in U.S. Family Law and Policy* (Cambridge: Cambridge University Press, 2018).

natural teachings further content and coherence. They need the help of stable institutions beyond the state–churches, schools, charities, hospitals, neighborhoods, and others. They need the help of service professionals beyond judges, lawyers, and state workers–preachers, teachers, doctors, mentors, counselors, therapists, accountants, coaches, and others. As Robert Bellah reminds us, while it takes a marriage to make a family, and a village to raise a child, it takes "a society to raise a family."[35]

The Role of the Church

The modern church plays a vital social role in raising a family and promoting healthy sexual morality in society. At minimum, the modern Christian church must be as zealous as the modern liberal state in establishing a basic sexual morality of duty–making compliance with current state sex crimes a condition for church leadership, if not membership. Some churches now do so in their canons of ordination and contracts of employment in sanctuaries, schools, charities, clubs, and service organizations.[36] But all churches should have clear, detailed, and enforceable sexual morality clauses with corresponding procedures for adjudicating complaints and cases.

This has become doubly imperative today given the grim reality of sexual abuse by some Catholic and Protestant clergy and cover-ups by some of their superiors. This fundamental sacrilege and betrayal of ordination vows has destroyed the lives of untold thousands of victims and has gravely harmed the moral standing and witness of the modern church throughout the world.[37] Churches must root out and drive out all clergy and other religious leaders who abuse their wives, children, students, clients, patients, or parishioners, as well as their accomplices after the fact who cover up these grave offenses. These are serious sex crimes whose perpetrators can and should find no refuge behind constitutional walls or sacramental veils. Clerical pederasts, in particular, should remember that Jesus has reserved a special place in hell for those who harm children (Mark 9:42; Luke 17:2). This biblical teaching merits regular repetition in churches and

---

35 Robert Bellah, "Epilogue: It Takes a Society to Raise a Family," in *Family Transformed: Religion, Values, and Society in American Life*, ed. Steven M. Tipton and John Witte Jr. (Washington, DC: Georgetown University Press, 2005), 286–98.

36 See examples in Norman Doe, *Christian Law: Contemporary Principles* (Cambridge: Cambridge University Press, 2015); Mark Hill, *Ecclesiastical Law*, 4th ed. (Oxford: Oxford University Press, 2018).

37 Dominic Legge, OP, "Cleansing the Church of Clerical Sacrilege," *First Things*, Aug. 16, 2018, https://www.firstthings.com/web-exclusives/2018/08/cleansing-the-church-of-clerical-sacrilege.

seminaries and ample elaboration in the church's law books and disciplinary codes.

Rather than just following the secular status quo, however, or seeking to establish spiritual norms by state positive law, modern churches in liberal societies should go further to teach a higher sexual morality of aspiration for their own voluntary communities, setting out the norms and habits of sexual purity, bodily integrity, and marital fidelity taught by scripture and tradition. Among the most likely moral standards to consider are the repeated biblical injunctions against adultery, bestiality, buggery, fornication, and sodomy. Some churches might also wish to add other long-standing sex prohibitions in the Christian tradition, such as abortion, contraception, prostitution, and concubinage. Some modern churches support the continued enforcement of these sexual prohibitions within the church–although same-sex relationships have been under hot theological dispute.

A church may view this aspirational sexual morality–however specified–as essential or optional for church life and membership. It may have formal or informal methods of adjudication and enforcement of those rules. In a liberal society, no citizen may be compelled to be part of a church nor barred from leaving it. But in a liberal society, every church has the right to maintain internal norms and procedures for its voluntary members without interference from the state, so long as there is no harm or threat to life and limb. Spiritual discipline in the form of fines, public confessions, mandatory charity, bans from the Eucharist, removals from church benefits or offices, shunning or ostracism from the community, and the like can pass muster in a liberal society. But hard coercive power against life or limb is reserved to the state alone under strict due-process constraints.

Churches need not, and in my view should not, banish from the pew, pulpit, lectern, keyboard, or choir bench every person who falls short of their community's sexual standards. Nor should churches indiscriminately shun modern science and new insights about sex and sexuality. But churches do have a right and responsibility to teach, counsel, and facilitate members to follow biblical teachings in their sex lives and to set realistic benchmarks for the spiritual growth of each member, with encouragement and appropriate consequences for those who fall short. This is doubly imperative for clergy and other religious leaders who are called to be faithful stewards of scripture and tradition, as well as moral exemplars and teachers in their communities.

Sexual liberty is a hard-won prize of modern liberal life whose protection has allowed liberal citizens to escape some of the patriarchy, paternalism, and plain prudishness of the past. But sexual violation and abuse remain a perennial reality of modern life, and sex crimes inflict some of the deepest scars on their victims. A liberal society must thus maintain minimum standards of sexual morality in its criminal law as a restraint on deviant and destructive "devices and desires" and as a bulwark against a society's slide into a sexual state of nature, where life can be "nasty, brutish, and short" for the most vulnerable. And a liberal society would do well to encourage its citizens and its communities of faith to pursue a higher morality of aspiration that views sex and the sexual body as a divine blessing to be enjoyed and exercised in loving service of God, neighbor, and self.

Part Three: Where Does Law Teach Values: Views from the Bench, Bar, Academy, and Conscience

The Clergy of Liberalism

Lawyers' Character, Virtue, and Moral Education in Pluralized Societies

Reid Mortensen

The Rival Judgments on Lawyer X

Melbourne barrister Nicola Gobbo is better known across Australia as "Lawyer X"–the pseudonym used by the media even after a court order suppressing the reporting of Gobbo's name was lifted.[1] The alias had to be used because of the "almost certain" risk of death that Gobbo confronted when, having represented criminal underworld figures in trials arising out of Melbourne's gangland wars between 1999 and 2009, it was revealed that she had also been an active registered informer with Victoria Police.[2] As a law student, Gobbo had herself been convicted of two drug offenses. Soon after, she was registered as a police informer. The convictions did not prevent her from securing admission as a lawyer, and within a year of beginning practice as a barrister she was defending significant underworld figures. Con Heliotis, QC, who led Gobbo in many of these trials, warned her not to "mix too much with clients" and, when the warnings went unheeded, said that "she wasn't smart enough, she was in too deep." Heliotis added: "There's no loyalty among [the drug clients] ... they will slice you up as soon as it suits them."

Gobbo had woven a tangled web. Through this period, she was informing on clients whom she was defending, unlawfully passing confidential information that she received from them on to the police. She was simultaneously tipping off underworld clients with information that she had learned about police investigations, and at least two gangland executions are alleged to have taken place as a result of these tips.[3] Gobbo was also sexually involved with drug traffickers and a

---

1 *AB v CD & EF* [2019] VSCA 28.

2 *AB v CD & EF* (2018) 362 ALR 1, 3.

3 Sarah Farnsworth, "Lawyer X Identified as Nicola Gobbo after Court Lifts Suppression Order on Informer 3838," *ABC News*, March 1, 2019, https://www.msn.com/en-au/news/australia/lawyer-x-identified-as-nicola-gobbo-after-court-lifts-suppression-order-on-informer-3838/ar-BBUe9TS; Chris Vedelago and Cameron Houston, "Gobbo Told Her

police officer. Her informing to police, nevertheless, helped secure the convictions and jailing of clients, including drug lord Tony Mokbel and at least six of his criminal associates.[4] Gobbo herself claimed to have given information that helped convict 386 people.[5] But when the evidence of the disclosures to police came before the courts, they regarded it as a serious corruption of the criminal justice system and ordered that Gobbo's clients be officially advised of her informing. The first of Gobbo's clients to have an appeal heard had his conviction for murder quashed in July 2019.[6] Mokbel and others are also pursuing appeals. A Royal Commission was established to investigate Victoria Police's informer program–particularly its use of a lawyer as an informer.[7]

The public narrative in Australia surrounding the "Lawyer X affair" exemplifies what Alasdair MacIntyre called the different rationalities that play out in a society of liberal democratic peoples.[8] First, there was the argument that Gobbo's informing had achieved a significant public good. The gangland wars between 1999 and 2009 involved a struggle for control of Melbourne's underworld that saw at least thirty-six people murdered. The informing therefore helped to realize substantive justice by assisting in securing the imprisonment of many seriously dangerous criminals.[9] Gobbo herself claimed to be frustrated with the inability of police to address the gangland crime problem; she believed that what she did was good and hoped that, if she also were to suffer a gangland execution, "nice things" would be said in her eulogy–although these may be rationalizations offered after news of the scandal broke.[10]

In contrast, the institutions of liberal democracy demonstrated a rationality that attributes a distinctive procedural morality to lawyers. A unanimous High Court of Australia said that Gobbo's actions when informing on clients "were fundamental and appalling breaches of [her] obligations to her clients and of [her]

Underworld Clients Hodson Was a Snitch," *The Age*, April 23, 2019, https://www.theage.com.au/national/victoria/gobbo-told-her-underworld-clients-hodson-was-a-snitch-20190423-p51gke.html.

4 *AB v CD & EF* (2018) 362 ALR 1, 3.

5 Farnsworth, "Lawyer X."

6 *Orman v The Queen* [2019] VSCA 163.

7 Margaret McMurdo, *Royal Commission into the Management of Police Informants–Progress Report, July 2019* (Melbourne: Government Printer, 2019), 14–15.

8 Alasdair MacIntyre, *Whose Justice? Which Rationality?* (South Bend, IN: University of Notre Dame Press, 1988), 343.

9 Australian Broadcasting Corporation TV News, Interview with Simon Rice on the Court Suppression Order on the Identity of "Lawyer X" Being Lifted, March 4, 2019.

10 Farnsworth, "Lawyer X."

duties to the court."[11] The Royal Commissioner, Margaret McMurdo, recognized the competition of the two rationalities:[12]

> Some members of the public may query the outrage expressed by the courts, professional associations and legal academics at the conduct of [Gobbo] and the police, arguing that it had a positive effect, namely, the conviction of serious offenders. But, as the courts have explained, these are matters of high principle, fundamental to our democracy. The Rule of Law requires that everyone (the rich, the disempowered, the poor, the mighty, individuals, governments and their agencies, police officers and corporations) everyone is answerable to the same laws before independent courts. Those charged with criminal offences are usually legally represented. Whether handsomely paid, on Legal Aid rates or acting without fee, the law requires lawyers to keep clients' confidences, act in the client's best interest, and disclose and avoid any potential or actual conflict of interest.

When addressing Gobbo's moral station, the High Court and the commissioner expressed no concern for the substantive justice of the outcomes of the gangland prosecutions. Instead, they presented lawyers as having a central, distinctive, and necessary moral purpose in a society of liberal democratic peoples. In MacIntyre's words, the court and the commissioner assume that "lawyers, not philosophers, are the clergy of liberalism."[13]

This chapter gives an account of the core rationality of liberal democracy and how it shapes, and yet relies on, the distinctive moral purpose and dispositions of the legal profession. Australia, which is by worldwide measures an old society of liberal peoples with settled democratic government, gives this account its legal, political, and social context. In the next section, I therefore deal with the place of lawyers and their moral dispositions in societies of liberal democratic peoples. This account addresses the central question of this volume, *The Impact of Law on Character Formation.* The chapter considers how *legal practice*, and not specifically the law, holds possibilities for the development of people of virtue and character. This argument might seem to have little prospect of success–but the aim is to explore how lawyers' character and the virtues that build it help to manage the religious and nonreligious pluralism that sustains a society of liberal peoples. The conclusion reflects on lawyers' moral development in law school and practice, and the role of the law school in educating in the distinctive moral commitments of the legal profession in liberal democracies.

11 *AB v CD & EF* (2018) 362 ALR 1, 4.

12 Emma Ryan, "Lawyer X Identity Confirmed," *Lawyers Weekly*, March 1, 2019.

13 MacIntyre, *Whose Justice*, 344.

The Lawyer in Liberalism

Liberalism as a Tradition

In calling lawyers "the clergy of liberalism," MacIntyre was marking them out as paradigmatic liberal citizens. He was not, however, intending a compliment. MacIntyre's early combination of broad Christian and Marxist positions, his later Catholicism and his debt to Aquinas have long led him to challenge liberalism and other consequences of the Enlightenment.[14] However, even when, as in this chapter, liberalism is addressed sympathetically, MacIntyre's critique helps to strengthen the philosophical case for the central importance of the legal profession in societies of liberal peoples, and for the distinctive role that the moral dispositions of lawyers have in liberalism. His earlier social construction of the virtues also explains how, despite conventional liberal understandings of lawyers' ethics, a scheme of virtues can, and should, develop with the lawyer's role in liberal democracy.

MacIntyre's critique of the Enlightenment project (including the role of liberalism in it) is the whole purpose of his ground-breaking *After Virtue.* I do not intend to explore this in any depth. However, two aspects of MacIntyre's account of liberalism are worth noting for the insight they give into the role morality of lawyers in liberal democracy. First, *After Virtue*'s criticism of the Enlightenment project is largely about the invention of the individual during the Enlightenment, its moral scheme of abstract human rights, and yet (as MacIntyre sees it) its failure to give a theoretical justification for them.[15] The moral structure of liberalism, in particular, is *procedural* in the sense that it is indifferent to achieving substantive moral outcomes–"ultimate goods." This insight is akin to John Rawls's later understanding of the "thin theory of the good," a societal recognition of individuals' equal claims to rights and opportunities that enable *individuals* to pursue different ultimate goods.[16] This kind of good demands a scheme of societal justice that is agnostic, and for which ultimate goods are indifferent things. As a result, the individual's personal commitment to an ultimate good and her commitment to the procedural goods of an agnostic constitution must involve rational debates of different kinds. The ultimate good of, say, an Anglican Christian might be faith in

---

14 J. L. A. Garcia, "Modern(ist) Moral Philosophy and MacIntyrean Critique," in *Alasdair MacIntyre*, ed. Mark C. Murphy (Cambridge: Cambridge University Press, 2003), 101–06; and for the principal criticisms, see MacIntyre, *Marxism and Christianity*, 2nd ed. (London: Duckworth, 1995); MacIntyre, *After Virtue*, 51–78; MacIntyre, *Whose Justice*, 326–48; MacIntyre, *Three Rival Versions of Moral Enquiry: Encyclopaedia, Genealogy and Tradition* (South Bend, IN: University of Notre Dame Press, 1990), 170–215.

15 MacIntyre, *After Virtue*, 61, 68–69.

16 John Rawls, *Political Liberalism* (New York: Columbia University Press, 1993), 178, 180.

the Holy Trinity, but in practicing liberal citizenship she could also commit to a thin theory of the good that *must*, so far as the political constitution is concerned, be completely indifferent to that. She therefore has to reject, or perhaps just ignore, her church's Reformation understandings that government should promote true religion and that it is even under an obligation to interfere in questions of faith.[17] As, in conditions of religious and nonreligious pluralism, individuals can realize different life plans only if they all have equal access to the social and economic goods of a large commercial commonwealth,[18] they must also demonstrate tolerance, respect, and a willingness to compromise toward those with different life plans and moral positions.[19]

Not without paradox, this agnostic political constitution is, as Jürgen Moltmann put it, not "an irreligious evil" but a "religious achievement." Perhaps more specifically, it is a Protestant achievement.[20] Catholicism certainly reached a *rapprochement* with it in the 1960 s,[21] but MacIntyre still found reason to object to the bifurcated rationality of liberalism because he considered it inconclusive–and inconclusive precisely because liberalism's political debate about societal justice cannot appeal to an ultimate good. And if it is also recognized that an important setting for determining disputes about justice is the legal system, then it, too, suffers from inconclusiveness. A liberal legal system is therefore *procedural* insofar as it resolves the disputes that come before it without reference to an idea of a substantive ultimate good. Importantly, MacIntyre recognizes that the liberal legal system is not morally neutral but promotes, to use Rawls's term, a "thin theory of the good."[22]

A second aspect of MacIntyre's critique of liberalism is his recognition that it has become a "tradition." MacIntyre's idea of a tradition has evolved, but in *After Virtue* it is "an historically extended, socially embodied argument, and an argument precisely in part about the goods that constitute that tradition."[23] A tradition

---

17 *Book of Common Prayer*, 611 (Article I), 627–28 (Article XXXVII).

18 For the idea of "a large commercial republic," see James E. Fleming, "Are Constitutional Courts Civic Educative Institutions," in this volume.

19 John Rawls, *The Law of Peoples* (Cambridge, MA: Harvard University Press, 1999), 14.

20 Jürgen Moltmann, *God for a Secular Society: The Public Relevance of Theology* (London: SCM Press, 1999), 211–12.

21 Ibid., 212; Austin Flannery, ed., *Vatican II: The Conciliar and Post Conciliar Documents* (Collegeville, MN: Liturgical Press, 1975), 799–812 (*Dignitatis Humanae*).

22 MacIntyre, *Whose Justice*, 343–45, 367.

23 MacIntyre, *After Virtue*, 222. For the following account of a tradition, see Reid Mortensen, "The Lawyer as Parent: Sympathy, Care and Character in Lawyers' Ethics," *Legal Ethics* 12 (2009): 1–34, at 8–9; Jean Porter, "Tradition in the Recent Work of Alasdair MacIntyre," in Murphy, *Alasdair MacIntyre*, 38. The idea of a tradition evidently owes much to

is the dominant philosophy that, in the earlier MacIntyre, structures communities, but in his later thought tradition seems to encompass the larger social and economic system. It gives a communal and historical setting for moral reasoning but is "living" in the sense that it may have grown out of, and still bear the influence of, earlier traditions. A tradition allows debates about and revisions of its understandings and aims to give coherence to its inner rationality. As such, a tradition provides the goods that ultimately shape the distinctive set of moral virtues that a community or society will honor. The archetypes for MacIntyre are the Augustinian and Thomist traditions of medieval Christendom. However, liberalism is also a tradition of this kind–the prevailing Western tradition and, as such, spawning its own moral practices and scheme of virtues.[24]

Lawyers' Ethics: Foundations and Pillars

The analogy between the role of clergy in medieval Christendom and the role of lawyers in liberalism is a compelling one for a number of reasons. There is the close identity of the moral dispositions, habits, and discipline of the profession with the moral purposes promoted by the *polis.* The moral dispositions of the profession in question are *necessary* if the political community is to realize its moral purposes. In an important sense, the relevant profession is also the gatekeeper of the primary goods that the political and social tradition offers to its members. To give this context, at least in the modern common law tradition, the distinctive moral commitments and discipline of the legal profession march closely with liberalism's thin theory of the good, and they *must do so* if the citizen is to have access to the kind of good life that is promised by a society of liberal peoples and the large commercial commonwealth that sustains it. These goods are social and economic: individual liberty, moral choice, nondiscriminatory access to opportunities for economic security and affluence, and a productive working life. Not only is the lawyer the paradigmatic citizen in a society of liberal peoples, but the ethics of her profession *require* the lawyer to be the paradigmatic liberal citizen–putting the legal profession in a position that is shared perhaps only with the civil service (at its best) and the judiciary. In these respects, the lawyer's importance in liberalism parallels that of the medieval clergy, whose moral commitments and discipline made them an expert grouping distinct from lay believers, and through whom the church gave the laity access to the divine. And finally, the professional

---

the idea of a scientific paradigm: Thomas Kuhn, *The Structure of Scientific Revolutions,* 2nd ed. (Chicago: University of Chicago Press, 1970), 43–51.

24 MacIntyre, *After Virtue,* 221–25; MacIntyre, *Whose Justice,* 146–208, 326–48, 356–57; Pinkard, "MacIntyre's Critique of Modernity," in Murphy, *Alasdair MacIntyre,* 193–94; Porter, "Tradition," 38, 55.

group's central functional role in the tradition means that it is needed for more than the core practice of its profession. Medieval churchmen filled most roles in temporal government, the secular courts, and education. Lawyers in liberal democracies fill parliaments and offices in executive government; they are prevalent in business and diplomacy. Liberal peoples can be understood as making up societies that are under lawyers.[25]

In the common-law world, the professional ethics of lawyers are tied closely to the ordering principles of the liberal political constitution. Lawyers' ethics, when understood as moral dispositions or habits, can generally be reduced to three pillars: (1) *partisanship* or the single-minded representation of an individual client's interests; (2) *procedural morality*, by which the lawyer is obliged to undertake any lawful cause on behalf of the client, even if it conflicts with the lawyer's personal moral beliefs; and (3) *procedural moral accountability*, under which the lawyer is not taken to have any moral responsibility for the substantive outcomes of her lawful work, but is exposed to professional discipline if she fails to discharge the procedural morality of the profession. The interrelationship among these pillars is complex, and to some extent partisanship presents tensions with the other two. Focusing on the claim that a lawyer carries no moral responsibility for the outcomes of her legal work, legal ethics scholars usually refer to procedural moral accountability as "moral non-accountability."[26] This view, nevertheless, is an incomplete account of the lawyer's moral responsibility, as it ignores the moral discipline that is exercised when a lawyer fails to maintain her partisanship or the standards of procedural morality. The Australian High Court, after all, described Nicola Gobbo's double-dealings as "fundamental and appalling breaches of [her] obligations to her clients and of [her] duties to the court"[27]–moral opprobrium expressed for Gobbo's stepping outside her procedural morality, but language that is also completely indifferent to the substantive justice that she claimed to be serving.

This pillar of accountability is also sometimes folded into the second pillar, procedural morality, as accountability is a possible consequence of the lawyer's "morally neutral" role as the instrument by which the client will achieve his pur-

---

25 For the United States, see Mary Ann Glendon, *A Nation under Lawyers: How the Crisis in the Legal Profession Is Transforming American Society* (New York: Farrar, Strauss and Giroux, 1994).

26 Bradley Wendel, *Lawyers and Fidelity to Law* (Princeton, NJ: Princeton University Press, 2010), 6, 29–30; Richard Wasserstrom, "Lawyers as Professionals: Some Moral Issues," *Human Rights* 5 (1975): 1–24, at 18; David Luban, "Tales of Terror: Lessons for Lawyers from the 'War on Terrorism,'" in *Reaffirming Legal Ethics: Taking Stock and New Ideas*, ed. Kieran Tranter et al. (Abingdon, UK: Routledge, 2010), 56, 57.

27 *AB v CD & EF* (2018) 362 ALR 1, 4.

poses. Indeed, scholars usually call the second pillar "moral neutrality."[28] However, as MacIntyre has rightly pointed out, moral neutrality is a pipedream–the lawyer is really giving effect to the procedural moral structures of liberalism, the thin theory of the good, even if those structures are firmly agnostic and themselves bereft of ultimate goods. Procedural morality nevertheless recognizes "a special relationship between lawyers and the value of legality ... a fidelity to law,"[29] in that the measure of the lawyer's obligation to give effect to client preferences is that the law makes those preferences available. Procedural morality also implies an obligation on the lawyer to represent all comers, regardless of the substantive justice of their cause–an obligation that Lord Hobhouse called "a fundamental and essential part of a liberal legal system."[30]

The combination of partisanship, procedural morality, and procedural moral accountability gives rise to a distinctive set of moral commitments that are pinned to the lawyer's "station and duties"[31]–the expression which philosophers use for role moralities of different kinds.[32] The contrast of the contemporary lawyer's role morality with her belief in an ultimate good is necessarily stronger than that which clergy experienced in medieval Christendom, although our Anglican Christian can be comforted that the language of "station and duties" is drawn from social commitments set out in *The Book of Common Prayer.*[33] The recognition of this distinctive role morality has typically been credited to the needs of the lawyer's role in common law adversarial trial processes. An important criticism has therefore been directed more fundamentally at what are argued to be the shortcomings of adversarial systems of justice (especially as compared with civilian inquisitorial processes).[34] And, certainly, by the eighteenth and early nineteenth centuries

---

28 Wendel, *Fidelity to Law*, 29–30; Luban, *Lawyers and Justice*, 7, 154–55, 402–03; Murray Schwartz, "The Professionalism and Accountability of Lawyers," *California Law Review* 66 (1978): 669–97, at 673; Monroe Freedman and Abbe Smith, *Understanding Lawyers' Ethics*, 5th ed. (Newark, NJ: LexisNexis, 2004), 46–51, 71–72.

29 Wendel, *Fidelity to Law*, 8, 9.

30 *Arthur JS Hall & Co (a firm) v Simons* [2000] 3 WLR 543, 610. This is the "cab-rank rule" of the common-law barrister: see, for example, *Legal Profession Uniform Conduct (Barristers) Rules 2015* (NSW) r 17.

31 Luban, *Lawyers and Justice*, 116–25, 137–39.

32 Ibid.; see also Thomas Hill Green, *Prolegomena to Ethics (Cambridge: Cambridge University Press, 1883)*; Francis Herbert Bradley, *Ethical Studies, 2nd ed. (Oxford: Oxford University Press, 1927).*

33 *Book of Common Prayer*, 292–93 (Catechism).

34 Luban, *Lawyers and Justice*, 50–103; Luban, "Twenty Theses on Adversarial Ethics," in *Beyond the Adversarial System*, ed. Helen Stacy and Michael Lavarch, 134–54 (Sydney, NSW: Federation Press, 1999); Wasserstrom. "Lawyers as Professionals,"12–13; cf. Freedman and Smith, *Lawyers' Ethics*, 13–43.

the needs of adversarial justice, specifically in criminal defense, were invoked to defend the three pillars.[35] The criminal trial presents the strongest example of conditions in which a liberal political constitution gives effect to the procedural rights of an individual as a free and equal citizen, and where the lawyer's three moral pillars are necessary if that purpose is to be achieved. As the Lawyer X affair shows, it is in criminal defense that the most social disruption can occur if the role morality of the lawyer's station is not respected. However, the attempt to build the three pillars from the system of adversarial justice remains an incomplete explanation of lawyers' ethics.

The system of adversarial justice can, in fact, be understood as a distinctive English-speaking expression of liberalism. As a result, Stephen Pepper's insight is that it is liberalism itself that is more immediately the foundation for the three pillars of lawyers' ethics. Liberalism therefore also gives an account of the moral dispositions of lawyers when practicing in the more usual legal business of transactions and outside the context of adversarial prosecutions or civil litigation.[36] Pepper grounds the lawyer's procedural morality on the individual and the individual's entitlement to free and equal access to those goods of a large commercial commonwealth that allow him to pursue his own idea of the ultimate good. A legal system in societies of liberal peoples therefore includes choice-enabling institutions like contracts, trusts, companies, and wills that give the individual the means of planning his affairs in ways that others might pursue differently. This legal system represents a social structure that prioritizes individual autonomy. Although it does so unevenly and with inconsistencies and anomalies, the legal system helps to realize the individual's choices. Its complexity means that the goods it gives access to are often available only with expert assistance–the gatekeeping role that the legal profession carries. Pepper draws an analogy between the lawyer and a skilled machinist:[37]

---

35 For partisanship, see Henry Brougham in *The Queen's Trial* (1820) 1 St Tr (NS) 1348. For procedural morality and substantive moral non-accountability, see Samuel Johnson's comments in 1773, in James Boswell, *The Journal of the Tour to the Hebrides* (Harmondsworth, UK: Penguin, 1985), 168–69; and Thomas Erskine's comments in *R v Thomas Paine* (1792) 22 St Tr 357, 412.

36 Stephen Pepper, "The Lawyer's Amoral Ethical Role: A Defense, a Problem, and Some Possibilities," *American Bar Association Research Journal* (1986): 613–35. For the following, see also Reid Mortensen, "Agency, Autonomy and a Theology for Legal Practice," *Bond Law Review* 14 (2002): 391–413, at 395–403.

37 Pepper, "Lawyer's Amoral Ethical Role," 623–24.

> [T]he image ... is that of the individual facing and needing to use a very large and very complicated machine (with lots of whirring gears and spinning data tapes) that he can't get to work. It is theoretically there for his use, but he can't use it for his purposes without the aid of someone who has the correct wrenches, meters and more esoteric tools, and knows how and where to use them.

If the legal system is a machine, then the lawyer is probably better pictured as one of the whirring gears or cogs.[38] The system is a complex organization of people in different stations with structured roles, and lawyers are the most important agents in those roles. The system is not perfect, and in a society of liberal peoples the market that most lawyers work in means that the access that the lawyer gives usually comes with a hefty fee. However, in the lawyer's role in the legal system, the pillar of procedural morality is necessary if the individual client's access to the goods he is pursuing is to be formally equal with others' access. The lawyer is the means to achieving the client's good, but in conditions of pluralism it is essential that, when acting in her professional role, the lawyer is consistently indifferent to those ultimate goods.

The Possibility of the Virtuous Lawyer

A deeper question raised by the three pillars of lawyers' ethics is the extent to which the lawyer's engagement by the client is limited to legally determined advice and representation–or whether, compatibly with the lawyer's procedural morality, broader moral dispositions than those embedded in law might be important in the counselling and representation of the client. Serious arguments have been presented that anything other than a legally defined agency is dangerous and risks the lawyer imposing her own ideas of the ultimate good on the client.[39] This view is compatible with liberal philosophies' tendency to articulate personal morals as rules, rights, and duties. It also has implications for legal education and whether that should be limited to the learning of professional codes. However, the mere observation of the legal profession's moral habits suggests that this, too, is an incomplete account of lawyers' ethics. Often, a lawyer's advice to a client will amount to no more than telling him, "Don't be such a damned fool."[40] The warning is not typically about the client's legal entitlements. It is often given for financial

38 Mortensen, "Agency, Autonomy," 400.

39 Tim Dare, *The Counsel of Rogues? A Defence of the Standard Conception of the Lawyer's Role* (Farnham, UK: Ashgate Publishing Limited, 2009); Dare, "Virtue Ethics and Legal Ethics," *Victoria University of Wellington Law Review* 28 (1998): 141–55, at 143.

40 James Moore, "Lawyer Independence: Being Able to Tell the Client 'You are a Damned Fool,'" *New York State Bar Journal* 71 (1999): 5.

reasons, but it may also be given to guard the client's reputation or, despite the lawyer's partisanship, to plead with the client to consider the welfare of others.

The moral habits and discipline of lawyers do suggest that their procedural morality is thicker than the law. First, the exercise of the legal profession's discipline is generally by reference to an evaluation of a lawyer's character and repute, rather than of her compliance with professional rules.[41] To some extent, this may be a lingering inheritance of the classical and Christian traditions that predated liberalism. The ongoing "debate" (conducted through ever-changing legislation and adjudication) about ethical measures for the contemporary profession is certainly seeing greater recognition of the role of rules in the discipline of lawyers. However, even at that point the question is, having broken the rules, what does breaking them indicate about the character of the lawyer.[42] Assessments whether an individual has the character expected of a lawyer, and particularly traits implicating truthfulness, are even made by reference to considerations other than the law.[43]

Second, accepting MacIntyre's concession that liberalism has become a tradition brings with it the place that a tradition has in structuring a distinctive scheme of virtues. *After Virtue*'s critique of liberalism suggests that it dislodges the virtues from any commitment to the good and, at times, may amount to nothing more than a disposition to follow rules. Again, this is not the place to articulate a full liberal scheme of virtues. The religious and nonreligious pluralism characteristic of liberal societies will itself see liberalism accommodate different communal schemes of virtues. There will also be an inherited societal recognition of virtues that are more easily traced to pre-Enlightenment traditions. However, the critical point for the moral role of the lawyer in liberalism is the extent to which the three pillars of lawyers' ethics may structure a procedural virtue that is encouraged by the ordinary business of legal practice. In short, it is possible, adapting MacIntyre, to describe the moral dispositions of lawyers as one of "station and

41 The record is extensive. It is even the standard recognized in statute: for example, *Legal Practitioners Act 1898* (NSW) s. 9; *Legal Profession Act 1987* (NSW) s. 11. See *Ex Parte Brounsall* (1778) 2 Cowp 829, 830; 98 ER 1385, 1385; *In re Pyke* (1865) 34 LJQB 121, 123; *Stephens v Hill* (1842) 10 M & W 28, 32, 34, 35; 152 ER 368, 370, 371; *Incorporated Law Institute v Meagher* (1908) 9 CLR 655, 664–6; *Ziems v Prothonotary of the Supreme Court of New South Wales* (1957) 97 CLR 279, 285–6, 288, 297–8; *A Solicitor v Council of the New South Wales Law Society* (2004) 216 CLR 253, 267.

42 Cf. *Council of the Law Society of New South Wales v Parente* [2019] NSWCA 33, [9]-[13]; and see *Legal Profession Uniform Law 2015* (NSW) s. 298.

43 For example, where there is evidence of misconduct as a law student: *Re AGJ* [2004] QCA 88; *Re Liveri* [2006] QCA 152; *Re OG (A Lawyer)* (2007) 18 VR 164; Francesca Bartlett, "Student Misconduct and Admission to Legal Practice–New Approaches," *Monash University Law Review* 34 (2008): 309–30.

virtues" rather than of "station and duties."[44] It may also help to realize, for lawyers, MacIntyre's hope that the Aristotelian tradition and its scheme of virtues can be presented anew to help make liberalism more intelligible.[45]

The suggestion is that practical judgment or prudence–*phronēsis*–is an important virtue that helps promote the procedural goods of a liberal society. Practical judgment is naturally a virtue that has long been a significant moral aspiration for lawyers–Chaucer's sergeant-at-law was "war and wys."[46] Even in Aristotle, practical judgment serves procedural purposes. It gives unity to the virtues in that it amounts to the ability to deliberate well about, and apply, any other virtues (say truthfulness and justice) that are implicated when a decision has to be made.[47] So far as the legal profession is concerned, Anthony Kronman gave a central yet procedural role to practical judgment in the development of the good lawyer: the lawyer as a wise counselor or *phronimos.* Indeed, Kronman argued that the intrinsic nature of traditional legal practice encouraged the lawyer to develop practical judgment, the capacity for choosing well between "incommensurable values" held by the parties to a transaction or dispute. These incommensurable values may include, we can infer, differing ultimate goods.[48] "[T]he practice of law tends to promote the development of this same trait," *phronēsis.* The relevant aspects of legal practice that habituate in judgment include legal advising, putting transactions together, and advocacy. The practical judgment that may develop is a personal capacity, certainly, but it is also an intellectual and moral virtue.[49]

The development of this kind of practical judgment in contemporary common law practice is motivated by the two moral pillars of partisanship and procedural morality. It demands that the lawyer both sympathize with–or *feel*–the strength of the client's interests and adopt a detached stance in a dispassionate evaluation of the client's legal position independently of his preferences. The tension between partisanship and procedural morality, between sympathy and detachment, certainly makes practical judgment difficult, but intellectual effort and habitua-

---

44 Alasdair MacIntyre, "My Station and Its Virtues," *Journal of Philosophical Research* 19 (1994): 1–8, at 3–4.

45 MacIntyre, *After Virtue*, 228–33, 251–52, 259.

46 That is, cautious and prudent: Chaucer, *Canterbury Tales* (London: J. M. Dent & Sons, 1958), 10 (Prologue 309).

47 "Now it is thought to be a mark of a man of practical wisdom to be able to deliberate well about what is good and expedient for himself, not in some particular respect ... but about the sorts of thing that to the good life in general": Aristotle, *Complete Works of Aristotle*, ed. Jonathan Barnes (Princeton, NJ: Princeton University Press, 1984), 1800 (1140a 25–28).

48 Anthony Kronman, "Living in the Law," *University of Chicago Law Review* 54 (1987): 835–76, at 848.

49 Ibid., 863, 865–67, 870–01; see also Richard Sorabji, "Aristotle on the Role of Intellect in Virtue," *Proceedings of the Aristotelian Society* 74 (1974): 107–29, at 118–24.

tion over many years in the ordinary business of legal practice encourage its development. Temperance and, yes, truthfulness would also be expected to develop.[50] Practical judgment, however, does not necessarily see the lawyer impose her own moral values on the client's work and thereby risk betrayal of procedural morality. Instead, it recognizes a moral habit that is needed to promote procedural morality and to enable the choices that the law makes available to the individual. It is therefore a specifically liberal structure of *phronēsis.* It is in this connection that the Lawyer X affair suggests the need for a lawyer-*phronimos* in the defense of serious criminal charges, if that is to be handled capably and without compromising the lawyer's role or integrity. A newly admitted barrister like Nicola Gobbo is a surprising choice as a lawyer for underworld clients. Mixing too much socially with them, she had not appreciated the importance of detachment to the liberal system of justice and to the security of its agents. She did not foresee the dangers of being so casual about compromising her partisanship and her procedural obligations of confidentiality—let alone that her compromises could allegedly contribute to at least two murders. And, if Heliotis was right, even if Gobbo had been given more time, she may not have had the temperament to develop the necessary *phronēsis* for the kind of legal practice she was undertaking.

Second, Kronman sees that an important aspect of the development of practical judgment, temperance, and other virtues is that the lawyer would need to have a commitment to the public good. Kronman tends to see this commitment fulfilled by elite lawyers who, having developed *phronēsis* in legal practice, can make a larger contribution to the well-being of the nation in problem-resolving careers in politics, government service, higher education, diplomacy, and (more predictably) judicial office. Hence, he calls the elite professional with this kind of character the "lawyer-statesman."[51] Australian lawyer-*phronimoi* (and judges) who also contributed to the development of the nation and its democracy, politics, education, and diplomacy could include, for instance, William Charles Wentworth, Edmund Barton, Samuel Griffith, Owen Dixon, Robert Menzies, Roma Mitchell, and Robert J. L. Hawke. These lawyers practiced law as "a craft" that successfully blended a professional grounding in common law reasoning, utilitarian systematization, and compromise for the public good.[52] However, the lawyer-*phronimos* contributing to the public good in the civil society of suburban and regional communities should also be regarded as a lawyer-statesperson. Kronman

---

[50] Kronman, "Living in the Law," 853; Anthony Kronman, *The Lost Lawyer: Failing Ideals of the Legal Profession* (Cambridge, MA: Harvard University Press, 1993), 15.

[51] Kronman, *Lost Lawyer*, 15, 383; William Rehnquist, "The Lawyer-Statesman in American History," *Harvard Journal of Law and Public Policy* 9 (1986): 537–57. There are seeds of the connection between knowing the law (that is, being a lawyer) and being a legislator in the *Nicomachean Ethics:* Aristotle, *Complete Works*, 1865–66 (1180a33–1181a12).

[52] Cf. Kronman, *Lost Lawyer*, 3, 11–12, 20–01.

gives only a reluctant nod to this,[53] but voluntary civil society in local communities is important to the cohesion and cooperative attitudes of pluralized societies. The extensive contribution, for instance, of lawyers in regional Australia who not only have held office in local government but also have managed churches, private schools, local corporations, Volunteer Defence Corps, and Returned Services Leagues, as well as sporting, cultural, and patriotic associations, has been said to be of "incalculable value to the country at large."[54] As was the case with the ordinary parish clergy in medieval Christian traditions, suburban and regional lawyers are well positioned, as important instruments for the realization of the goods of a large commercial commonwealth, to develop the capacities necessary to contribute comprehensively to the functioning of the *polis.* The professional habit of undertaking "the compassionate survey of alternatives viewed simultaneously from a distance" can train the lawyer to address, and often resolve, the conflicting requirements that individuals have in societies marked by extensive religious and nonreligious pluralism, and to live with the inevitable inconclusiveness of liberal democracies and the unresolved tensions that arise within them.[55]

The Seminary of Liberalism

It takes long and varied life experiences for the development of *phronimoi* and, so too, for lawyer-statespeople to develop.[56] Kronman considers that it is only through decades of general legal practice with a broad and diverse clientele that the practical judgment that marks the lawyer-statesperson can arise. He also argues that there are strong "antiprudential" forces in modern legal practice and education that compromise the structures needed for habituation in practical judgment and undermine the intellectual grounding needed to put the lawyer on the path to virtue.[57] There is tension here with MacIntyre's idea that liberalism, as a tradition, must inevitably develop its own scheme of virtues. However, in addition to that, legal practice and education may differ between liberal democracies to the extent that the prospects for cultivating lawyer-statespeople may not be as gloomy as Kronman considers is the case in the United States.

53 Ibid., 379–80.

54 J. M. Bennett, with A. M. Minchin and Anthony Fisher, *A History of Solicitors in New South Wales* (Sydney, NSW: Legal Books, 1984), 262; Reid Mortensen, "The Moralities of Australian Bush Lawyers," in *The Place of Practice: Lawyering in Rural and Regional Australia*, ed. Trish Mundy, Amanda Kennedy, and Jennifer Nielsen, 20–44 (Sydney, NSW: Federation Press, 2017), at 29–31.

55 Kronman, "Living in the Law," 853.

56 Kronman, *Lost Lawyer*, 12; Aristotle, *Complete Works*, 1742 (1103a16–17).

57 Kronman, *Lost Lawyer*, 165–313, 351–52, 379–80.

Large commercial law firms have nurtured the American legal elite and, according to Kronman's assessment, many of its lawyer-statespeople. His concern is that, in large law firms, increasing specialization and an extensive division of labor—other consequences of liberalism and market capitalism—have undermined the conditions necessary for the development of practical judgment. Questions may be asked whether legal practice in those firms is as mechanical and transactional as Kronman claims it to be. He also admits that opportunities for broadening life experience, which are not available through practice as a narrow specialist, are nevertheless still available to the large-firm lawyer through reading and travel.[58]

However, there are different patterns of legal practice in the United Kingdom and the larger Australian states, where the most consciously elite branch of the profession is concentrated in the Independent Bar—the barristers' branch—and particularly in the ranks of Queen's Counsel. Early in the development of legal specialization, solicitors' practices were much more likely to see specialists emerge than the Bar was—although, as the Lawyer X affair showed, criminal defense specialization is relatively more common among barristers.[59] The solo nature of practice at the Bar and the strong professional obligation to take all comers means that even a QC of recognized expertise and eminence is unlikely to practice exclusively as a specialist—except, perhaps again, in criminal law. As a consequence, Kronman's pessimism about the ability of legal elites to contribute to the well-being of a society of liberal peoples may not be as justified in the United Kingdom or Australia. However, it is a mistake to assume that, throughout the common-law world, it is only lawyers in elite legal practice who can contribute to the regular healthy working of the *polis*. Even if reluctantly, Kronman concedes that general practitioners in suburban and regional communities still practice law in conditions that make the development of practical judgment and of lawyer-statespeople possible.[60] And, as we have seen, there is good reason to conclude that the lawyers who contribute to civil society in suburbs, regional cities, and towns have also been of "incalculable value" for the governance and cohesion of societies of liberal peoples.

Although the development of *phronēsis*—even the procedural *phronēsis* that is structured by the liberal tradition—requires extensive professional and life experience, the lawyer's formal education can still have a critical role in its ultimate development. In liberal societies, the contemporary lawyer begins professional life at a university law school, and the university is important, as John Henry New-

---

58 Ibid., 271–313.

59 Julian Disney et al, *Lawyers*, 2nd ed. (Sydney, NSW: Law Book Company, 1986), 123–48, 152–53; cf. Ainslie Lamb and John Littrich, *Lawyers in Australia* (Sydney, NSW: Federation Press, 2011), 61.

60 Kronman, *Lost Lawyer*, 379–80.

man noted, as a place where "a habit of mind is formed which lasts through life."[61] Kronman is again skeptical that the modern American law school can give this grounding, specifically because he observes "antiprudential" themes in legal education when the theoretical predominates in the syllabus. His particular concerns are ideologies of the left that treat law as merely politics-by-other-means, and those of the right that treat it as economics-by-other-means.

MacIntyre and Moltmann express disquiet about a contrary trend that is equally antiprudential, although a concern for the development of virtue does not expressly underlie Moltmann's criticism. They argue that academic disciplines and professional schools have tended to isolate themselves from other disciplines and broader philosophical and theological enquiry.[62] Unsurprisingly, a prudential professional education demands a syllabus that sits between the two extremes–a moderate position that centers on the distinctive methodologies and objects of the discipline,[63] but that encourages an appreciation of its relationships and connections with philosophy, theology, history, political economy, and other disciplines. All of this is reflected in the concern in virtue ethics for an education that helps to broaden life experience "vicariously by reading," and which is undertaken "in a more serious spirit, for the sake of education, in order to expand one's horizon of knowledge and experience."[64] Harper Lee gives the most celebrated lawyer-*phronimos* in literature, Atticus Finch, a dim view of university legal education, but also a prudential position on the importance of broad reading when, in *Go Set a Watchman*, he says:[65] "[I]t took at least five years to learn law after one left law school: one practiced economy for two years, learned Alabama pleading for two more, reread the Bible and Shakespeare for the fifth. Then one was fully equipped to hold on under any conditions."

Kronman's and Lee's skepticism may not be justified for law schools in all liberal societies, but there are inherent limitations in what the law school can achieve in moral education simply because it is engaged in *university* education.

---

61 John Henry Newman, *The Idea of a University* (New York: Doubleday, 1959), 129 (I.V.1).

62 Kronman, *Lost Lawyer*, 165–270; Anthony Kronman, *Education's End: Why Our Colleges and Universities Have Given Up on the Meaning of Life* (New Haven, CT: Yale University Press, 2007); Alasdair MacIntyre, *God, Philosophy, Universities: A Selective History of the Catholic Philosophical Tradition* (Lanham, MD: Rowman & Littlefield, 2009), 15–16; Moltmann, *God for a Secular Society*, 255.

63 See the chapter by Patrick Parkinson, "Law, Morality, and the Fragility of the Western Legal Tradition," in this volume. He refers to the disciplinary distinctiveness of law as its "autonomy."

64 Kronman, *Lost Lawyer*, 305.

65 Harper Lee, *Go Set a Watchman* (London: William Heinemann, 2015), 33–34; cf., ibid., 53. See Thomas Shafer, "The Moral Theology of Atticus Finch," *University of Pittsburgh Law Review* 42 (1981): 181–224.

While Newman's *Idea of a University* promotes a university's capacity to develop the mind, it equally cautions that we can make only modest claims for its capacity to develop moral qualities. The purpose of the university is to extend knowledge by teaching and research. Importantly for law schools, that includes knowledge as professional skill.[66] This means that, in short, the university is not there to make people good. As Newman put it, "knowledge is one thing, virtue is another."[67] That does create a tension when educating for a profession, like law, that has an important role in giving effect to the procedural moral structures of liberal democratic societies, and for law schools that are expected to educate graduates who must commit to the thin theory of the good if they are to perform that role.

There is little question that the university law school develops in its students a "habit of mind ... which lasts through life," and therefore that it can influence the development of the moral station and virtues of lawyers-to-be. In Australia, law schools are more integral to the process of qualifying individuals to practice law than are their counterparts in the United States and Britain. This is because Australian legal professions exercise effective control over the core of the syllabus in the nation's law schools, prescribing "areas of knowledge" in private, public, and adjectival law with a strong emphasis on the study of the doctrines of the common law and the interpretation of statutes. The little space left over, and on which the law schools themselves have prescribed standards, holds an equally strong emphasis on technical professional skills.[68] This puts the distinctive doctrinal methodologies of the law at the heart of legal education and brakes the possibility that a syllabus could be over-theorized or captured by ideology in the sense critiqued by Kronman. The greater risk, in Australia at least, is the intellectual isolation of legal education from the other humanities and slavish devotion to "the current practice of the profession."[69] The moderate center point in legal education could therefore be maintained through a syllabus that recognizes that the procedural

---

66 Newman, *Idea of a University*, 127–47 (I.V), 170–92 (I.VII). See also Jaroslav Pelikan, *The Idea of the University: A Reexamination* (New Haven, CT: Yale University Press, 1992), 99–109.

67 Newman, *Idea of a University*, 144 (I.V.9).

68 Academic qualifications for admission to practice law in all Australian states are university degrees approved by an agency of the relevant state Supreme Court: see, for example, *Legal Profession Uniform Admission Rules 2015* (NSW) s. 7, sch. 1. And see Learning and Teaching Academic Standards Project, *Bachelor of Laws*, 10 (3.2); Learning and Teaching Academic Standards Project, *Juris Doctor*, 3–4. This compounds for law schools the common criticism of the "sameness" of Australian universities: Glyn Davis, *The Australian Idea of a University* (Melbourne: Melbourne University Press, 2017), 99–103; cf. Glyn Davis, "Universities in the Service of the Nation," *Melbourne University Law Review* 38 (2015): 861–72.

69 Pelikan, *Idea of the University*, 105–06.

morality of the legal profession is thicker than the law. Such a syllabus would therefore also address legal and constitutional history, Western legal and moral philosophy (including theologies), and an understanding of ethics that makes the political constitution of a liberal society intelligible to the aspiring lawyer. The study of professional ethics should certainly involve more than learning the professional codes.

Australian law schools, nevertheless, have given themselves self-regulatory standards that prescribe one *moral* commitment: "The law school's mission encompasses a commitment to the rule of law, and the promotion of the highest standards of ethical conduct, professional responsibility, and community service."[70]

It is in respect of this procedural morality that the Australian law dean Michael Coper described law schools as "institutions of moral purpose."[71] Although it may well trip over the doubtful capacity of universities to make people virtuous, the standard's commitment to the rule of law aligns closely with the political constitution's thin theory of the good and the lawyer's station in giving effect to that. It is express recognition of the "special relationship between lawyers and the value of legality,"[72] and it is precisely the commitment to procedural morality that is *required* of lawyers in societies of liberal peoples.

The Australian law school standard, nevertheless, did at one point threaten overreach, initially adding to its commitment to the rule of law an expectation that law graduates show an awareness and "internalisation" of the values underlying professional ethics. Against Newman, it therefore assumed that law schools could extend knowledge *and develop virtue.* However, it would be imprudent of law schools to *assure* that lawyers will internalize the rule of law and the pursuit of the distinctive liberal virtues that are needed to sustain it. The standard that the law school should aim to secure students' internalization of values was therefore, quite properly, later qualified with the proviso–"so far as is practicable."[73] This is not just to escape responsibility for educating a Lawyer X. To the contrary, it is hoped that law graduates will internalize the rule of law that sits behind a liberal legal system and, as presented in this chapter, the virtues that are necessary to give it effect. That is the role of law schools, as institutions of moral purpose in the service of societies marked by extensive religious and nonreligious pluralism.

---

70 Council of Australian Law Deans, *The CALD Standards for Australian Law Schools* (Council of Australian Law Deans, 2009), https://cald.asn.au/wp-content/uploads/2017/11/CALD-Standards-As-adopted-17-November-2009-and-Amended-to-March-2013-1.pdf, 3 (1.3.3).

71 Michael Coper, "Legal Knowledge, the Responsibility of Lawyers, and the Task of Law Schools," *Australian Legal Research Series* (2006): 2.

72 Wendel, *Fidelity to Law*, 8.

73 Council of Australian Law Deans, *Standards*, 5 (3.2.1[d]).

Legal Representation and the Character Formation of Lawyers and Clients

Robert F. Cochran Jr.

> [T]he goal and purpose of a virtuous life in a profession is to help others become good persons.[1]
>
> –Thomas L. Shaffer, *American Lawyers and Their Communities*

As other chapters in this collection have suggested, to some extent law both is formed by and forms the character of a people. But for law to influence character, people must learn of its requirements, and ordinary people do not sit around in the evenings and read statutes and legal opinions. They learn about some aspects of law through the media and through word of mouth, and this will influence moral values in a jurisdiction where law is respected. People also learn about law when they consult a lawyer. Lawyers advise clients about law, sometimes in anticipation of a client's actions, sometimes in response to a lawsuit. Almost all decisions made in a law office affect people besides the client and lawyer and therefore have moral implications. These decisions are likely to move the client's and the lawyer's character in a good or bad direction.

In this chapter, I consider the impact of decisions made in the law office on the character of lawyers and clients. I first consider whether legal representation is a good thing. Do lawyers who represent clients generally add to human flourishing in the world? Second, I consider the impact of legal representation on the character of the lawyer. Does handling legal cases result in lawyers becoming better or worse people? Finally, I consider the moral impact of legal representation on clients, and the ways lawyers might make clients better or worse people.

---

1 Thomas L. Shaffer, *American Lawyers and Their Communities* (Notre Dame, IN: University of Notre Dame Press, 1992), 94.

The Moral Value of Ordinary Law Practice

The reputation of lawyers in most cultures is not very good.[2] My students often report that when they decided to go to law school, members of their community, church, or synagogue asked, "Why would a nice girl [or boy] like you go to law school?" Some lawyers see no connection between their law practice and their moral values. Other lawyers envision their moral values and their work being at odds with one another. They hope that the good they do on the weekend in their communities and families will make up for the harm they do during the rest of the week.[3] Such lawyers live morally schizophrenic lives, with one set of values at work and another set at home. My hope is that this chapter will help lawyers nurture a vision for how their law practice might serve a moral end.

I title this section of my chapter "the moral value of ordinary law practice." By that, I do not intend to denigrate ordinary law practice or those who engage in it. I intend "ordinary" to signal that I am not talking about specialty areas of practice such as poverty law, nonprofit representation, and civil-rights advocacy that have an obvious connection to morality. Not many lawyers have the opportunity to engage in these types of practice full-time. In this chapter, I consider whether there is a connection between one's moral and religious convictions and what Tom Shaffer used to refer to as what ordinary lawyers do in ordinary law offices on ordinary Wednesday afternoons.

Many ordinary lawyers, when asked why they practice law, talk about good things they can do while they are practicing law, rather than about the practice of law itself. While at the office, they can be good to secretaries, fellow lawyers, and clients. With the proceeds of their practice, they can provide a good living for their families and support charitable organizations. But is there something inherently good about what they do as lawyers? In considering this question, I start with a story told by John Witte, which on its face does not appear to have anything to do with the practice of law:

> In 1415, a traveler came to the French town of Chartres to see the great cathedral that was being built there. He arrived at the cathedral just as the workmen were leaving for home. He asked one man, covered with dust, what he did there. The man replied that he was a stonemason. He spent his day carving rocks. Another man, when asked, said he was a glassblower, who spent his days making slabs of colored glass. Still another workman replied that he was a blacksmith who pounded iron for a living. Wandering

---

2 Substantial portions of this section are adapted from Robert F. Cochran Jr., "Can the Ordinary Practice of Law be a Religious Calling? Symposium Introduction," *Pepperdine Law Review* (2005): 373

3 See Joseph Allegretti, *The Lawyer's Calling: Christian Faith and Legal Practice* (New York: Paulist Press, 1996), 1.

> into the deepening gloom of this unfinished edifice, the traveler came upon an old widow, armed with a straw broom, sweeping up after the day's work. "And what are you doing?" he asked her. The woman paused, looked up, and said proudly: "Me? Why, I am building a cathedral to the glory of Almighty God."[4]

In order to see this as a story that tells us something about lawyers, we must first ask whether practicing law is anything like building a cathedral. What is the cathedral in which lawyers invest so much labor? I think that for many lawyers, it is the law itself. These lawyers shape the law through drafting legislation, trying cases, arguing appeals, writing opinions, and advising clients to comply with the law. Other lawyers serve commerce—they draft contracts, organize corporations, and put together deals. Their cathedral is the cathedral of commerce. Of course, the work of many lawyers overlaps, adding to the structure of both law and commerce. It seems to me that the work on each cathedral is justified if it serves the good of other people.[5] What lawyers do is meaningful if the legal and commercial structure they build and maintain enhances human flourishing. Does law or commerce, on balance, serve the good of the neighbor?

First, consider the cathedral of law. Lawyers play many roles in building and maintaining the law. Although there are many laws with which I and other people disagree, on balance I think most legal systems are worthy of protection. The value of law is most obvious when we look at nations that do not have the rule of law. The experience of Rwanda, Bosnia, Afghanistan, and Iraq in recent decades testifies to the value of a strong legal system. And a strong legal system would not be possible without the work of lawyers. The role lawyers play most often, advising clients how to comply with law, is essential to the functioning of the legal system. A lawyer's greatest service to the law probably comes not in dramatic courtroom scenes, but in the privacy of the law office, as she counsels clients to act within legal parameters. But, of course, lawyers also serve as advocates. One may rightly criticize the excesses of lawyer advocacy—advocacy that distorts or conceals, rather than clarifies truth—but I believe that most advocacy, most of the time, is beneficial. Lawyers' arguments generally increase the possibility that judges and juries will discover truth and that law will be just. Legal argument sharpens judges' and juries' thinking by providing a variety of viewpoints.

Second, the cathedral of commerce. In most commercial systems, there are injustices that need correcting through changes in the law, but here as well I believe that, on balance, most commercial systems are a force for good. They provide jobs that enable people to feed and provide shelter for themselves and their families. Commercial systems produce some trashy products, but, on balance, most

---

4 John Witte Jr., "Kuyper Lecture: God's Joust, God's Justice: The Revelations of Legal History," *Princeton Theological Seminary Bulletin* 20 (1999): 295, 312–13.

5 Lev. 19:18; Matt. 19:19; Mark 12:31; Luke 10:27; Rom. 13:9; Gal. 5:14; James 2:8.

products serve individuals and society in good ways. Working within a commercial system that meets the needs of our neighbors is a means of serving and loving our neighbors.

In my view, most lawyers, most of the time, serve God and neighbor. It is not always easy to see the connection between one's work and one's commitment to God. Philosopher Lee Hardy gives the following example: Christians wake in the morning and pray, "Give us today our daily bread."[6] God gives us our bread, but generally it does not appear magically. At the very time that we pray, the baker is already awake, kneading the dough, and preparing the bread. The baker does God's work.[7] But even if one is serving others, that does not mean that one is going to find one's work meaningful. In the Chartres Cathedral story, the stonemason, the glassblower, and the blacksmith were all, like the sweeper woman, building a cathedral to the glory of God, but their work did not seem to provide meaning to their lives as hers did for her. They were focused only on the immediate task at hand. Whether the workers found meaning in their work depended in large part on their perception. Each may have been doing just as good a job as the other, but the stonemason, the glassblower, and the blacksmith focused on their little corner of the cathedral, while the widow saw her part in the whole project. Each little part of the work, by itself, might have had very little significance, but the sweeper saw the broader picture. She envisioned the entire cathedral, the people who would worship there, and the God it would glorify.

In an earlier day, it may have been easier for some people to see a connection between their work, their neighbor, and, ultimately, God. The baker was able to see the people he served. This no doubt gave him great pleasure. The practice of many lawyers is like this. Some see individual clients every day, and their service –drafting legal wills or representing individual clients in court–gives them a direct picture of the good they do. But much of the work of lawyers is more like work on a cathedral. They work on a little part of a bigger project. Today, many lawyers (as well as bakers) are far removed from the people who benefit from their work. This distance is one of the sources of the alienation many people feel from their work. But that distance does not make their service any less valuable. The lawyer who drew up the contract for the transportation of the bread and the lawyer who drew up the articles of incorporation for the supermarket chain that sells the bread should both take pride in their work. God provides bread, not only through the hands of the baker but also through the hands of the lawyer who drafted the documents necessary for its sale.

In my view, most lawyers, most of the time, should see themselves as building a cathedral to the glory of God, even if they have only a small part in its develop-

---

6 See Matt. 6:11.

7 Lee Hardy, "A Larger Calling Still: Can the Ordinary Practice of Law be a Religious Calling?," *Pepperdine Law Review* (2005): 383.

ment and are far removed from the people who benefit from their work. As U.S. Supreme Court Justice Oliver Wendell Holmes noted the lawyer's monument "is the body of our jurisprudence ... to which the least may make their contribution and inscribe it with their names. The glory of lawyers ... is more corporate than individual. Our labor is an endless organic process."[8]

But, of course, finding meaning in building a cathedral to the glory of God requires that the cathedral be to the glory of God. The clients a lawyer accepts and what she does for them are important. If a client is using the lawyer's services to produce a destructive rather than a beneficial product, it is hard to argue that the lawyer is building a cathedral that glorifies God. The lawyer who wants to find meaning in work must build something worthwhile. Some lawyers need to take another look at the clients they represent, the projects they further, and the way they practice, but many lawyers just need to take another look at the work that they already do. They need to look up and see the fruits of their labor. They are building a cathedral to the glory of God.

Lawyers, Virtues, and Vices

Many would scoff at the idea that legal representation has anything to do with virtue.[9] Indeed, observers of the legal profession see a growing preoccupation with making money, an increase in litigiousness, and greater incivility and misuse of legal procedure. I argue, however, that legal representation can and should encourage the virtues of truthfulness, courage, justice, and mercy, and that the virtue of practical wisdom should underlie legal representation. In addition, I explore in this section one of the moral risks in legal representation–that the habitual nature of advocacy in law practice may lead to the development of vices.

---

8 Oliver Wendell Holmes, "The Profession of the Law," in *The Occasional Speeches of Justice Oliver Wendell Holmes*, ed. Mark DeWolfe Howe (Cambridge, MA: Belknap Press, 1962), quoted in Mary Ann Glendon, *A Nation under Lawyers: How the Crisis in the Legal Profession Is Transforming American Society* (Cambridge, MA: Harvard University Press, 1992), 92.

9 For further development of the themes explored in this section, see Robert F. Cochran Jr., "Lawyers and Virtues: A Review Essay of Mary Ann Glendon's *A Nation under Lawyers: How the Crisis in the Legal Profession Is Transforming American Society* and Anthony T. Kronman's *The Lost Lawyer: Failing Ideals of the Legal Profession*," *Notre Dame Law Review* 71 (1996): 707. See also Anthony Kronman, *The Lost Lawyer: Failing Ideals of the Legal Profession* (Cambridge, MA: Belknap Press, 1993); Thomas L. Shaffer and Robert F. Cochran Jr., *Lawyers, Clients, and Moral Responsibility* (St. Paul, MN: Thomson/West, 1994), 40–92 (discussing the place of the virtues of friendship, loyalty, justice, mercy, and truthfulness in the lawyer–client relationship).

Virtue ethics is an alternative to Enlightenment liberalism's principles ethics. Advocates of virtue ethics suggest that morality is a matter of exercising virtues or good habits that enable people to reach human nature's fullest potential.[10] Virtues include truthfulness, courage, justice, and mercy. In contrast to virtue ethics, principle ethics sees the moral life as a matter of applying a complex moral code. The focus of virtue ethics is on being a person of character, rather than making right choices. Principles can be important pointers, but there is no code that answers every moral problem.

Virtue ethics has its roots in Greek culture, especially the writings of Aristotle. Philosopher Alasdair MacIntyre describes Aristotle's concept of a virtue as follows:

> Aristotle tries to use the notion of a mean between the more or the less to give a general characterization of the virtues: courage lies between rashness and timidity, justice between doing injustice and suffering injustice, liberality between prodigality and meanness. For each virtue therefore there are two corresponding vices. And what it is to fall into a vice cannot be adequately specified independently of circumstances: the very same action which would in one situation be liberality could in another be prodigality and in a third meanness. Hence judgement has an indispensable role in the life of the virtuous man which it does not and could not have in, for example, the life of the merely law-abiding or rule-abiding man.[11]

Anthony Kronman notes the place of practical wisdom in the life of American lawyers.

> [E]arlier generations of American lawyers conceived their highest goal to be the attainment of a wisdom that lies beyond technique–a wisdom about human beings and their tangled affairs that anyone who wished to provide real deliberative counsel must possess. They understood this wisdom to be a trait of character that one acquires only by becoming a person of good judgment, and not just an expert in the law.[12]

Practical wisdom is a dispositional trait that requires one "to entertain the widest possible diversity of points of view, and to explore these in a mood of deepening

10 For thoughtful discussion of virtue ethics, see, for example, Alasdair MacIntyre, *After Virtue: A Study in Moral Theory*, 2nd ed. (Notre Dame, IN: University of Notre Dame Press, 1984); Gilbert C. Meilaender, *The Theory and Practice of Virtue* (Notre Dame, IN: University of Notre Dame Press, 1984); Martha C. Nussbaum, "Non-Relative Virtues: An Aristotelian Approach," *Midwest Studies in Philosophy* 13 (1988): 32.

11 MacIntyre, *After Virtue*, 154.

12 Kronman, *The Lost Lawyer*, 2.

sympathy, while retaining the spirit of aloofness on which sound judgment also crucially depends."[13]

Though she does not use the term "practical wisdom," Mary Ann Glendon identifies lawyer qualities that are part of practical wisdom: the lawyer's eye for the issue, a feel for common ground, an eye to the future, problem-solving abilities, tolerance, and recognition of the value of incremental change.[14] Law practice can (and should) be an opportunity for lawyers and clients to develop the virtues as they address particular problems and seek to make wise choices in particular situations.

One insight from virtue ethics is a troubling one for lawyers. Virtue ethics teaches that the moral life, both virtues and vices, is largely a matter of habit. Though some of the habits of lawyers can develop and reinforce virtues, others can develop and reinforce vices. In law school, we train lawyers to be advocates, to forcefully argue the positions of their clients. Such a disposition is likely to carry over into other aspects of one's life. I often ask my students whether their family members find that they have become more argumentative since going to law school. Many smile sheepishly.

In addition, the practice of law commonly involves (and teaches) some level of deception–or at least a failure to be forthcoming. Lawyers learn things from clients, and these things are protected by rules of confidentiality. At trial, lawyers do their utmost to convince judges and juries that they believe in their cause, whether they do or not; lawyers do what they can to keep out damaging, even truthful (maybe especially truthful), testimony; lawyers do what they can (within the bounds of the law) to keep the other side from gaining access to damaging evidence; lawyers make arguments to judges based not on what they believe the law should be but on the interpretation of the law that is in the client's interest; and in negotiations, lawyers commonly lie about their and their clients' true valuation of claims.

There are two justifications for such advocacy. One is instrumental: in litigation, if both sides have aggressive advocates, they will present the best possible case, and judges and juries will be able to make wise decisions.[15] The other is deontological: advocacy protects the autonomy of the client.[16] In the following section, I consider whether the advocacy system yields justice and protects autonomy. For present purposes, I assume that such advocacy is justified. My purpose here is to explore the effects of such advocacy on a lawyer's character.

---

13 Ibid., 304.

14 Glendon, *A Nation Under Lawyers*, 102–08.

15 See, for example, Lon L. Fuller and John D. Randall, "Professional Responsibility: Report of the Joint Conference of the ABA and AALS," *A.B.A. Journal* (1958): 1159, 1160–61.

16 See, for example, Monroe H. Freedman and Abbe Smith, *Understanding Lawyers' Ethics*, 5th ed. (Durham, NC: Carolina Academic Press, 2016), 45–57.

The adversary system, which requires lawyers to do things that seem intuitively wrong (whether they are wrong or not) carries moral risk. There is a danger that the lawyer who is deceptive to juries or to opposing lawyers today will be deceptive to clients, partners, family, and friends tomorrow. Actions affect character.

These ethical issues for lawyers can be analogized to those faced by Dietrich Bonhoeffer, the pacifist Lutheran pastor who joined a plot to kill Adolf Hitler. (Bonhoeffer was executed for his involvement.) While working in the resistance, Bonhoeffer said:

> We have learnt the art of deception and of equivocal speech. Experience has made us suspicious of others and prevented us from being open and frank. Bitter conflicts have made us weary and even cynical. Are we still serviceable? It is not the genius that we shall need, not the cynic, not the misanthropist, not the adroit tactician, but honest, straightforward men. Will our spiritual resources prove adequate and our candor with ourselves remorseless enough to enable us to find our way back again to simplicity and straightforwardness.[17]

Note several things about Bonhoeffer's experience. First, the decision to assist in the plot to kill Hitler put some of the virtues in tension with others. Some virtues would support participation in the plot (justice, mercy toward the oppressed, courage); others would not (truthfulness, mercy toward Hitler). Virtues also often pull an attorney in different directions when faced with decisions during representation. The virtue of practical wisdom enables one to consider all of the virtues in making a decision.

Second, in the section quoted above, Bonhoeffer notices the moral cost to himself and his comrades–he notices that what they do will create moral hazards. Deception or harming others, even in a good cause, even when it is the best decision, may become a habit. If our work as attorneys calls on us to do what in other circumstances would be wrong, the danger is that it will become a habit.

Finally, because Bonhoeffer recognizes the moral dangers he and his comrades face, he is able to ask whether they will be able to overcome those dangers. "Will our spiritual resources prove adequate and our candor with ourselves remorseless enough?" Lawyers do not often ask such questions in professional-responsibility classes or at bar association meetings. It may be that we are unaware of the problem, but just recognizing the problem may enable lawyers to resist its influence on their character.

---

17 Dietrich Bonhoeffer, *Prisoner for God: Letters and Papers from Prison* (New York: Macmillan, 1958), 27, quoted in Meilaender, *The Theory and Practice of Virtue*, 10.

Lawyers, Clients, and Character Formation

As the prior sections have noted, legal representation affects the character of lawyers. Legal representation also affects the character of clients.[18] Many law students and lawyers ask, "Can I be a lawyer and a good person?" One way that a lawyer can be a good person is by helping the client who wants to know, "Can I be your client and a good person?"

Law office conversations are almost always moral conversations. This is so because they involve law, and law is generally a claim that people make on one another. The moral content is often implicit, but it is always there. Legal claims rest on normative considerations as well as objective rules. Almost all decisions made in the law office will benefit some people at the expense of others. Will the client assert or resist a claim? In a divorce, will the client take actions that will harm a child or spouse? In structuring a business deal, or writing a will, who will benefit? Who will lose? Will the officers of a corporation consider the effects of its actions on workers, on consumers, on competitors, on the environment, on the community? As to most law-related questions, lawyers and clients have substantial discretion. As Thomas Shaffer has said, "If it is possible for a serious conversation, between a lawyer and a client, in a law office, to be without moral content, I cannot think of an example."[19]

One of the common challenges of law practice arises when the client's moral values are different from those of the lawyer. We can examine that issue by asking two questions:

(1) Who controls decisions during legal representation? and
(2) Are the interests of people other than the client taken into consideration?

I will explore the four possible combinations of answers that might be given to these questions. Professor Shaffer and I have suggested metaphors for the lawyers who adopt each of those combinations:

(1) The Hired Gun defers to the client and ignores the interests of others.
(2) The Godfather controls the representation and ignores the interests of others.
(3) The Guru controls the representation and considers the interests of others.
(4) The Friend defers to the client but engages the client in consideration of the interests of others.

I will examine these possibilities in the context of the story of a lawsuit that arose in Boston in the early part of the twentieth century.

---

18 For further development of the themes explored in the following section, see Shaffer and Cochran, *Lawyers, Clients, and Moral Responsibility.*

19 See Thomas L. Shaffer, "The Practice of Law as Moral Discourse," *Notre Dame Lawyer* (1979): 231, 232.

The Warren family was one of the most prominent families in Boston. Mr. Warren died and left the family business in a trust for the benefit of his widow and five children. Sam, the oldest son, had had the most experience in business and the trust of everyone in the family. He was placed in charge of the business and the family trust. Ned, a younger brother, moved to England and lived off of his trust income.

After many years, there were difficulties with the business, and Ned began to suspect his older brother Sam of bad faith. Ned went to one of Boston's finest lawyers and shared his suspicions. His lawyer filed a complaint in equity, charging Sam with a breach of trust. On the same day on which the complaint was filed, Ned wrote Sam a letter in which he stated:

> The phrases are such as in a legal document I have felt obliged to sign, but are very far from representing my feelings toward you ... Let us try to agree; it would be much pleasanter.
>
> Your affectionate brother, E. P. Warren[20]

As you might imagine, Sam was deeply offended by the allegations in the complaint. The two brothers went to court. During the trial, Ned's lawyer subjected Sam to rigorous cross examination. After several days on the witness stand, Sam committed suicide. The effect of the litigation on Sam was dramatic, and unusual, but it illustrates the stress and anxiety that people go through (and put one another through) in law cases.

The Lawyer as Hired Gun

We often hear lawyers referred to as "hired guns." In some respects, Ned's lawyer acted as the hired gun of classic American western movies–he attacked someone for the client. But in other respects, Ned's lawyer was different, and more dangerous, than the hired gun. The hired gun acts at the direction of the boss, and the boss assumes responsibility for what the hired gun does. If Ned's lawyer had acted as a hired gun, he would have looked to Ned to control the representation. But Ned's letter indicates that he deferred to his lawyer, despite his misgivings about the suit.

---

20 For additional discussion of this case, see John T. Noonan Jr. "Distinguished Alumni Lecture–Other People's Morals: The Lawyer's Conscience," *Tennessee Law Review* (1981): 234–36 (citing *Warren v. Warren*, No. 14630, Massachusetts, December 13, 1909).

The Lawyer as Godfather

Ned's lawyer more closely resembled another classic figure from American film, the godfather. Like Don Corleone, Ned's lawyer controlled the action and ignored the interests of other people. No one dealt with the moral question whether they should accuse Sam of a breach of trust. It appears that Ned turned the problem over to the lawyer, and the lawyer deferred to his role as advocate. This is not an uncommon role for lawyers. In Douglas Rosenthal's classic study of lawyer-client relations, he interviewed one client who had suffered fairly minor injuries in a traffic accident. The lawyer persuaded the client to embellish his claim for damages. The client said:

> [T]he lawyer is a reassuring presence who takes away your guilt feelings. He says, "Hey, this is the way the game is played; you take as much as you can get; it's what they expect; it's the way it's done." [The lawyer] takes upon his own shoulders the burden of your guilt–he's the professional.[21]

Hired-gun lawyers and godfather lawyers are likely to defend their attacks on other people based on their role in the adversary system–if both sides have aggressive lawyers who present their cases well, judges and juries will be able to decide wisely. It is a theory that works well in many cases, but as every lawyer knows, it does not work well in many other cases. Often lawyers are not equally effective, and, increasingly, one side in a conflict is unable to afford the expense of a lawyer. In addition, decisions made during litigation often affect people who are not present in court. Furthermore, lawyers and clients often make decisions in the privacy of the law office, where the judge is not present as an arbiter of justice.

The other argument for lawyer advocacy is that lawyer advocacy protects client autonomy. But again, what of other people who are affected by lawyer advocacy? What of their autonomy? What about communities that are damaged by the pursuit of client autonomy? Aggressive representation may protect the client's autonomy at the expense of people who have no lawyer to protect them. There are places for aggressive advocacy, but a lawyer and client cannot put the blinders on and assume that advocacy will always yield justice.

Indiscriminate lawyer advocacy not only harms other people; it harms clients and lawyers. Clients are deprived of the opportunity for moral reflection about the issues they face. Some lawyers suffer moral pain. In an interview conducted by Rand Jack and Dana Crowley Jack, a lawyer named Diana Cartwright reports, "I have to contradict myself depending on the role I'm taking .... It's sort of profes-

---

21 Douglas Rosenthal, *Lawyer and Client: Who's in Charge?* (New Brunswick, NJ: Transaction Books, 1977).

sional prostitution."[22] Other lawyers distance themselves from what they do–they try to live divided lives, with one set of morals for the office and another set for home, but as noted in the prior section, life at the office is likely to infect their lives at home.

The Lawyer as Guru

An alternative to the injustice and moral schizophrenia yielded by unreflective lawyer advocacy is presented by the traditional American lawyer. David Hoffman, who in the 1830 s drafted the first guidelines for American lawyers, said, "[The client] shall never make me a partner in his knavery."[23] Clement Haynsworth put it, "[T]he lawyer must never forget that he is the master. He is not there to do the client's bidding. It is for the lawyer to decide what is morally and legally right."[24] Elihu Root said, "About half the practice of a decent lawyer consists in telling would-be clients that they are damned fools and should stop."[25] The traditional lawyer acts as guru, taking control of the representation and making decisions based on what he or she thinks to be right. Such lawyers do not live divided lives. A guru lawyer in the Warren case might have told Ned that he should not sue his brother.

But there is a danger that the guru (and the godfather) lawyer will be guilty of paternalism. As Richard Wasserstrom put it:

> [T]he professional often, if not systematically, interacts with the client in both a manipulative and a paternalistic fashion .... [F]rom the professional's point of view the client is seen and responded to more like an object than a human being, and more like a child than an adult. The professional does not, in short, treat the client like a person; the professional does not accord the client the respect that he or she deserves.[26]

Whereas there is no place in the office of the godfather or the hired-gun lawyer for the morals of the lawyer, there is no place in the office of the guru lawyer for the morals of the client. Guru lawyers assume that the client will be a moral problem

---

22 Rand Jack and Dana Crowley Jack, *Moral Vision and Professional Decisions: The Changing Values of Women and Men Lawyers* (Cambridge: Cambridge University Press, 1989), 112.

23 David Hoffman, "Resolutions on Professional Deportment," in id., *A Course of Legal Study*, 2nd ed. (Baltimore: J. Neal, 1836) 752–75.

24 Clement F. Haynsworth, "Professionalism in Lawyering," *South Carolina Law Review* (1976): 628.

25 Glendon, *A Nation Under Lawyers*, 37.

26 Richard Wasserstrom, "Lawyers as Professionals: Some Moral Issues," *Human Rights* 5 (1975): 1, 19.

for the lawyer and that they can be a source of moral wisdom for the client. Such lawyers show admirable concern for others and for client rectitude, but they show little respect for the client and little recognition that clients can be a source of moral wisdom for the lawyer. Humility is justified when approaching the moral issues that arise in the law office. These issues are likely to be difficult. People disagree over what sound ethics require. None of us has the perfect ability to discern correct moral standards or to determine how they should apply. There is a danger that lawyers will be confident of their moral judgment when their confidence is not justified. Two consciences, in conversation, are more likely to get to moral truth than one.

The Lawyer as Friend

Thomas Shaffer's and my preferred alternative for lawyers is the lawyer as friend, based on Aristotle's notion of friendship as a virtue. The notion that friendship would have a moral component may sound odd to modern ears. Robert Bellah explores the moral character of friendship:

> For Aristotle and his successors, it was precisely the moral component of friendship that made it the indispensable basis of a good society. For it is one of the main duties of friends to help one another to be better persons: one must hold up a standard for one's friend and be able to count on a true friend to do likewise. Traditionally, the opposite of a friend is a flatterer, who tells one what one wants to hear and fails to tell one the truth.[27]

Lawyers cannot become a friend to every client, but they can discuss moral issues with a client in the way they would discuss moral issues with a friend: not imposing their values on the client, but exploring the client's moral values, and not being afraid to influence the client.

As Anthony Kronman argues, the advice of friends and lawyers is of great value to their friends and clients because they combine a commitment to the interests of the client/friend with detachment. Both friends and lawyers bring sympathetic detachment to the relationship. Both are looking out for the interests of the client/friend, but both also bring objectivity to issues that arise. Here is Kronman:

---

27 Robert N. Bellah et al., *Habits of the Heart: Individualism and Commitment in American Life* (Berkeley: University of California Press, 1985), 115.

> Friends take each other's interests seriously and wish to see them advanced; it is part of the meaning of friendship that they do. It does not follow, however, that friends always accept uncritically each other's accounts of their own needs. Indeed, friends often exercise a large degree of independent judgment in assessing each other's interests, and the feeling that one sometimes has an obligation to do so is also an important part of what the relation of friendship means. What makes such independence possible is the ability of friends to exercise greater detachment when reflecting on each other's needs than they are often able to achieve when reflecting on their own. A friend's independence can be of immense value and is frequently the reason why one friend turns to another for advice. Friends of course expect sympathy from each other: it is the expectation of sympathy that distinguishes a friend from a stranger. But they also want detachment, and those who lack either quality are likely to be poor friends.[28]

Friends raise moral issues without imposing their values on each other. As Jeremy Taylor, a seventeenth-century bishop and Cambridge fellow advised:

> Give thy friend counsel wisely and charitably, but leave him to his liberty whether he will follow thee or no: and be not angry if thy counsel be rejected .... He that gives advice to his friend and exacts obedience to it, does not the kindness and ingenuity of a friend, but the office and pertness of a schoolmaster.[29]

A friend is unlikely to impose his or her will on a friend, but neither will a friend sit by and let a friend go down a wrong path. A lawyer as friend will raise and discuss moral issues with clients in a way that takes those issues seriously, without imposing the lawyer's values on the client.

There are two places, in particular, in the client-counseling process where the interests of other people might be considered. The first is the point where the lawyer and client are determining the potential consequences of alternative courses of action. Some client-centered counselors suggest that the lawyer and client consider only consequences to the client. But moral discourse will consider the consequences to other people as well. The lawyer and client should consider all the consequences that might arise from various alternatives. This can be as simple as the lawyer asking the client what effects various alternatives will have on other people.

The second place where the lawyer should raise the interests of other people is at the point of decision-making. Once the alternatives are identified, the client

---

28 Kronman, *The Lost Lawyer*, 131–32.

29 Jeremy Taylor, *A Discourse of the Nature, Offices and Measures of Friendship* (1657), 97 (quoted in Robert J. Condlin, "'What's Love Got To Do With It?'– 'It's Not Like They're Your Friends for Christ's Sake': The Complicated Relationship Between Lawyer and Client," *Nebraska Law Review* 82 (2003): 263.

must choose between them. Among the many questions the lawyer as friend might ask at this point, one is, "What would be fair?" Note that this question does not impose lawyers' values on clients; it calls on clients to draw on their own sources of moral values.

Most decisions made in the law office are decisions over which reasonable people might disagree. So long as the client does not ask the lawyer to do something the lawyer believes to be wrong, generally I think the lawyer should defer to the client. If the client asks the lawyer to do something the lawyer believes to be wrong, I believe the lawyer should withdraw from representing the client, but that will be the unusual case. As lawyer and client discuss the issues they face, they are likely to reach agreement as to the direction to take. If they do this well, both are likely to emerge from the experience as better people.

Law, Conscience, and Character Formation

A South African Case Study in Ricœurian Perspective

Robert Vosloo

Introduction

In 1975 the International Commission of Jurists published a book titled *The Trial of Beyers Naudé: Christian Witness and the Rule of Law*. In the editorial note, the secretary-general of the commission, Niall MacDermot, warrants the publication by stating that the evidence given at the trial by Beyers Naudé–an influential Afrikaner pastor and antiapartheid activist–provides "a remarkable account by an outstanding Christian leader of the way in which he was led by deep religious convictions into conflict with the apartheid policies of the South African government."[1] MacDermot also alludes to the legal interest that the trial could evoke, since it showed how a "careful and impressive judicial system is able to exist side by side with a system of detention without trial, banning orders, and secret inquisitions, over which the judiciary has little power or no control."[2] In addition, an account of the trial illustrates how "legal decisions often depend on the importance which judges attached to the rights of the individual and to the powers and prerogatives of the executive."[3]

The charge against Naudé was straightforward: in September 1973 he was summoned, together with others working for the Christian Institute–an ecumenical institute committed to unity and reconciliation, of which Naudé was the director–to testify before a commission of inquiry into antiapartheid organizations (officially named the Commission of Inquiry into Certain Organizations, but informally known as the Schlebusch Commission, in reference to its chair, Alwyn Schlebusch, a member of Parliament). At this occasion, Naudé refused to take the oath before answering the questions, and since this was a punishable offense, he

---

1 The International Commission of Jurists, Geneva, ed., *The Trial of Beyers Naudé: Christian Witness and the Rule of Law* (London: Search Press; Johannesburg: Ravan Press, 1975), editorial note.

2 Ibid.

3 Ibid.

was liable to a fine or up to six months' imprisonment. The case centered on Naudé's claim that his refusal was justified, and actually required, on grounds of conscience. Hence the defendant, as Professor A. N. Allot pointed out in his discussion of the legal background to the trial, justified the refusal to take an oath "both in conscience and in law."[4] In the process, the defendant's beliefs, as well as what were viewed as principles of the Gospel, the attitudes of churches, the constitution and functioning of the commission, and the principle of South African law with regard to the defense of conscience, all became relevant in November 1973 within the overcrowded magistrate's court in Pretoria. During the trial, Naudé even quoted as part of his testimony a whole sermon he had preached in 1963 in the Dutch Reformed congregation of Aasvoëlkop in Johannesburg, in which he made it clear that he sadly could not continue his ministry with a clear conscience.[5] Using Acts 5:29 ("We must obey God rather than men") as text, Naudé stated that the choice for him to leave the congregation was not a choice between the church and the Christian Institute. Rather, the decision went deeper as a choice "between religious conviction and submission to Christian authority; by obeying the latter unconditionally I would save my face but lose my soul."[6]

It is not the aim of this chapter to go into all the details of this trial, but rather to use it to amplify and problematize the complex and much-discussed relationship between law and conscience, or more broadly, between legality and morality. What is clear from the trial of Beyers Naudé is the often-made assertion that legality is not the same as legitimacy. In the eyes of many, the apartheid government often acted within the bounds of legality but lacked legitimacy on the grounds of what was understood as principles of morality and justice. Therefore, some have argued, it was not really Beyers Naudé who was standing as the accused in the dock, but rather the South African apartheid government.[7] Yet the trial of Naudé also raises questions about the limits of the appeal to conscience in legal proceedings.

---

4 Ibid., 18.

5 For the text of the sermon as read in court, see *The Trial of Beyers Naudé*, 68–74.

6 Ibid., 71. From his sermon it is also clear that Naudé was conscious that it is not straightforward to say one is obeying God rather than other authorities. As Naudé states: "But how does the person know that it is God who speaks? And how do we know that our conscience is always right? How did Peter know this? How could he prove this? The fact is that he could not, he stands defenceless before his judges and before the people. All that he has as anchor is that inner assurance of faith which God has given him through his Spirit." Ibid., 69.

7 Cf. Robert Birley's introduction to *The Trial of Beyers Naudé*, 14. Birley notes how in the trial of Beyers Naudé the tables were slowly turned: "it is the South African government and, to Dr. Naudé's obvious deep sorrow, his own Church, who have to answer the charges" (14).

Against this backdrop–to which many other concrete examples from various times and contexts can be added–the need for greater conceptual clarity regarding the relationship between law and conscience remains as more than merely of academic interest. I propose in this chapter that in speaking of the impact of the role of law on the complex processes of character formation, one should indeed consider the aspect of conscience and, in particular, its role as part of the internalization and problematization of law(s). Drawing in part on the work of the French philosopher Paul Ricœur, the chapter seeks a way beyond viewing law and conscience in terms of a stark polarity. I also argue that one should guard against viewing conscience in a reductive way as merely a faculty of the autonomous individual vis-à-vis a repressive state or other authority, but should rather affirm the relational and societal aspect of conscience (as con-science, knowing with), especially if one wants to give an adequate account of the interrelation between law and conscience with questions of character formation in mind.

Law and Conscience: Beyond a Restrictive Dilemma

In his essay "Conscience and the Law: The Philosophical Stakes" (published as the last essay in his book *The Just*), Ricœur points to what he describes as the restrictive dilemma that arises when law is seen as "immutable, universal, constraining, and objective" and set in opposition to conscience, which is then held to be "variable, circumstantial, spontaneous, and eminently subjective."[8] For the purposes of rethinking the relationship between law and conscience and its role concerning character formation, Ricœur's refusal to succumb to this apparent dilemma and his attempt to think toward a plausible and constructive model of correlating law and conscience are instructive.

Ricœur's discussion, moreover, can be set against the backdrop of the broader relationship between law and morality. One should surely guard against setting up a false dichotomy between law and morality, avoiding in the process what

8 Paul Ricœur, *The Just* (Chicago: University of Chicago Press, 2000), 146. In what follows I will draw mainly on this essay. In the last decade or so before his death, Ricœur wrote several essays in which he undertook, as the preface to *The Just* notes, "to do justice to the question of right and law, to do justice to justice" (ix). For further relevant discussions by Ricœur on conscience, also with theological implications, see the section on the testimony of conscience in his essay "The Summoned Subject in the School of Narratives of the Prophetic Vocation," in Paul Ricœur, *Figuring the Sacred: Religion, Narrative, and Imagination* (Minneapolis: Fortress Press, 1995), 262–74, esp. 271–74. Cf. also his discussion on conscience (partly in conversation with Heidegger) in Paul Ricœur, *Oneself as Another* (Chicago: University of Chicago Press, 1992), especially 341–55.

Cathleen Kaveny calls "two opposite and equally damaging extremes." As she notes:

> We should not make the mistake of assuming that law and morality are co-extensive, on the one hand, or of maintaining that they should have as little as possible to do with each other, on the other. In very different ways, both mistakes can be traced to the same fundamental problem: ignoring the full range of ways in which moral considerations enter into wise lawmaking.[9]

In his discussion of the relationship between law and conscience, Ricœur likewise aims to keep the tension between these notions real without allowing the polarity to become a schism. Ricœur starts his discussion on the relationship between conscience and law by placing at the pole of law the most basic discernment between good and evil.[10] Following Charles Taylor's expression of "strong evaluations," Ricœur argues that such evaluations express the fact that life is not morally neutral. In our ordinary speech we easily use pairs of terms such as honorable and shameful, worthy and unworthy, admirable and abominable. We approve of what we view as the better and disapprove of what we view as the worse. This presents a way of speaking about the normative sense attached to the idea of the law. At the other pole, on the side of conscience, Ricœur–this time following Taylor's pairing of the idea of the self with the idea of the good–places the question "Who am I?" as a way of orientating ourselves within moral space.[11] As Ricœur states: "As a moral being, I am someone who assumes an orientation, takes a stand, and maintains himself in moral space. And conscience, at least at the first level, is nothing else than this orientation, this stance, and this holding on."[12] In this regard, Ricœur thus follows the neo-Aristotelian line of reasoning in which the question "What ought I to do?" is secondary to the question of my identity as a moral agent. On a basic level, then, Ricœur sets up the polarity of law and conscience in terms of the pair "strong evaluations–strong adherence."[13]

---

9 Cathleen Kaveny, *Law's Virtues: Fostering Autonomy and Solidarity in American Society* (Washington, DC: Georgetown University Press, 2012), 45 (Kindle edition).

10 This first level can be seen as related to the category of "the good" as expounded upon in his "little ethics," as he refers to the last section of his book *Oneself as Another*. The second and the third levels, as we shall see, correlate roughly with his categories of "the right" (or the norm) and "the wise." Cf., in this regard, Bernard P. Dauenhauer, *Paul Ricœur: The Promise and Risk of Politics* (Lanham, MD: Rowman and Littlefield Publishers, 1998), 235–40.

11 Ricœur, *The Just*, 148.

12 Ibid.

13 Ibid.

Ricœur proceeds in his analysis–on a second level–with reference to three features of the normative dimension of the law that should be considered in the reflection on the dialectic between law and conscience. The first aspect relates to interdiction as the stern face of the law (one can think, for instance, of the Ten Commandments with their grammar of negative imperatives). But Ricœur is quick to point out that we should guard against viewing these prohibitions as necessarily repressive. The prohibition against false testimony, for example, protects the institution of language and thus helps to establish a bond of mutual trust within a linguistic community. Ricœur also highlights–as a second feature–the aspect that the juridical and the moral norms claim universality. That it is only a "claim" to universality, and therefore has a factual relativity, does not detract from the fact that in principle, universal validity is intended. The prohibition of murder, for instance, would lose its normative character if it were not applicable to everybody and every circumstance. Our attempt to justify exceptions (through, say, positing examples in which somebody's life is in danger, or with regard to defending a just war or the death penalty for serious crimes) in a way already pays tribute to the universality of the rule. As a third feature regarding the law, Ricœur points to the connection between the norm and what he terms "human plurality" (which refers to the self in relation to others). What is forbidden by the law, one can say in this regard, is a whole series of wrongs done to others. It assumes the fragile interhuman bond, and one of the basic functions of the law is therefore to protect the separation of what is mine from what is yours.

How do these three features of the law relate to conscience? With regard to interdiction, Ricœur underscores the idea that legality demands external obedience. Furthermore, physical force is authorized as a way to restore the law. Conformity to the law is hereby often linked to a fear of punishment. The passage from legality to morality then requires a process of internalizing the norm that points to the role of conscience. With regard to universality, the second feature, the external legislator (demanded by legality) is replaced by personal autonomy (which is linked to conscience). As Ricœur writes: "Through autonomy, a rational will emerges from a merely arbitrary one, by placing itself under the synthesis of freedom and rule-governedness."[14] The third feature of legality, described by Ricœur with the phrase "human plurality," points to the dialogical and conversational aspect of the norm. Here the idea of justice and the need for mutual respect between people comes into play.

For Ricœur, legality is raised to the level of morality through a process of internalization that is completed in moral conscience. But it is important for Ricœur to note at this stage that this internalization is not a negation of the law, since "conscience is nothing other than an inward, willing obedience to the law *as law*, through pure respect for it and not out of the mere conformity to the statement of

---

14 Ibid., 150, 151.

the rule" (my emphasis).[15] Therefore, the voice of conscience, too, is the voice of prohibition, universality, and impartial justice to others. Any false juxtaposition or strict separation between legality and morality, or between law and conscience, should be resisted.

What is decisive for our purposes here in the light of Ricœur's analysis is that it makes clear that we should not set up law (also with regard to the various aspects related to its normative character) over against conscience, as if conscience –including what is often described as religious conscience–can function as a merely spontaneous and subjective network of processes that can be abstracted from features such as moral rigor, universal intent, and impartial justice. In this way, law plays a vital role in cultivating conscience and forming moral persons, to infer the point from the title of a book by Lyn Stout.[16] As she writes in *Cultivating Conscience: How Good Laws Make Good People:* "Law can reward and punish, but it can do more as well. If we gain a better understanding of the ways in which law can activate–or disengage–the force of conscience, we can not only understand the law better, we can use it more effectively."[17]

We should therefore emphasize not merely the limitations of law when discussing the relationship between law and character formation, but also its impact and potential. The South African theologian Dirkie Smit states this positive transformational role of law as follows:

> Law can even fulfil the role of moral education, formation, and transformation. Morality changes, and very often it changes as a result of legal changes. Experience amply shows that forms of racism, sexism, homophobia, prejudice and discrimination, disregard for human dignity, violations of human rights, slavery, abuse, and in fact many practices of corruption, nepotism, and exclusion often first have to be prohibited by law, before a major part of the population will change their minds to accept and share these convictions. In this sense, living in a city with just laws is indeed an important form of moral formation–as the Greek philosopher already taught.[18]

---

15 Ibid., 150.

16 Cf. Lyn Stout, *Cultivating Conscience: How Good Laws Make Good People* (Princeton: Princeton University Press, 2011). In her book, Stout describes conscience as "an internal force that inspires unselfish, pro-social behavior" (6). Since law, too, is mostly about the promotion of unselfish, prosocial behavior, law and conscience are tightly intertwined.

17 Ibid., 17.

18 Dirk J. Smit, "What abou' the lô? Adam Small on Law and Morality," in *Remembering Theologians–Doing Theology: Collected Essays*, ed. Robert Vosloo (Stellenbosch: Sun Press, 2013), 402–03.

Law, Smit affirms, may help to make societies more moral. In this sense, it is certainly apt to speak, with Cathleen Kaveny, of law's virtues.[19]

Between Legality and Conviction

Ricœur, moreover, extends his discussion on the relationship between law and conscience to a third level that might also be relevant for discussions of the role of law in processes of character formation. In the light of the emphasis on the acting subject (the capable human being) in Ricœur's broader philosophical project,[20] it is not surprising that he turns to the question of the complex operation of making moral judgments in particular situations. For Ricœur, however, it would be a mistake to think that the idea of law has disappeared from the process of making a judgment in a concrete situation. The question is rather what law is applicable in the specific situation, and often this might not be that difficult to ascertain. But Ricœur is also aware that there are often "a number of more embarrassing situations where it is the very reference to the law that causes the problem."[21] One can therefore also think of cases–as seen, for instance, in Greek tragedy–when norms clash or become incompatible. These tragic dimensions then call for the need to act wisely, to embody the virtue of *phronesis/prudentia.* Ricœur speaks in this regard of practical wisdom, or more precisely, "wisdom in judgment."[22]

---

19 For Kaveny this reference to "law's virtues" has a dual meaning. On one hand, the argument is put forward that law can function as a teacher of virtue (also in pluralistic Western societies), supporting, for instance, autonomy and solidarity as aspects of the virtues of prudence and justice, respectively. On the other hand, Kaveny adds, "good law must possess attributes–virtues–in addition to encouraging the citizenry to act virtuously" (Preface, Kindle edition loc 90 of 7012). For a description of these attributes, she quotes approvingly–following Aquinas–from Isidore of Seville's *Etymologies:* "Law shall be virtuous, just, possible to nature, according to the custom of the country, suitable to place and time, necessary, useful; clearly expressed, lest by its obscurity it lead to misunderstanding, framed for no benefit, but for the common good" (Kaveny, *Law's Virtues*, Preface, Kindle edition loc 90 of 7102).

20 With regard to the centrality of human capability in Ricoeur's thought, David Kaplan writes: "Ricœur's readers ... are quick to agree that the notion of human capability (*l'homme capable*) is the guiding thread that runs through Ricoeur's philosophical career, unifying his seemingly disconnected works... . To be human being is to be able to initiate new actions that are immutable to one as freely chosen activities." See Richard Kaplan, ed., *Reading Ricoeur* (Albany: State University of New York Press, 2008), 2-3.

21 Ricœur, *The Just*, 154.

22 Ibid.

For Ricœur, it is the tragic dimension of action that is left out in wholly formal conceptions of moral obligation.[23] But, writes Ricœur, "the tragedy that has been pushed out the door comes in again through the window once the irreducible diversity of basic social goods is taken into consideration."[24] In these contexts, we are confronted with what Rawls calls "reasonable disagreements," an expression that for Ricœur captures nicely something of the need for the virtue of prudence.[25] The complexity arising in this regard is thus not merely about respect (or the lack thereof) for norms, but follows from the fact that the norms themselves are part of the debate. Ricœur comments:

> Wisdom in judging consists in elaborating fragile compromises where it is less a matter of deciding between good and evil, black and white, than between gray and gray, or, in the highly tragic case, between bad and worse.[26]

In the discussion on the law and character formation, this aspect of the limitations of the normative dimensions of the law with regard to conscience and morality, as highlighted by Ricœur, should be acknowledged. Something of this is reflected in a story from the Talmud, also often quoted by the sociologist Zygmunt Bauman:

> Ulla bar Koshev was wanted by the government. He fled for asylum to Rabbi Joshua ben Levi at Lod. The government forces came and surrounded the town. They said: "If you do not surrender him to us, we will destroy the town." Rabbi Joshua went up to Ulla bar Koshev and persuaded him to give himself up. Elijah used to appear to Rabbi Joshua, but from that moment on he ceased to do so. Rabbi Joshua fasted for many days, and finally Elijah revealed himself to him. "Am I supposed to appear to informers?" he asked. Rabbi Joshua said: "I followed the law." Elijah retorted: "But is the law for saints?"[27]

---

23 This point is also made by the theologian Stanley Hauerwas. See, for instance, Stanley Hauerwas, with Richard Bondi and David B. Burrell, *Truthfulness and Tragedy: Further Investigations into Christian Ethics* (Notre Dame: University of Notre Dame Press, 1977), 18–21.

24 Ricoeur, *The Just*, 154.

25 Ibid., 155. Ricoeur writes: "The fragmentation of political ideas, of spheres of justice, and, even in the juridical domain, the multiplication of sources of law and the blossoming of codes of jurisdiction invites us to take seriously the idea of reasonable disagreement."

26 Ibid.

27 Cf. Zygmunt Bauman, *Postmodern Ethics* (Oxford: Blackwell, 1993), 81. In the light of this story from the Talmudic sages (*Trumot* 8:10), Bauman comments: "Saints are saints because they do not hide behind the Law's broad shoulders. They know, or they feel, or they act as if they felt, that no law, however generous and humane, may exhaust the moral duty." Ibid., 81.

Is the law for saints? If one thinks about the relationship between law and conscience, this story and Elijah's question could have a disruptive effect. It seems to suggest that the moral or religious life is determined by more than mere obedience to the law. In fact, it could be that, because of one's moral or religious convictions, one must in certain circumstances even break the law. This sensibility that character and conscience might require at times the transgression of the law can of course take on many forms. It can, for instance, result in acts of civil disobedience to the laws of the state. It might also happen that one could be disobedient because one claims obedience to a higher authority, namely one's conscience or reason or God. One can think in this regard of the trial and example of Beyers Naudé referred to in the Introduction.[28] Or, famously, one can recall Martin Luther's response before the emperor at the Diet of Worms in 1521, when he was asked to retract his writings: "Unless I am convinced by the testimony of scripture or by clear reason, I am bound by the scripture I have quoted, and my conscience is captive to the Word of God. I cannot and I will not retract anything, since it is neither right nor safe to go against conscience."[29] These kinds of response reiterate the need in the discussion on law and character formation to ask: "Whose law? What law?"[30]

---

28 In a similar way as Naudé's appeal to conscience and obedience to God, the antiapartheid theologian Allan Boesak wrote an open letter to Alwyn Schlebusch, then the minister of justice, dated August 24, 1979. The letter was a reply to Schlebusch's response after the South African Council of Churches' resolution on civil obedience and amounted to a warning to church leaders "to stay out of politics." In his letter, Boesak writes: "The believer in Christ not only has the right, but also the responsibility, should a government deviate from God's law, to be more obedient to God than to government." See Allan Boesak, *Black and Reformed: Apartheid, Liberation and the Calvinist Tradition* (Johannesburg: Skotaville Publishers, 1984), 36–45, at 39. And toward the end of the letter, Boesak adds that he is aware that the decision to resist the forces of government cannot be an easy one, and then quotes a decision from the Dutch Reformed Mission Church at its 1978 synod meeting: "If a Christian is bound by his conscience to follow the way of criticism, which brings him in conflict with the state, then he should obey God more than humans. In this case, however, he must be prepared to accept suffering in the spirit of Christ and his apostles." Ibid., 44.

29 Quoted in Randall C. Zachman, *The Assurance of Faith: Conscience in the Theology of Martin Luther and John Calvin* (Minneapolis: Fortress Press, 1993), 22.

30 The reference to these questions here is drawn from an Afrikaans poem by the South African poet Adam Small. The poem deals with an interracial relationship between Martin and Diana, which was not permissible under apartheid's laws. In this poem we read: "Diana was a wit nôi [Diana was a white girl]/ Martin was a bryn boy [Martin was a brown boy]/ dey fell in love [they fell in love]/ sê Diana se mense [say Diana's people] / sê Martin se mense [say Martin's people]/ sê almal se mense [say everybody's people]/ what about the lô [what about the law]/ sê Martin sê Diana watte lô/ God's lô/ man's lô/ devil's lô/

Yet the question remains, also for Ricœur, whether the emphasis on wisdom in judgment does not reduce our conscience to arbitrary responses. Are we then not back again to a position in which the relationship between law and conscience is polarized in line with the polarities of dogmatism and situationalism? Ricœur answers in the negative, since "the ethicist, faced with the tragic dimension of action, states *the better or the less bad*, as it appears at the end of a debate where norms weigh no less than people" (my emphasis).[31] Inner conviction thus has its objective correlate in what is apparent as the better thing to do in a particular circumstance.

Ricœur is clearly aware of the complex and often tragic nature of our judgments (even if it is the better, or the less bad, judgment in the light of the circumstances), but he ends his discussion with an emphasis on the need for our judgments to be accompanied by argumentation and interpretation in counsel with others. As he writes:

> Wisdom in judging must always involve more than one person. Then conscience truly merits the name *conviction*. Conviction is the new name that the strong adhesion of our first analysis now receives, after having traversed the rigor, intransigence, and impartiality of abstract ethics, and having confronted the tragic dimensions of action.[32]

The point that Ricœur underscores is that conscience is not an arbitrary faculty of the autonomous individual that functions in isolation from, and in ignorance of, the law and the counsel of others. Robert Vischer makes a similar point in his book *Conscience and the Common Good: Reclaiming the Space between Person and State*. With reference to America's cultural and legal landscapes, Vischer warns against restricting the right to conscience merely to the right to individual autonomy. As he writes, "Our failure to break conscience out of its individualist framework affects our understanding of the interplay between the individual and the state in a variety of intermediate institutions such as voluntary associations, social service providers, corporations and even the family."[33] Vischer's aim is not to oppose the view of conscience as an individual person's judgment regarding right and wrong, but he does not want us to lose sight of the earlier meaning of con-

---

watte lô [says Martin, says Diana what law? God's law? Man's law? Devils law? What law?"). For a discussion that uses this poem as a springboard to discuss the relationship between law and morality/religion, see Smit, *Remembering Theologians–Doing Theology*, 399–409.

31 Ricoeur, *The Just*, 155.

32 Ibid.

33 Robert Vischer, *Conscience and the Common Good: Reclaiming the Space between Person and State* (Cambridge: Cambridge University Press, 2010), 2.

science as knowledge shared by several people (con-science). Hence his plea that we should recover the relational dimension of conscience. As he puts it:

> Conscience, by its very nature, connects a person to something bigger than herself, not only because we form our moral convictions through interaction with the world around us, but also because we form our moral convictions with real-world authority in ways that are accessible, if not agreeable, to others.[34]

One should further note that conscience, understood in its relational dimension, is not a passively held belief, but a belief applied to conduct. "To a significant extent, the acting, not the intellectual choosing, makes up personhood and justifies the state's respect for conscience."[35] Understood in this way, we can say that conscience is not merely a means of expressing our character and identity, but also a means of forming it within a social environment. As Vischer states: "Respect for conscience also entails respect for the relationships through which consciences are formed."[36]

This emphasis on the intersubjective framework of conscience is also affirmed by Ricœur in his discussion of what he calls "the summoned subject."[37] This self, Ricœur writes, is "already a self in relation, and, in this way, a self in the position of respondent."[38] The summoned self (as in response to the prophetic call or in conformity with the Christ figure, to use the examples that Ricœur draws upon), is thus a dialogical and responding self. As Ricœur writes within the context of Christianity: "Far from undertaking a polemic against this conquered autonomy won by conscience, I would like to show that it opens new possibilities for interpretation for the dialogical structure of Christian existence."[39]

In summary, one can say that Ricœur's discussion of the relationship between conscience and law emphasizes the need to take the long route from law to conscience (and back) through a confrontation with law's normative aspects as well as the tragic aspects of our communal existence. Law's role in this process should therefore be neither minimized nor absolutized. The polarity should not

---

34 Ibid., 3.

35 Ibid.

36 Ibid., 307. Vischer concludes his book on a thought-provoking note by reiterating again the intersubjective nature of moral claims: "Conscience, and the self-transcending paths by which it forms the common good, bear a legitimacy founded on human nature and the inescapable intersubjectivity of moral claims. This legitimacy warrants the state's deference, but should not require its approval." Ibid., 310.

37 See his essay "The Summoned Subject in the School of Narratives of the Prophetic Vocation," in Ricoeur, *Figuring the Sacred*, 262–75.

38 Ibid., 262.

39 Ibid., 271.

become a schism; the tension should remain creative. This implies the need for wisdom in judgment, which affirms, in turn, the intersubjective nature of conscience and moral formation.

Conclusion

In the introduction, I referred to the court case in which Beyers Naudé was on trial for refusing to testify before a commission of inquiry of the apartheid government. As stated in *The Trial of Beyers Naudé*, the court could follow two lines of approach in dealing with this case:

> Either they could see if the particular person called as a witness, given his background, beliefs and fears, had sufficient cause to refuse–this is the *subjective* test, and implies that an accused person can escape punishment if he did not have a guilty mind, because in his own mind he was justified in refusing. Or the courts could follow the *objective* test, disregard the actual state of the defendant's mind, and lay down general categories of excuse.[40]

The outcome of the case was that Naudé was found guilty and imposed a fine of R50 or a sentence of one month's imprisonment. Naudé's defense could not prove sufficient cause for his refusal to testify before the commission. His counsel immediately gave notice of appeal, which went to the Transvaal Supreme Court, and the outcome was that the appeal was successful on grounds of a technicality regarding the way in which the commission was constituted.

One can certainly understand that the appeal to conscience in this setting was problematic on legal grounds, also given the implications if subjective appeals to conscience would prevail in legal settings in multicultural and multireligious societies. To quote Dirkie Smit again:

> Merely the fact of different religious communities with diverse understanding of divine law and revelation in the same pluralist society calls–at least according to democratic philosophical and legal traditions–for ways of separation between legality, that is universal, fair, procedural, on the one hand, and the claims of particular moral and religious views, on the other hand.[41]

The plurality of expressions of conscience indicates therefore that the reference to, and the respect for, conscience indicates part of our challenge, rather than merely our solution to the dilemma. Yet it is also important to note how for Naudé,

---

40 *The Trial of Beyers Naudé*, 34.

41 Smit, *Remembering Theologians*, 405.

for instance, it was important to give an account of himself, also in a legal setting–and thus to witness to what was perceived (by himself and others) as a stance for justice and truth. His witness, with others, in this setting cannot be separated, moreover, from the way in which his character was formed in a myriad of complex ways that also included the inculcation of specific moral and religious convictions. The need to witness in this way probably also had to do with the fact that it served as a public challenge to the legitimacy of the apartheid government. This explains, in part, the extensive statement the defendants compiled, titled *Divine or Civil Obedience?*, on the reasons why they decided not to testify before the commission–a document rich in quotations from the Bible and theological sources, including the work of Karl Barth.[42]

For Naudé, as for many others, resistance against apartheid was justified with reference to a higher obedience than merely to the law. An understanding of the relationship between law and character formation that does not also take into account the intricacies associated with conscience will be reductive, or so this chapter argues. This said, one can also point to many other examples in which people, motivated by concrete and traumatic experiences, have called, also in the name of conscience and justice, for due process, for rules and laws not be set aside but followed and enforced. Any stark binary construction of the relationship between law and conscience, therefore, should be problematized and rejected in favor of accounts that allow the tension between law and conscience to be constructive and transformative.

---

42 This document is included as an appendix in *The Trial of Beyers Naudé*, 153–63. It was also later published and distributed as a pamphlet by the Christian Institute. The statement is introduced as follows: "A witness in the name of Jesus Christ to the commission of inquiry into certain organizations concerning the refusal to testify because of obedience to God as the highest authority."

Law, Values, and Moral Influence

Kenneth John Crispin, QC

In most Western countries, the legal conservatism of earlier generations has been progressively challenged, and some laws once seen as bulwarks of social decency have been repealed. For example, damages are no longer available for breach of promise or "criminal conversation," and people no longer face prosecution for blasphemy or homosexual activity between consenting adults. However, such challenges have prevailed over earlier conceptions of moral orthodoxy largely because of increasing social recognition of other moral principles, such as respect for individual freedom and the rights of minorities. The debates between those manning the barricades of conservatism and those pressing for change have sometimes been rancorous, but the competing arguments have reflected a common underlying assumption that the law should reflect moral values. But what is the relationship between law and morality? And is the converse also true? Do our laws and legal systems influence moral consciousness, community values, and perhaps even character formation?

The Influence of Moral Beliefs

Many people still seem to assume that the legitimate scope of the law extends to enforcement of traditional moral standards. This assumption has been displayed in opposition to same-sex marriage, some drug-law reform proposals, and so-called victimless crimes, such as prostitution and attempted suicide. It is also reflected in much of the rhetoric of those agitating for legal reform. Yet, in theory at least, law and ethics are substantially separate realms: ethics is concerned with how people should behave, while law is concerned with how they should be required to behave. But what values should influence our laws, and where should the line between morality and law be drawn?

Religious Influences

Earlier generations shaped their laws by reference to religious precepts. This may have seemed a laudable approach, but it involved recourse to some disturbing precedents. The Old Testament patriarchs had insisted that people be executed for a wide range of offenses, including cursing a parent, adultery, homosexual acts, witchcraft, working on the Sabbath, and being a newly married woman unable to produce "tokens of virginity."[1] Later jurists limited the application of the death penalty, but religious belief continued to shape law and legal practice. Saint Paul had proclaimed that the secular authorities were God's agents of punishment, and the Church Fathers, notably Saint Augustine of Hippo and Saint Thomas Aquinas, insisted that the temporal law be subordinate to the eternal law of God.[2] Early writings on the English common law all had a strong religious flavor,[3] and Blackstone's commentaries conceded the supremacy of "divine law."[4] Christianity was accepted by Lord Eldon and other judges as part of the law of England,[5] though the demands of the faith for justice and mercy sometimes fell on deaf ears. Lord Eldon opposed laws for the abolition of slavery, the closure of debtors' prisons, and the emancipation of Roman Catholics. He reportedly wept in court when informed that the death penalty would no longer be available for petty larceny. It was said that he feared "an ordered universe was shivering into fragments."[6] Women had limited rights of inheritance, and their husbands had substantial powers over their lives and property. Even slavery was defended as biblically authorized.[7]

Legal procedures were also shaped by religious beliefs. Some litigants were able to rely on compurgation, a process by which a defendant could obtain vin-

---

1 Lev. 20:9, 20:10, 20:13; Exod. 22:18, 35:2, Deut. 22:20; and Rom. 13:1–6.

2 There were significant theological differences between the Augustinian and Thomist conceptions of law: H. McCoubrey, *The Development of Naturalist Legal Theory* (London: Croom Helm with Methuen, 1987), 39–60.

3 David Melinkoff has cited Glanvil (twelfth century), Bracton (thirteenth century), Fortescue and Littlejohn (fifteenth century) and St. Germain (sixteenth century): David Melinkoff, *The Conscience of a Lawyer* (Los Angeles: West 1973), 145.

4 William Blackstone, *Commentaries on the Laws of England*, ed. William Carey Jones (San Fransisco: Bancroft- Whitney Co, 1916; originally published 1765–69), 41–43.

5 Richard Whately, *Elements of Rhetoric* (New York: Sheldon & Co., 1872), 13. This view was effectively dispelled by the House of Lords in *Bowman v Secular Society Limited* [1917] AC 406.

6 F. E. Smith (Earl of Birkenhead), *Fourteen English Judges* (London: Cassell & Co Ltd., 1926), 237.

7 Lev. 25:44. See also R. Morrison, "The Religious Defense of American Slavery Before 1830," *The Journal of Religious Thought* 37 (1980–81): 16.

dication by taking an oath and having a number of others swear they believed what he had sworn was true.[8] Other cases were decided by ordeal. One form involved burning or scalding a person's hand to see if God would prevent festering. Another involved binding a person and throwing him into a river or pond. If he floated, he was presumed guilty and could be executed. If he sank, he would be presumed innocent,[9] though vindication often proved equally fatal. These practices waned after the Lateran Council in 1215 prevented the participation of clergy, but the cold-water ordeal was again used when women were accused of witchcraft, "drowning them to prove their innocence."[10] The Norman innovation of trial by battle was based on the belief that God would strengthen the arm of the righteous,[11] though women were permitted champions, and this option was later extended to men. Fear of God also influenced the emerging adversarial system of justice in English courtrooms. The jury system and insistence on proof beyond reasonable doubt seem to have been intended to protect judges from divine wrath for condemning the innocent.[12] Even the *peine forte et dure*, a practice which involved piling rocks on defendant until he entered a plea or died, was defended by reference to religious beliefs.[13]

It might be comforting to dismiss such practices as historical footnotes and assume that any Christian influences on our laws and legal systems would now be wholly benign. Yet, sadly, many who insist that the law should enforce Christian moral standards seem reticent about Christian emphases on compassion, and a disturbing number still support the use of torture and the death penalty. Of course, Christianity has also made many positive contributions to our laws, and while many people still seem to believe that their conceptions of morality should be legally enforceable, there is now general recognition of the need for separation of church and state, especially in pluralist societies where there may be differing moral beliefs and expectations. Furthermore, even those with similar religious beliefs sometimes disagree about moral issues and, as Samuel Beckett perhaps

---

8 L. M. Friedman, *The Legal System: A Social Science Perspective* (New York: Russell Sage Foundation, 1975), 272.

9 J. H. Baker, *An Introduction to English Legal History*, 3rd ed. (London: Butterworths, 1990), 5n12. See also R. Bartlett, *Trial by Fire and Water* (Oxford: Clarendon Press, 1986).

10 Blackstone, *Commentaries*, bk. 4, chap. 27, 337.

11 Winston Churchill, *A History of the English-Speaking Peoples* (New York: Dorset Press, 1990), bk. 1, 218.

12 J. Q. Whitman, *The Origins of Reasonable Doubt; Theological Roots of the Criminal Trial* (New Haven, CT: Yale University Press, 2008), chap. 5.

13 A report of the case against Robert le Ewer in 1322 notes that even if the accused was pressed to death, this was "healthy for the soul provided he bore it with resignation." M. Evans and L. Jack, *Sources of English and Legal Constitutional History* (Sydney: Butterworths, 1984),182.

ruefully observed, "God is a witness that cannot be sworn."[14] But if the law is not to be founded upon religiously based moral codes, what principles should shape its content?

The Philosophical Debate

Lawrence Solum has recently argued for an "aretaic" theory, in which the promotion of virtue would be accepted as the central aim of law. He accepts that there are different views about the nature of virtues, but he suggests that some common ground may be found in certain assumptions: humans flourish by rational and social activities that express excellences or virtues; virtues are dispositional qualities of mind or character; and virtues are both intellectual and moral.[15] These assumptions may be well-founded, but aretaic theories raise difficult questions. Can virtues really be promoted by the imposition of legal rules? Laws regulate conduct, not attitudes, and the concept of virtue surely requires more than compliance with legal obligations. As Solum suggests, the law may foster positive changes in attitudes by maintaining peace and prosperity and supporting families and educational institutions. But if the promotion of virtue were to be accepted as the "central aim" of the law, what implications might this have for individual rights and freedoms? To what extent would the laws based on such a philosophy differ from religiously based systems? How could any such system be justified in pluralistic societies, where there may be disagreement about what values should be given priority? And how could the legitimate scope of legal regulation be delineated?

Other legal philosophers have appealed to natural law, which is said to consist of objective and universal standards of moral behavior that may be deduced from the natural order.[16] Aquinas said that any human laws that conflict with such standards are "but a perversion of law,"[17] and Blackstone agreed that such laws are invalid. Some German laws that allegedly authorized Nazi atrocities were actually held to have been invalid on this basis.[18] However, the concept of natural

14 Samuel Beckett, *Watt* (London: Calder & Boyars, 1970), 6.

15 Lawrence B. Solum, "Virtue as the End of Law: An Aretaic Theory of Legislation," *Jurisprudence* 9 (2018): 6–18.

16 For a reasonably succinct discussion of natural-law concepts, see John Finnis, "Natural Law Theories," *Stanford Encyclopedia of Philosophy*, 2015.

17 Saint Thomas Aquinas, *Summa Theologica* ST I–II, Q.95, A.II.

18 In rejecting a contention that "experimental killings" had been sanctioned by the laws of the Third Reich, the *Oberlandesgericht* at Frankfurt said: "An accused may not justify his conduct by appealing to an existing law if this law offended against certain self-evident precepts of the natural law." See *Suddeutsche Juristen Zeitschrift* 2 (1947): 521 ff.

law has been resisted on various grounds, including its dependency upon what Richard Weaver describes as "an intuitive feeling about the immanent nature of reality."[19] Oliver Wendell Holmes Jr. famously dismissed the concept of natural law with the comment that "(t)he common law is not a brooding omnipresence in the sky,"[20] and the legal-positivist position that the validity of laws is not dependent upon moral considerations has generally prevailed.

There is greater support for natural rights, a concept that dates back to antiquity and was affirmed by the Stoics.[21] As Hugo Grotius explained, individuals have certain basic rights and should essentially be entitled to determine how they shall live.[22] John Locke maintained that some individual rights are inalienable and that there are moral limits to government power.[23] Such rights have been justified on various grounds, including Christian concepts of freedom and equality. Jeremy Bentham, another legal positivist, scoffed that "natural rights is simple nonsense: natural and imprescriptible rights, rhetorical nonsense–nonsense on stilts."[24] The positivists have generally prevailed, though many of the suggested rights are now constitutionally protected.

John Stuart Mill argued that "(t)he only purpose for which power can rightfully be exercised over any member of a civilized community against his will is to prevent harm to others. His own good, either physical or moral, is not a sufficient warrant. Over himself, over his own body and mind, the individual is sovereign."[25] This view was attacked on the ground that society had a duty to promote virtue and religion.[26] A century later, when the Wolfenden Committee recommended the decriminalization of homosexual acts in the United Kingdom, Lord Devlin argued that moral principles are essential to the survival of society and that even so-called harmless immoralities may weaken it. He defined immorality as "what every right-minded person is presumed to consider to be immoral," a definition that may send shivers up the spines of civil-libertarians, though he conceded that "[t]here must be toleration of the maximum individual freedom that is consistent

---

19 Richard Weaver, *Ideas Have Consequences* (Chicago: University of Chicago Press, 1948), 31.

20 *Southern Pacific Company v. Jensen*, 244 U.S. 205, 222 (1917).

21 Seneca, *De beneficiis*, III, 20.

22 *Hugo Grotius on the Law of War and Peace* [1625], ed. Stephen C. Neff (New York: Cambridge University Press, 2012).

23 John Locke, *Two Treatises of Government* [1690] (New York: Fordham University Press, 1995).

24 Jeremy Bentham, *Anarchical Fallacies* [1824], in *The Works of Jeremy Bentham*, vol. 2 (Edinburgh: William Tait, 1843).

25 John Stuart Mill, *On Liberty [1859] (London: Routledge, 2010).*

26 James Fitzjames Stephen, *Liberty, Equality, Fraternity* (New York: Holt & Williams, 1873).

with the integrity of society."[27] H. L. A. Hart strongly disagreed with Devlin's fundamental contention, arguing, *inter alia*, that social cohesion is not contingent upon public morality.[28] Others have also invoked societal needs as a yardstick. Lon Fuller suggested that the law should demand from individuals no more than is necessary to ensure the orderly functioning of society.[29] Edmund Cahn argued that it should enforce only those standards of moral behavior that are indispensable for its existence.[30] Whatever the merits of these propositions, the underlying assumption that the needs of society should delineate the legitimate scope of the law is not wholly persuasive. It is true that some form of social regulation is required, but societies may exist and function efficiently notwithstanding widespread infringements of human rights. It has even been argued that in the antebellum era (circa 1780–1861) of the southern United States of America, slavery was "the thread that held the fabric of society together."[31]

Another suggested yardstick is social-contract theory,[32] which postulates a notional contract under which individuals are taken to have agreed to relinquish some rights and to accept regulation in order to enjoy the benefits of society. In essence, one asks whether the consent of reasonable people affected by particular laws might fairly be assumed. Jean-Jacques Rousseau argued that this theory justified punishing serious offenders by exile or death.[33] It has even been suggested that Socrates accepted execution to comply with his social contract with Athenian society. The theory may be defensible, but it offers only limited practical guidance. Proponents of proposed laws often seem convinced that the consent of reasonable people could fairly be assumed, while their opponents are equally convinced that reasonable people should be outraged by the proposed laws.

---

27 Patrick Devlin, *The Enforcement of Morals* (Oxford: Oxford University Press, 1965).

28 H. L. A. Hart, *Law, Liberty, and Morality* (Oxford: Oxford University Press, 1963). See also H. L. A. Hart, "Social Solidarity and the Enforcement of Morality," in H. L. A. Hart, *Essays in Jurisprudence and Philosophy* (Oxford: Clarendon Press, 1983), 248–62.

29 Lon L. Fuller. *The Morality of the Law* (New Haven, CT: Yale University Press, 1964).

30 Edmund Cahn, *The Moral Decision* (Bloomington, IN: Indiana University Press, 1955).

31 Erin R. Mulligan, "Paternalism and the Southern Hierarchy: How Slavery Defined Antebellum Southern Women," *Armstrong Undergraduate Journal of History* 2 (Aug. 2012) https://www.armstrong.edu/history-journal/history-journal-paternalism-and-the-southern-hierarchy-how-slavery-defined#:~:text=In%20the%20antebellum%20South%2C%20slavery,and%20defined%20the%20southern%20woman.&text=This%20sense%20of%20superiority%20and,paternalism%2C%20and%20in%20effect%20maternalism.

32 J. W. Gough, *The Social Contract* (Oxford: Clarendon Press, 1936); T. M. Scanlon, *What We Owe to Each Other* (Cambridge, MA: Harvard University Press, 1998).

33 Jean-Jacques Rousseau, *On the Social Contract, or Principles of Political Right* [1762], ed. Donald A. Cress and David Wootten (Indianapolis, IN: Hackett, 2019).

Perhaps the most creative contribution has been made by John Rawls, who posited an "original position" in which those making political decisions imagine that they are subject to a "veil of ignorance" depriving them of all knowledge of their own personal characteristics and social and historical circumstances. What laws would you support if you did not know whether you were young or old, male or female, rich or poor? He argues that most people would accept two principles: the first guaranteeing equal basic rights to "the most extensive basic liberty compatible with a similar liberty for others"; and the second, providing for inequalities to be so arranged as to provide most benefit for the least advantaged in society, and for everyone to have equal opportunities for obtaining jobs and other social positions.[34] The "golden rule"–some form of which is recognized in most of the world's religions–requires us to do unto others as we would have them do unto us. Rawls's formulation invites us to try to move beyond our own perceptions and imagine what it would be like to be the others. It asks us to consider what laws would seem to be fair and appropriate if we were to stand in their shoes.

In reality, of course, our laws are not simply the product of jurisprudential reflection; they are shaped by many factors, including populism and political opportunism. In recent years, however, there has been increased legal recognition of equal rights and basic freedoms. Unfortunately, some politicians seem intent upon undermining them. We are invariably told that restriction is necessary for our safety, but, as William Pitt the younger once said, "Necessity is the plea for every infringement of human freedom."[35] It is obviously true that some restrictions have to be imposed to ensure social order and promote the interests of the common good, but this can also be invoked as a plea for unwarranted infringements of human rights. In my view, the common good is served by Rawls's ideals of equality of rights and opportunity and care for those less advantaged. It is not served by the maintenance of a rigid social conformity or by undermining the rights of dissidents and minorities. On the contrary, governments in democratic societies should be alert to the risk of what Alexis de Tocqueville has called "the tyranny of the majority." Our autonomy should not be restricted without sufficient justification, such as the need to protect others from harm or deprivation, and even then, the degree of restriction should be limited to what is reasonably necessary.

---

34 John Rawls, *A Theory of Justice, rev. ed. (Cambridge, MA:* Harvard University Press, 1999).

35 William Hague, *William Pitt the Younger* (New York: HarperPerennial, 2005).

The Influence of Law and Legal Systems on Character Formation, Ethical Education, and Values

While Aquinas thought law was conducive to virtue,[36] others have insisted that it merely reflects social values and attitudes; it does not to shape them.[37] Moral values and beliefs are more obviously influenced by enculturation, religious beliefs, political inclinations, and temperament. Even those inclined to assume that their values reflect objective consideration of the relevant issues may ruefully concede that we are all affected by our experiences and emotional responses, and that the full impacts of such effects are not always recognized. In contrast, legislative amendments may seem likely to evoke few moral epiphanies. Yet it seems clear that character is strongly influenced by the institutions of political, economic, and family life,[38] and they are all affected by our laws.

The Maintenance and Shaping of Society

Perhaps most fundamentally, law is essential for the maintenance of a just and ordered society, within which the institutions of political, economic, and family life may be strengthened and character development fostered.[39] Of course, decency and compassion may flourish within even the most lawless communities, but character formation is influenced by the social environment. The importance of laws that effectively uphold rights, protect the vulnerable from violence or oppression, and ensure that provision is made for those in need can be seen in the prevalence of criminal offenses committed by people with a history of social deprivation.

---

36 Saint Thomas Aquinas, *Summa Theologiae* (London: Blackfriars, 1975), I–II, q. 92, a. 1. For a brief account of Aquinas's reasoning, see Joseph M. Magee, "Aquinas on Virtue in Relation to Law," https://www.disruptivetruth.com/aquinas-on-virtue-in-relation-to-law/.

37 G. N Rosenberg, *The Hollow Hope: Can Courts Bring about Social Change?* (Chicago: University of Chicago Press, 1991); Lawrence M. Friedman, *A History of American Law*, 3rd ed. (New York: Simon & Schuster, 2005).

38 Marcia Homiak, "Moral Character," *The Stanford Encyclopedia of Philosophy* (Summer 2019), ed. Edward N. Zalta, https://plato.stanford.edu/archives/sum2019/entries/moral-character/.

39 For an account of how social institutions may enable people to live virtuously, see Marcia Homiak, "Yes, We Can Live Reasonably Decently and Flourish in an Imperfect World," in *The Value of Time and Leisure in a World of Work*, ed. M. Haney and A. D. Kline (Lanham, MD: Rowman and Littlefield, 2010), 61–88.

The Rule of Law

The rule of law reflects a moral judgment that, as Aristotle put it, "It is more proper that law should govern than any one of the citizens."[40] Fuller argues that the rule of law itself has both instrumental and noninstrumental moral value,[41] although this is disputed by Joseph Raz and is the subject of continuing debate.[42] Of course, the law can be used for base purposes and even as a means of oppression, as it was during the apartheid era in South Africa, but it is an essential concomitant of democratic societies that provides mechanisms of accountability and checks on abuses of state power.[43] Hence, the law affirms the primacy of common human rights over privilege. Its influences on community values may be largely unrecognized, but they are nonetheless profound.

Law as an Exemplar

Cicero described law as "the fountainhead of justice," and, despite political opportunism and compromises, the laws in Western democracies generally reflect high ideals. The extent to which any legal system may exemplify moral values is obviously limited, because the most noble human aspirations and actions invariably involve going beyond the demands of law or even moral duty. Yet research suggests that laws change behavior, not only by deterrence but also by the expression of values.[44] This may be seen in the repeated citations of famous statements, such as the proclamation in the American Declaration of Independence of the "self-evident" truths that "all men are created equal, that they are endowed by their Creator with certain unalienable rights, that among these are Life, Liberty and the

---

40 Aristotle, *Politics*, ed. Rackham (Cambridge, MA: Harvard University Press, 1959), 3.16.

41 Fuller, *Morality of Law.*

42 Joseph Raz, *Authority of Law* (Oxford: Clarendon Press, 1979), 226. See also T. R. S. Allan, *Constitutional Justice: A Liberal Theory of the Rule of Law* (Oxford: Oxford University Press, 2003); and Colleen Murphy, "Lon Fuller and the Moral Value of the Rule of Law," *Law and Philosophy* 24 (2005): 239–62.

43 Guillermo O'Donnell, "The Quality of Democracy: Why the Rule of Law Matters," *Journal of Democracy* 15 (2004): 32–46; Kevin Lingren, *The Rule of Law: Its State of Health in Australia*, Rule of Law Institute of Australia, https://www.ruleoflaw.org.au/what-is-the-rule-of-law/.

44 Cass R. Sunstein, "Social Norms and Social Roles," *Columbia Law Review* 96 (1996): 903–68; Robert Cooter,"Expressive Law and Economics," *Journal of Legal Studies* 27 (1998): 585–608; R. H. McAdams, "The Origin, Development, and Regulation of Norms," *Michigan Law Review* 96 (1997): 338–433; and R. H. McAdams, "An Attitudinal Theory of Expressive Law," *Oregon Law Review* 79 (2000): 339–90.

pursuit of Happiness," or the affirmation in the French Declaration of the Rights of Man and of the Citizen that "men are born and remain free and equal in rights." Of course, most people recognize that there is some discordance between the expression of these noble sentiments and the reality that confronts them in their daily lives, but this does not mean that they are not influenced by these ideals. In fact, there is some evidence that laws can be especially effective in the development and reinforcement of moral norms.[45] While some changes to the law may have little, if any, impact,[46] legal reforms do seem to influence public opinion about social issues if the reforms are generally in line with community sentiments.[47] It has even been suggested that learning law facilitates character development in prisoners.[48]

The Provision of Information and Conscience Stirring

Many people resolve ambiguity or uncertainty by seeking information about the views of others.[49] Since our laws are generally seen as reflecting widely held values and ethical principles, they are an obvious source of such informational conformity. Of course, not all laws reflect a social consensus, but those enacted by a duly elected government may nonetheless be seen as reflecting widely held views. Yet research has shown that some people will agree even with statements that are obviously wrong rather than disagree with a majority view.[50] Laws prohibiting certain acts not only expose perpetrators to penal sanctions and deter

45 K. Bilz and J. Nadler, "Law, Moral Attitudes, and Behavioral Change," in *The Oxford Handbook of Behavioral Economics and the Law*, ed. E. Zamir and D. Teichman (Oxford: Oxford University Press, 2014), 107.

46 For example, abolition of a British law criminalizing attempted suicide apparently led to no discernible change in public attitudes to its propriety. N. Walker and M. Argyle, "Does the Law Affect Moral Judgements?" *British Journal of Criminology* 4 (1964) 570–81.

47 Bilz and Nadler, "Law, Moral Attitudes, and Behavioral Change," 107.

48 Jeremiah Phoenix explains, *inter alia*, that "reading cases can inspire self-reflection, contemplation, and reconsideration of long-held beliefs": "Beyond Bars: Law as a Pathway to Character Development," *Guild Notes*, https://www.nlg.org/guild-notes/article/beyond-bars-law-as-a-pathway-to-character-development/.

49 Saul McLeod, "What is Conformity?," *SimplyPsychology* (2007, updated 2016), https://www.simplypsychology.org/conformity.html; see also M. Sherif, "A Study of Some Social Factors in Perception," *Archives of Psychology* 27 (1935): 187.

50 S. E. Asch, "Studies of Independence and Conformity: I. A Minority of One against a Unanimous Majority," *Psychological Monographs: General and Applied* 70 (1956): 1–70; but see also S. Perrin and C. Spencer, "The Asch Effect: A Child of Its Time?," *Bulletin of the British Psychological Society* 32 (1980): 405–06.

potential defenders, they also proclaim that such conduct is regarded as morally unacceptable within the society. Informational conformity may be particularly effective in changing social attitudes when the law prohibits conduct, such as insider trading, that may not otherwise have been widely recognized as infringing moral standards, but the influence of information conformity is wide-reaching.

Changing Conduct and Circumstances

There is some evidence that moral sensibilities may be shaped by changes in conduct even if motivated only by fear of prosecution. People tend to draw inferences about what is appropriate from observing the conduct of others, and this may influence their own behavior and beliefs.[51] Of course, following the herd is obviously not an adequate substitute for reason and reflection, but moral beliefs and standards are influenced by perceptions of what others seem to find acceptable.

Changes in attitude may arise from intentional intervention, such as rehabilitation programs undertaken to avoid imprisonment. Attitudinal changes may also occur when people are forced to become familiar with people or situations that they had previously shunned. For example, the forced desegregation of American schools did seem to reduce racism and lead to greater acceptance of school busing.[52] Empathy may also be fostered by restorative-justice programs in which young offenders meet their victims under controlled conditions and are confronted by the loss and distress that has been caused by their conduct.[53]

Law also affects character development by suppressing violence and oppression, facilitating the provision of social benefits and contributing to changing attitudes. Mill, writing in 1860, suggested that women who had been legally and socially subordinated to men had become meek, submissive, self-sacrificing, and manipulative.[54] Feminist psychology now emphasizes social context and lived experiences,[55] and there have been substantial changes in the lives of women since Mill made his observation, due in part to legal reforms that have opened opportunities and provided greater protection. Unfortunately, domestic violence is still prevalent, and presentence reports regularly reveal that offenders bear the

---

51 Bilz and Nadler, "Law, Moral Attitudes, and Behavioral Change."

52 Howard Maniloff, "Community Attitudes toward a Desegregated School System: A Study of Charlotte, North Carolina," *Equity & Excellence in Education* 16 (Sept. 1978).

53 Heather Strang, *Restorative Justice Programs in Australia: A Report to the Criminology Research Council* (2001, updated 2014) http://crg.aic.gov.au/reports/strang/index.html.

54 John Stuart Mill, *The Subjection of Women*, ed. S. Okin (Indianapolis, IN: Hackett, Indianapolis, 1988), 86.

55 Judith Worell, "Feminism in Psychology: Revolution or Evolution?," *The Annals of the American Academy of Political and Social Science* (2000): 571.

emotional scars of sexual or other forms of abuse. Yet the legal and social changes do seem to have had a significant effect. For example, one recent study has found similar levels of assertiveness in male and female undergraduate students. [56]

Catalysts for Change

Proposed changes to the law frequently provide a catalyst for debate about potentially controversial issues, such as same-sex marriage, abortion, stem-cell research, or drug decriminalization. Public debate may be rancorous, and it may trigger strong emotional responses, but, as Robert Solomon has argued, emotions may lend a keenness to our perceptions and a readiness for insight and understanding that cannot be evoked by abstract reasoning alone.[57] The competing arguments are usually based upon strongly held moral contentions, and they are often accompanied by personal stories that reveal the implications of existing laws or likely effects of the proposed changes. While many people seem unwilling to reconsider entrenched views, this process does lead to changes in community attitudes.

Cases that attract widespread publicity and cause outrage may also provide catalysts for change. One striking example is offered by public response to what became known as the Zong massacre. In 1781 the captain and crew of a ship ran short of water and, after a number of slaves had died, another 150 were thrown overboard. The owners of the ship subsequently sued their insurers for loss of the value of their "goods." A London jury found in the owners' favor. During the subsequent appeal, Lord Mansfield said that the jury had had no doubt that the situation had been the same as if horses had been thrown overboard.[58] The decision was overruled, but on the ground that there appeared to have been no necessity for this action.[59] Despite the public disquiet generated by the case, there was no prosecution for murder.[60] The resulting publicity initially seemed to have little effect on public opinion, but attitudes changed over time as the case was repeatedly cited, and this led to a dramatic expansion in the abolitionist movement in

---

56 J. Parham et al, "Influences on Assertiveness: Gender, National Culture, and Ethnicity," *Journal of Management Development* 34 (2015): 421–39.

57 Robert Solomon, *A Passion for Justice: Emotions and the Origins of the Social Contract (Reading, MA:* Addison-Wesley, 1990).

58 James Walvin, *The Zong: A Massacre, the Law and the End of Slavery* (New Haven, CT: Yale University Press, 2011), 153.

59 *Gregson v Gilbert* [1783] 3 Douglas 232: 99 E.R. 62.

60 Walvin, *The Zong*, 167.

Britain.[61] More recently, inquiries into child abuse have revealed a shocking incidence of predatory conduct and fueled demands for legal reforms.

Judicial Rituals

Despite many differences, our modern systems of justice share fundamental objectives: the maintenance of rights, the ascertainment of truth, the application of just principles, the sublimation of conflict, the provisions of procedural safeguards, and the affirmation of justice. While particular legal judgments may prove controversial, our courts and the rituals provided by public trials offer public affirmations of the values underlying these objectives. There is no obvious means of assessing the impact on community attitudes, but it is likely to be substantial, even if largely unrecognized.

Problems and Scope for Improvement

The positive influences of law and legal systems might be enhanced in a number of ways.

Promoting Understanding

Misconceptions about law and justice abound. For example, many people wrongly believe that crime rates in Australia and other Western countries are increasing, and that sentences are becoming more lenient. Such misconceptions often fuel support for policies, such as mandatory sentencing, that can entrench injustice. The role of law in facilitating rehabilitation is often overlooked, and many people seem unable to recognize the importance of the procedural safeguards in our legal systems. Sadly, this often seems true of politicians on both sides of the political spectrum and also of law enforcement officers, many of whom seem to see procedural requirements as unnecessary hindrances.

The ethical bases and principles of the legal system clearly need to be better understood, but adequate public explanation is beyond the capacity of the legal profession alone. Discussions need to occur in schools and universities concerning the role of law and the maintenance of human rights in modern democracies.

---

61 S. Drescher, "The Shocking Birth of British Abolitionism," *Slavery & Abolition* 33 (2012): 571–93, at 575–76. Walvin, *The Zong*, 176–79; S. Swaminathan, "Reporting Atrocities: A Comparison of the *Zong* and the Trial of Captain John Kimber," *Slavery & Abolition 31* (2010): 483–99, at 485.

There is a need for regular consultation among lawyers, legal academics, those advising legislators, and people in other relevant disciplines. There is also a need for lawyers to engage with journalists about the importance of public discussion of controversial cases that moves beyond appeals to populism and actually engages with the legal and social issues involved.

Ensuring That Our Laws Are Just

The just resolution of contested issues often requires the balancing of competing considerations rather than the relentless application of a single principle. Hence, to quote Holmes again, "the life of the law has not been logic: it has been experience."[62] Experience may provide insight and wisdom, but it can also induce complacency about long-standing theories and approaches. Daniel Kahneman has cautioned against "theory induced blindness," explaining that "once you have accepted a theory, it is extraordinarily difficult to notice its flaws."[63] While paradigm shifts in science may nonetheless occur as a result of a single groundbreaking discovery or theory, tipping points usually arise only as groundswells of support for change gradually build up and eventually overcome the resistance offered by those keen to defend the status quo.

The law has been changing at an unprecedented rate since the 1960 s, as successive tipping points have been reached by waves of support for the civil rights movement, feminism, gay activism, and other social movements. Many laws that once permitted injustice have been amended, and new initiatives have been adopted to protect the vulnerable. Human-rights legislation in many jurisdictions has provided new remedies, and previously inflexible rules have been mitigated by initiatives such as legislation dealing with misleading and deceptive conduct and concepts of conscionability. Of course, there has been resistance to some changes. For example, even some people who abhor so-called hate speech fear that the breadth of new provisions proscribing statements capable of causing offense has unduly limited freedom of speech. Social activists frequently raise new issues about laws and legal practices, and there is a need for continual review. Fundamental principles of legal and social justice should obviously be staunchly defended, but orthodoxy should be held lightly and challenges to the status quo seriously considered. The moral effect of the law is obviously dependent upon the morality of its content.

---

62 Oliver Wendell Holmes Jr., *The Common Law* (London: Macmillan, 1882), 1.

63 Daniel Kahneman, "Bias, Blindness and How We Truly Think (Part 2)," *Bloomberg*, Oct. 26, 2011, https://www.bloomberg.com/opinion/articles/2011-10-25/bias-blindness-and-how-we-truly-think-part-2-daniel-kahneman; Daniel Kahneman, *Thinking Fast and Slow* (London: Penguin, 2011).

Providing Greater Access to Justice

While many lawyers accept some briefs on a pro bono basis, and legal aid is sometimes available, the vast majority of litigants without substantial savings or borrowing capacity are effectively denied legal representation. Unfortunately, few are capable of adequately presenting their own cases. Judges may explain relevant procedures and ask helpful questions, but their capacity to offer assistance is limited by various factors, including their duty to remain impartial. Furthermore, even litigants with legal representation are often unable to obtain a hearing within a reasonable time due to backlogs of cases. These problems could be ameliorated. Procedures could be reformulated with a view to reducing the cost to litigants, legal aid could be made more readily available, courts could be better funded, and more judges could be appointed. These measures would require further public expenditure, but if our laws and legal systems are to have a substantial impact upon moral consciousness and community values, they must be accessible.

Contributors

Rüdiger Bittner is Professor of Philosophy at Bielefeld University.

Brian H. Bix is Frederick W. Thomas Professor of Law and Philosophy at the University of Minnesota.

Frank Brennan, a Jesuit priest, is Rector of Newman College at the University of Melbourne, and Adjunct Professor of Law at Australian Catholic University.

Allen Calhoun is McDonald Distinguished Fellow at the Center for the Study of Law and Religion at Emory University and Adjunct Faculty Member in Philosophy at Averett University.

Robert F. Cochran Jr. is the Louis D. Brandeis Professor of Law, Emeritus, at Caruso School of Law, Pepperdine University, and Senior Fellow at the Institute for Advanced Studies in Culture at the University of Virginia.

Kenneth John Crispin was barrister, Queens Counsel, Judge of the Supreme Court of the Australian Capital Territory (ACT), and President of the ACT Court of Appeal.

Jean Bethke Elshtain (1941–2013) was Laura Spelman Rockefeller Professor of Social and Political Ethics at the University of Chicago.

E. Allan Farnsworth (1928–2005) was Professor of Law at Columbia University.

James E. Fleming is The Honorable Paul J. Liacos Professor of Law at Boston University.

M. Cathleen Kaveny is Darald and Juliet Libby Professor of Law and Theology at Boston College.

Ute Mager is Professor of Public Law at the Institute for German and European Administrative Law and Director of the Center for Lawyer-Oriented Legal Training at Heidelberg University.

Linda C. McClain is Robert Kent Professor of Law at Boston University School of Law and Affiliated Faculty, Kilachand Honors College and Women's, Gender, and Sexuality Studies Program at Boston University College of Arts and Sciences.

Reid Mortensen is Professor of Law and Head of School at the School of Law and Justice at the University of Southern Queensland.

Patrick Parkinson is Professor of Law at the TC Beirne School of Law at The University of Queensland.

Thomas Pfeiffer is Director of the Institute for Comparative Law, Conflict of Laws, and International Business Law at the University of Heidelberg.

Robert Vosloo is Professor of Systematic Theology at Stellenbosch University.

Michael Welker is Senior Professor of Systematic Theology and Director of the FIIT-Research Center International and Interdisciplinary Theology at the University of Heidelberg.

John Witte Jr. is Robert W. Woodruff Professor of Law, McDonald Distinguished Professor of Religion, and Director of the Center for the Study of Law and Religion at Emory University.

Index